# *Recreating Utopia in the Desert*

# Recreating Utopia in the Desert

## *A Sectarian Challenge to Modern Mormonism*

Hans A. Baer

STATE UNIVERSITY OF NEW YORK PRESS

Published by
State University of New York Press, Albany



Printed in the United States of America



For information, address State University of New York Press, State University Plaza, Albany, N.Y., 12246

**Library of Congress Cataloging in Publication Data**

Baer, Hans A., 1944-
Recreating utopia in the desert.

Bibliography: p.
1. Aaronic Order. 2. Church of Jesus Christ of Latter-Day Saints. 3. Mormon Church. I. Title.
BX8680.A24B34 1984 306′.6 87-10133
ISBN 0-88706-681-X
ISBN 0-88706-682-8 (pbk.)

10 9 8 7 6 5 4 3 2 1

# *Contents*

# Figures and Tables

FIGURES



TABLES

# Preface

Mormons are often portrayed as a highly cohesive people who embody what many regard the finest virtues of American life. This image is not only held by the public at large but often is conveyed in the work of both Mormon and non-Mormon scholars. Perhaps partly as a consequence of this perception, observers of the Mormon scene tend to overlook the plethora of sects which have emerged directly or indirectly out of its mainstream. Over one hundred religious groups (many of which no longer exist) can be traced back to the church established by Joseph Smith, Jr., on April 6, 1830.

The focus of this book is one of these groups, namely, the Aaronic Order or, as it is more commonly called, "the Levites of Utah." The Levite sect is a small millenarian and communal group that emerged out of the Mormon Church during the early 1930s under the guidance of Maurice L. Glendenning, a self-proclaimed prophet who was a relative newcomer to the Intermountain West. Claiming to be a "first-born son" of Aaron, Glendenning's message struck a responsive chord among certain working class Mormons in the urban areas of northern Utah during the height of the Depression. While Glendenning was born and reared in the Midwest, most of his early followers were Utah Mormons. Based upon Glendenning's revelations, which were recorded in three sacred books, members of the Aaronic Order believe that they are patrilineal descendants of Aaron and/or Levi of Old Testament times, and that they are to perform special priestly duties prior to the Second Coming of Jesus Christ, which it is claimed will occur before AD 2000.

After residing in several midwestern and western states, Glendenning, his wife and daughter moved to Provo, Utah in 1929, and subsequently joined the Mormon Church. Shortly thereafter, Glendenning told various individuals that he had been receiving revelations from a supernatural voice. On July 16, 1930, he received a Writing in which the voice identified itself as the "Elias who should come in the last days" (Book of Elias 1944, sec. 166).

Between the early 1930s and 1942, small groups in northern Utah met to discuss the Levitical Writings which Glendenning periodically received. After participating in an unsuccessful communal venture in southwestern Utah during the early 1930s, Glendenning worked at various jobs in southern Utah and Nevada; eventually he established a chiropractic practice in Los Angeles. Some of his followers contacted him, expressing a desire to create a formal organization based on the Writings, and, in late November 1942, consecrated their belongings for the establishment of the Aaronic Order.

Despite the fact that there are striking similarities between Levite and Mormon theology, members of the Aaronic Order vehemently deny that their organization is a Mormon "offshoot." They maintain that their church and the Levitical priesthood were established in 1736 B.C. by Jesus Christ (also believed to be Jehovah) when Levi was consecrated a priest (Glendenning 1955, 10–13).

In the spring of 1949, the Levites established their first desert community, called Partoun, in western Juab County and only a few miles from the Utah-Nevada border (See Figure 0.1 for locations of the branches of the Order). They, along with a few non-Levites, applied for thirty-seven homesteads (each one hundred sixty acres). Several individuals and families, most of them elderly, still live at Partoun, certain that some day this section of the Great Basin will be populated by thousands of refugees from the cities. In 1955 the Levites, some of whom were residents of Partoun, established the Eskdale commune in western Millard County which is also only a few miles from the Utah-Nevada border. Eskdale gradually grew into an agricultural community of close to one hundred individuals. In addition to Partoun and Eskdale, the Aaronic Order has two additional branches: (1) a congregation located in a suburb of Salt Lake City and serving the Salt Lake Valley and (2) a congregation located in Springville and serving the Utah Valley (Provo-Orem area). Whereas Eskdale and Partoun are situated in the remote Snake Valley of the Great Basin, the Salt Lake and Springville branches are located in the urban Wasatch Front area where approximately three quarters of Utah's population resides. Most Levites live in Utah; the Order also has members in Idaho, Wyoming, Oregon, Colorado, Arizona, and Nevada.

Glendenning, the Levite prophet, died in 1969, and passed his leadership of the Order to Robert Conrad, who is also referred to as the Chief High Priest. Despite its membership of only a few hundred members, the significance of relating the story of the Aaronic Order goes beyond presenting an account of what might seem to many to be an obscure religious sect. I believe that the Levite sect serves as a reflection of the often overlooked contradictions that exist in modern Mormonism—a religious movement that has often been viewed as the most successful utopian venture in American history.

New religions throughout history have emerged as responses to social disequilibrium resulting from external or internal societal

Figure 0–1
Branches of the Aaronic Order

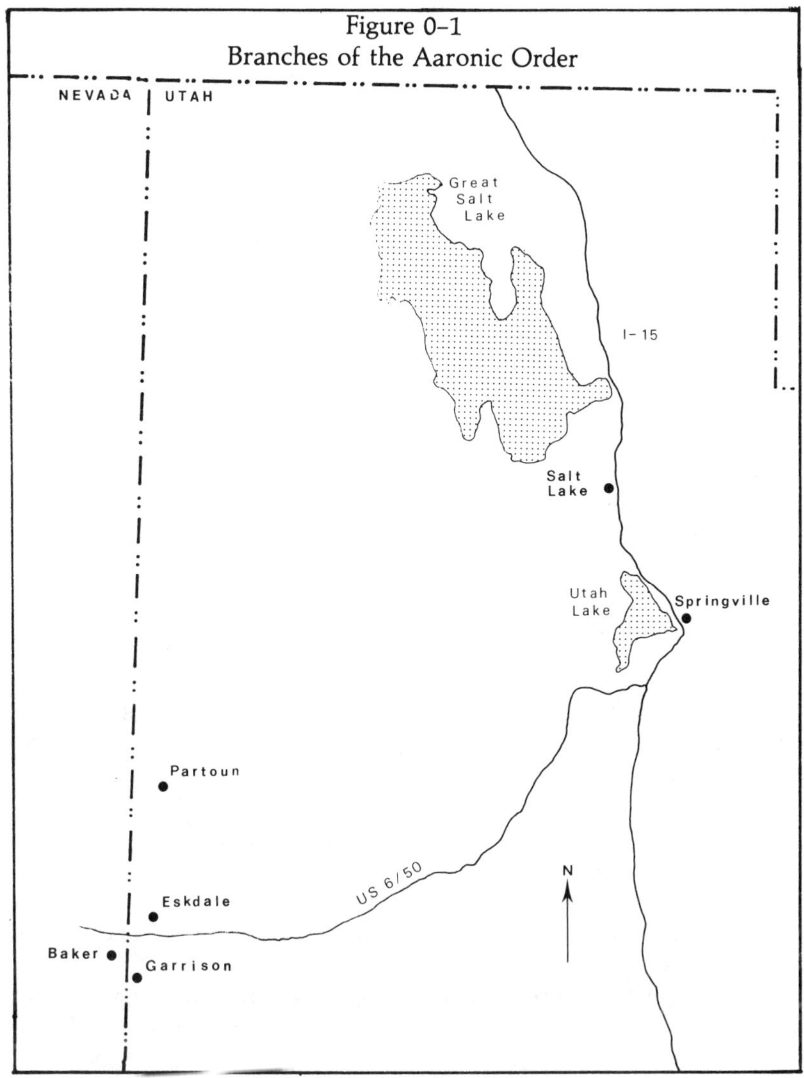


pressures. In the case of primitive societies, these arise in situations of conquest and subjugation by more technologically developed societies. The appearance of similar movements occurs among populations that constitute the subordinate segments of complex societies. Anthropologists, sociologists, and historians have referred to such developments by a wide variety of terms—"nativistic movements," "messianic sects," "cargo cults," "millenarian movements," "crisis cults," and so forth (Linton 1943; Aberle 1972; Worsley 1968; Cohn 1970; LaBarre 1972; Wilson 1973). Even Marx, who regarded religion as the "opium of the people," was cognizant of the revolutionary potential of religious ideas under certain social conditions (Marx and Engels 1964). Anthony F.C. Wallace is among those who recognize the redemptive aspects of religion during periods of social upheaval. In his now classic article, Anthony F.C. Wallace (1956a, 265) refers to these expressions of religious protest as "revitalization movements."

> A revitalization movement is defined as a deliberate, organized, conscious effort by members of a society to construct a more satisfying culture. Revitalization is thus, from a cultural standpoint, a special kind of culture change phenomenon: the persons involved in the process of revitalization must perceive their culture, or some major areas of it, as a system (whether accurately or not); they must feel that this cultural system is unsatisfactory; and they must innovate not merely discrete items, but a new cultural system, specifying new relationships as well as, in some cases, new traits.

Wallace (1956a, 267) maintains that "most denominational and sectarian groups and orders budded off after failure to revitalize a traditional institution," and suggests that perhaps all religious groups emerge as revitalization movements. While many of these groups abort at some point in their evolution, a successful revitalization movement will become an institutionalized part of its larger sociocultural environment.

This book deals with the processes of revitalization and institutionalization that have occurred within Mormonism. The Mormon religion emerged as an attempt by its initial members to adjust to the social strain and dislocation that existed among a certain segment of the new American republic. It managed to incorporate many aspects of popular thought and the religious and utopian movements that existed in American society during the first half of the nineteenth century. Mormonism emerged as a religious utopia in the Midwest, was transformed into a theocratic commonwealth on the periphery of an increasingly industrializing state, and was finally absorbed by the latter (Leone 1979). The price that it paid for its success was accommodation to the political, economic, and social institutions of its parent society. Whereas Mormonism grew up as a unique species of religious communitarianism, in time it developed into one of the staunchest defenders of the capitalist system that it had once so vehemently rejected.

This social transformation provided the impetus for the emergence of various sectarian groups within modern Mormonism. While these were by no means the first schisms from the Mormon mainstream, their character was different from their nineteenth century counterparts in that they tended to emphasize a return to egalitarian and communitarian ideals. Despite a greater rejection of its Mormon roots than some other groups, especially the polygynist ones, the Levite sect also was established on the basis of these ideals. It will be argued that the Aaronic Order, like many Mormon sects, emerged as a response to various social structural and ideological tensions within Mormonism. A central theme of this book is the proposition that the Order emerged as a revitalization movement that attempted to resurrect a sense of community, or what the German sociologist, Ferdinand Töennies, called *Gemeinschaft*, which its early adherents perceived Mormonism to have had in the nineteenth century, but which they believed had been lost in the present one. Whether or not Mormonism was ever characterized by such an ethos is of secondary importance. What is of primary significance is that certain people felt that Paradise had been lost and that they wished to restore it. At any rate, the transformation of Mormonism into an elaborate theocratic bureaucracy, which in many ways resembles the modern corporation, prompted some working class Mormons to attempt to rejuvenate their church.

The strong emphasis of the Levites on social equality, communalism, millenarianism, and modern revelation indicates their strong desire to revitalize twentieth century Mormonism. These features are also emphasized by various Mormon sects which maintain that the leaders of the Mormon Church have made unacceptable compromises with the larger society.

I am concerned with the roots of dissatisfaction motivating certain people, such as the Levites, to attempt to rejuvenate modern Mormonism. The early followers of Glendenning were not particularly interested at first in breaking away from the Mormon Church, irrespective of Glendenning's sentiments in this regard. It was over a decade after Glendenning began to proclaim the revelations which he had received from the Angel Elias that a religious group disclaiming any direct affiliation with the Mormon Church was formally established by the Levites. During this interim period, the Levites genuinely believed that the Mormon Church would eventually accept their claims and petitions for reform.

I believe that certain individuals were attracted to and eventually joined the Levite sect because modern Mormonism increasingly became oriented to its middle class constituency. Whereas nineteenth century Mormonism had exhibited many sectarian features, twentieth century Mormonism took on an appreciable number of denominational or ecclesiastical features. Mormonism was transformed from a utopian sect and a radical critic of its parent society into a full-fledged participant in corporate capitalism and a bastion of conservative American values. Only by considering the process of this transformation may we begin to comprehend the emergence of the Aaronic Order and various other modern Mormon schismatic groups.

Once a religious group comes into existence and becomes somewhat established in terms of its social structure and ideology, its development is dependent upon forces very different from those responsible for its origin. Some of these arise from interactions with the larger society, and others stem from the internal dynamics of the group itself. Although the Levite sect exhibits many aspects of Mormonism, it has incorporated certain features of evangelical Protestantism. In this regard, the Levite sect is unique when one considers the beliefs of many Mormon sects, most of which continue to look primarily to the revelations of Joseph Smith, Jr., for their inspiration. While some Levites, particularly older ones, place a great deal of stock in the Mormon scriptures, these have been superseded in the minds of most members by the revelations that Glendenning received.

In attempting to account for the ideological shift of the Order away from Mormonism and toward evangelical Protestantism, I will consider a number of external and internal factors, including the relationship of the Levite sect with the Mormon Church, the charismatic leadership of Maurice Glendenning, the group's contact with various Protestant groups and individuals, and the process of sectarian stagnation that accompanies the institutionalization of new religious groups.

Also, my study will deal with the conversion experience of thirty-five individuals to the Levite sect, some of whom joined the group at a relatively early stage in its development and others who joined it more recently. Concerning the value of examining the process of conversion to sectarian groups, Ellsworth Faris (1955, 89) notes the following:

> The most fruitful field for study would seem to lie in the securing of complete and adequate life histories of sectarians, including new converts to the sect, members who have always been in it, and dissidents and deserters who have gone out from it. For the intimate life histories will give light on the actual product that the sect is responsible for and afford material for the accurate answering of the problems at the present unresolved.

I hope that a study of the Levite conversion experience will not only contribute to the growing literature on religious conversion in general, but that it will add to our understanding of the factors that propelled various alienated working class Mormons to leave their church and to join a sect that was attempting to resurrect the former's earlier communitarian goals.

## *Fieldwork among the Levites*

I, like most Americans (especially those who reside east of the Rockies), grew up with only a superficial knowledge about Mormons. My curiosity about Mormonism was first aroused when in the summer of 1967 I passed through Mormon country enroute to a new job in Seattle, Washington. Never once in my wildest imaginings did I suspect that I would return six years later not only to live in the Mormon Mecca of Salt Lake City, but also shortly thereafter to study one of its spin-offs, or, in the disparaging terminology of the Mormons, a group of "apostates."

My interest in communitarian societies and the factors that contribute to their maintenance or collapse first drew my attention to the Aaronic Order. Because of work that I had done intermittently between November 1970 and April 1973 among the Hutterites of South Dakota, Seymour Parker suggested the possibility of my studying the Levites of Utah (Baer 1973, 1976). It was not until later that I became interested in the emergence and development of the Aaronic Order and factors leading various people to convert to it. Shortly after I learned about the Levites, I met in early October 1973 with Dr. Robert Conrad, the Chief High Priest of the Order. Upon obtaining a brief sketch about the Order, I requested his permission to attend religious and study meetings at the Salt Lake branch. After I attended a few meetings in Salt Lake, I visited the Eskdale branch with my ex-wife for a weekend in mid-November 1973. Shortly following this visit, I obtained permission from Robert Conrad and the Acting Priest at Eskdale to conduct an in-depth study of the Aaronic Order. The period between my initial contact and this request provided the Levites, at least those who met me, an opportunity to "look me over" and alleviate possible reservations about my motives.

While I believe that most Levites came to accept my presence among them, some remained skeptical about the merits of my study. Early on, a Levite woman asked me if I was going to look at them "through a microscope." On my first visit to the Eskdale commune, a prominent resident of the Eskdale commune asked me if I planned to conduct research on Eskdale or was I "just visiting." Since I had not yet asked the leaders of the Order for permission to undertake a study of the group, I was taken somewhat aback by her question. I replied that I was "just visiting," but that I eventually would have to conduct research for my dissertation on some topic. She complained that various people misrepresented the Levites after short visits to Eskdale. As I learned more about the development of the Aaronic Order and the background of Maurice Glendenning and his followers, it became clearer to me that, following Wallace (1956a), the Levite sect could be viewed as a revitalization movement that emerged as a response to certain changes in Mormonism. In light of this question, it indeed seems ironic that in the spring of 1975 a middle-aged man said to me during an interview, "I wish I could read your mind; I wonder if you think that the Aaronic Order is like early Mormonism."

I gathered most of the data for this study between October 1973 and November 1975. This research was followed up with interviews of some members after a major schism that occurred following the expulsion of the leaders of a Pentecostal movement within the Order. Between January 1975 and June 1975 I was involved in full-time fieldwork among the Levites. During this time I frequently visited the desert communities of Eskdale and Partoun, attended worship services and study classes at the Salt Lake and Springville branches, and interviewed members in all the branches. Unless specified otherwise, this period will serve as the "ethnographic present" in my discussion of the social structure and ideology of the Levite sect.

I gathered most of my data through participant-observation. From the very beginning of my study, I kept a log of my observations and conversations and interviews with the Levites. This portion of my field notes came to nearly five hundred single-spaced, typed pages. I created an index system to find material quickly on specific topics in my notes, particularly in identifying those requiring additional data. I also created an index system for my biographical notes about members of the Order. I wrote these notes while alone, either at home after religious or study meetings at the Salt Lake and Springville branches, or else during visits to the desert communities. While I generally waited until the end of the day to record my notes when I stayed at the Eskdale commune, I sometimes was able to do this during the day.

I also conducted interviews with the leaders and middle-aged and elderly members—many of whom had been affiliated with the group since the 1940s, and some of whom were followers of Glendenning in the 1930s prior to the formal incorporation of the Order. I generally took notes during formal interviews and usually did not use a tape recorder. With the exception of some Levites (generally the leaders), I found that those members whose comments I wished to tape generally felt uncomfortable about it. Some expressed concern that they would be directly quoted, that their comments would be taken out of context, or perhaps that others in the Order would learn about their comments.

Given the small size of the Order, I became acquainted with most active adult members as well as some of its semi-active and inactive members. My key informants included high ranking members as well as peripheral ones. The generally favorable (but never completely glowing) accounts given by the former were counterbalanced by the more critical and sometimes bitter accounts given by the latter, and vice versa. While most of my informal and formal interviews were with adult Levites, the fact that I often slept in the school dormitory and spent many of the evening hours there brought me into considerable contact with the younger Levites. I also occasionally visited their classes and even taught a high school class once.

While formal interviews with various Levites provided me with useful information, I feel that an even more important source of data were casual conversations during work, in people's homes, after religious and study meetings, and during long drives between Salt Lake City and Eskdale. As Julia B. Crane and Michael V. Angrosino (1974, 57), "Most anthropologists freely admit that a surprisingly large part of their information—sometimes the *best* information" comes from informal or impromptu interviews.

I collected data in both formal interviews and casual conversations with over thirty-five converts to the Aaronic Order. I asked these individuals about certain factors that contributed to their decision to join the group. Potential factors leading to conversion were identified from the following sources: (1) a review of the social scientific literature on religious conversion (2) casual conversations with some Levites about their conversion experiences and (3) consideration of the sociocultural milieu in which the Order developed. I asked semi-structured questions to determine whether these factors were present in the conversion experience of specific Levites during formal interviews. To ensure that each informant was asked questions on the same topics, I kept a list of items before me to be covered during the interview. Each convert was asked questions about the following items:

1. Vital statistics, such as age, education, occupation, and previous religious affiliations
2. Background of their parents
3. Degree and source of their early religious socialization
4. Manner in which they became affiliated with the Order
5. Length of time that they spent investigating the order, and the date when they formally joined
6. Feelings of deprivation prior to conversion
7. Presence of life crises prior to conversion
8. Influence of significant others in the decision to join
9. Relationships with non-Levites during the period of their investigation of the Order
10. Influence of significant others in the decision to join
11. Aspects of the Order that they perceived as attractive.

I attempted to interview most converts who were active in the Aaronic Order during 1975, but several of these individuals chose not to discuss their conversion experience. Since some converts lived a long distance from Utah, I was unable to interview them. Other converts provided only fragmentary and vague evidence that was insufficient for analysis. I could not interview several converts because of old age and physical impairments.

I tape recorded only one interview with a convert. When she appeared to be uncomfortable about being taped, I wrote down her responses. Due to the apparently sensitive nature of the data being collected, I pursued the same technique with other interviewees. Although I asked all converts specific questions, I did not do so in the same order or wording in each case. Instead I allowed the interviewee to discuss his or her conversion in an open-ended manner, asking specific questions at the appropriate moment. My notes on the details of the conversion experiences of the thirty-five informants in my sample total some 140 single-spaced, typed pages. As Leon Salzman (1953) observes, the conversion experience is difficult to analyze. Individuals often overlay their decision to convert with ideological rationalizations and may consciously or subconsciously repress various details essential to a complete analysis. I hoped that the semi-structured, open-ended interview style would put subjects at ease and provide them with ample opportunity to 'free associate.'

A fair amount of the information presented in this book was obtained from Aaronic Order "in-house" booklets, letters, newsletters, and scriptures which were given or loaned to me by various Levites or available in the Church Historian's Office of the Church of Jesus Christ of Latter Day Saints in Salt Lake City. A National Endowment for the Humanities Fellowship to participate in a seminar, conducted by Professor John F. Wilson at Princeton University during the summer of 1977, permitted me to conduct library research on the roots of Mormonism and various Mormon sects.

While I attempted to make the Levites aware that, as an anthropologist, I was interested in conducting a social scientific study of their group, a fair number of Levites apparently viewed me as a prospective member. My own research in more recent years with the Spiritual movement among Afro-Americans and my conversations with a number of colleagues who have been involved in the study of sectarian groups indicates that this is an almost inevitable consequence of such research (Baer 1984). A number of Levites insisted that my real motives for studying the Order were spiritual, even if I was not fully aware of this. A Levite man lamented in September 1975 that I had failed to make a commitment to the Gospel of Jesus Christ, despite much exposure to testimonies and discussion of this matter. Robert Conrad told me early in my study that my discovery of the Order was the will of the Lord. An elderly Partoun resident told me that my "bull-headed" attitude prevented me from realizing that I was a lineal descendent of Aaron, and a Levite woman predicted that I eventually would be a high ranking member of the Order, adding that perhaps then someone would understand her. Several other members suggested that I would eventually reside at one of the desert communities, or at least become a Levite. Some members insisted that I could not possibly understand the Order unless I made a total commitment to the Lord. In March 1975 several Levites prayed during a "prayer circle," consisting of twenty-five participants, including myself, that my family and I would join the Order, and for an end to my "intellectual" approach to life. For the most part, however, efforts to proselytize me were minimal.

In December 1986 I revisited the Levites at the Eskdale commune and the Salt Lake branch for several days in order to update myself on changes that have occurred in the Aaronic Order over the past decade. I will summarize the findings of this visit in an epilogue at the end of the book. Since the mid-1970s, many of the early or "pioneer" Levites, including a man who I refer to as Henry in the text, have passed away. Conversely, many of the Levites who I first met as children and adolescents are now adults, many with families of their own. Despite a schism by the charasmatics from the Order during 1975–1976, a reconciliation of sorts has occurred between them and the main body of the Order since then. As I will note in greater detail in the Epilogue, the Aaronic Order has continued to shift away from its Mormon roots towards evangelical Protestantism, particularly the neo-Pentecostal or charismatic variant.

The fact that I am a non-Mormon (or a Gentile) was probably conducive to conducting field work among the Levites. Since the Mormon Church had condemned the Aaronic Order and had excommunicated many middle-aged and elderly members of the group, there tended to be an apprehension among the Levites toward Mormons expressing a scholarly interest in them. Unfortunately, I fear that some Levites expected me to write an apology for their religion. Undoubtedly many Levites will disagree with much of my analysis of their group and its relationship to Mormonism. Despite such perceptual differences, I would like to add that their ideals of egalitarianism and communalism are ones toward which I am deeply sympathetic.

# *Acknowledgements*

I am indebted to many individuals for their role in bringing this book to fruition. First of all, I am grateful to Seymour Parker in the Department of Anthropology at the University of Utah for encouraging me in the early fall of 1973 to conduct fieldwork among the Levites of Utah. My ability to find a topic of research almost from the beginning of my program of study facilitated my completion of my doctoral work within a relatively short period of time. Laurence Loeb, from whom I took two classes in religion, and Patricia Albers, who acquainted me with the complexities of fieldwork, also served as valuable guides in my study of the Levites. Lenore Hirsh and Eric, our son who was born during the course of my fieldwork among the Levites, often accompanied me to Levite activities at the Salt Lake branch and several times to the Eskdale commune. The rapport that they both developed with the Levites played a significant part in facilitating my research efforts.

I would like to thank Seymour Parker, Laurence Loeb, Patricia Albers, Lenore Hirsh, John F. Wilson, Ino Rossi, Merrill Singer, Mark Leone, Armand Mauss, O. Kendall White, and Brigham Madsen for having read earlier drafts and providing valuable suggestions for revising the manuscript which resulted in *Recreating Utopia in the Desert.* Armand Mauss, Professor of Sociology at Washington State University, deserves a special note of gratitude since he read several versions of my manuscript, and made numerous recommendations on improving the final product. I also would like to give special thanks to Rosalie Robertson, Acquisitions Editor at the State University of New York Press and an anthropologist in her own right, for the role that she played in the completion of the book. Finally, I would like to thank Gerald Hanson, a colleague at the University of Arkansas at Little Rock, for drawing the maps in the final manuscript.

My greatest expression of gratitude must go the the subjects of this book, the members of the Aaronic Order who permitted me to enter their lives. Robert Conrad, the Chief High Priest of the Order, facilitated my entree into the group and served as an inside critic of my work. Many other individuals—many of whom continue to be active members of the Order, others who left the group, and still some who are now deceased—patiently tolerated my presence at their branches and communities, welcomed me into their homes, and answered my numerous questions about their way of life and commitment. I sincerely hope that in some small way my study sheds insights that will assist the members of the Order in achieving their ideals of communalism, social equality, and spirituality.

My research among the Levites, as well as among Black churches in the United States, has alerted me to the complexities of conducting ethnographic fieldwork among religious groups. Given the focus of religious groups on ultimate concerns, the social scientist finds himself or herself in a highly ambigious and paradoxical relationship with his/her subjects. There is often a fundamental tension between the social scientific perspective and the religious perspective. I doubt whether many, if any, Levites will agree with my interpretation of their culture and religion. The possibility that the end product of my research may offend some, or even most, members of the Order troubles me. Yet, I genuinely hope that something positive emanates out of the dialectic of our contrasting perspectives. Only time will tell whether my desire will be fulfilled.

# 1

# *The Rise and Institutionalization of Mormonism*

Scholars interested in the American religious scene often note that Mormonism, along with the Adventist movement, Christian Science, Pentecostalism, and the Jehovah's Witnesses, emerged on American soil rather than in Europe (Pearsons 1958, 183). Joseph Smith, the founder of the Church of Jesus Christ of Latter-day Saints (commonly referred to as the Mormon Church), was born in Sharon, Vermont, in 1805. In 1816 Joseph's family moved to Palmyra, a village in Genesee County in upper state New York. Because of intense revivalism during the early decades of the nineteenth century, the vicinity around Palmyra was referred to as the "Burned-over District" (Cross 1950). Joseph's mother, Lucy Mack Smith, joined the Presbyterians, and Joseph evinced some interest in the Methodists but never actually joined them (Bushman 1984, 53–54). Being a farm boy of humble origins, Joseph felt confused by the claims of the competing religious groups evangelizing in the area, and prayed as to which one he should join. In a series of visions during the early 1820s, various supernatural personages appeared to Joseph, urging him not to join any of the existing sects but to restore true Christianity. The angel-prophet Moroni, who according to Mormon belief had served in mortality as the last in a series of chroniclers recording the history of the ancient civilizations in the Americas, directed Joseph to golden plates which had been hidden beneath a large rock near the Smith homestead. In time Joseph, with the assistance of trusted scribes, translated these ancient records (first published in 1830 as the Book of Mormon). The plates told about the oceanic migration of Lehi, an Israelite prophet, his six sons, and their families from Palestine to the New World around 600 B.C. Whereas Nephi and his brothers, Samuel, Jacob, and Joseph, followed the righteous way of their father, Laman and Lemuel disregarded his prophecies. Over the next millennium, the Nephites and the Lamanites frequently warred against each other. Nonetheless, following his crucifixion, Jesus Christ appeared in the Americas and brought peace between the Nephites and the Lamanites for nearly 200 years. Finally, in the vicinity of the Hill Cumorah near Palmyra, New York, the Nephites were annihilated by the wicked Lamanites, who in time degenerated into the many American Indian cultures.

Mormons regard their religion as the restoration of the biblical priesthoods and the church established by Christ in both Palestine and the Americas. In May 1829, John the Baptist ordained Joseph Smith and Oliver Cowdery into the Aaronic priesthood, and later that summer the Apostles Peter, James, and John restored the Melchizedek priesthood. On April 6, 1830, a group of six elders and about fifty others met in Fayette, New York, for the organization of the Mormon Church (Bushman 1984, 143).

Mormonism thus appeared shortly after the birth of the American nation and moved westward as part of America's territorial expansion. Mormonism probably embodies more traditional American values and ideals than any other religion. O. Kendall White, Jr., (1969, 44) refers to it as a "nineteenth-century heresy" since it challenged the basic assumptions of Protestant Christianity. For example, Alexander Campbell (1832, 13), the founder of what became the Disciples of Christ denomination, wrote that the Book of Mormon provided final answers to every theological question of the early nineteenth century, including "infant baptism, ordination, the trinity, regeneration, repentance, justification, fasting, penance, church government, religious experience, the call to the ministry, the general resurrection, external punishment, who may baptize, and even the question of freemasonry [sic], republican government and the rights of man."

Despite the exaggeration of this statement, Joseph Smith also provided other theological "answers," some of which diverged from those in the Book of Mormon, in the form of more than one hundred revelations, many of which have been compiled into another Mormon scripture known as the Doctrine and Covenants. In essence, like other new religions, Mormonism syncretized the elements of older religious traditions so as to create something new. Walter Franklin Prince (1917), Thomas F. O'Dea (1957), and others discuss how the Book of Mormon reflects the common belief in the Hebraic origins of American Indians and specific events in Joseph Smith's life.

Mormon theology exhibits several obvious links with New England Puritanism revealed by its emphasis on providential history, the covenant, intelligence, and ideal theocracy, the church of saints, the establishment of the Kingdom of God on earth, and various other Hebraic themes. Conversely, Mormonism contains a strong streak of Arminianism in its emphasis on the concept of "free agency" and the belief that human beings have the potential eventually to become gods. Its rejection of certain aspects of Calvinism is further indicated by its negation of original sin and predestination and by its doctrine of practical universal salvation.

Dean DePew McBrien (1929, 71–75) suggests that Mormonism may have been influenced by the doctrines and practices of the various denominations that were evangelizing in the Burned-over District. Like the Baptists, Mormonism incorporated a closed communion ritual and congregational voting; it rejected infant baptism. Early Mormonism was very much influenced by the primitivist movement, which apparently was not only found among the Disciples of Christ on the western frontier, but also emerged independently in other parts of the nation (Hill 1969). Joseph's parents held a primitivist outlook as did some of the early converts to Mormonism. In fact, the infant church did not begin to see any marked growth until it moved from western New York to the Western Reserve where it merged with the congregation of a former Campbellite preacher, Sidney Rigdon. During the early years of the Mormon Church, Rigdon served as Joseph Smith's chief counselor, scribe and spokesman.

Finally, an important ideal in the air when Mormonism arose was that of religious communitarianism. As section forty-nine of the Doctrine and Covenants indicates, Smith was aware of the Shaker community at Sodus Bay on Lake Ontario, thirty miles from Palmyra. Although Jemmima Wilkinson died in 1819, the core of her community at Seneca Lake in the Burned-over District continued until 1843; she made an indelible impression upon the area (Cross 1950, 33–34). While the Book of Mormon mentions the concept of "all things in common," Joseph Smith never indicated any intention to turn his church into a communal society until he met Sidney Rigdon. Shortly after he came in contact with Rigdon's tiny communitarian group in Kirtland, Ohio, Joseph received a revelation to establish a new version of communalism called "the Order of Enoch" or "United Order."

## *Mormonism as a Nineteenth Century Revitalization Movement*

While the view that Mormonism served as an answer to the theological controversies of the day has merit, an alternative but not necessarily contradictory interpretation must consider its social roots in the new republic. As Richard L. Bushman (1984, 7–8) argues, Mormonism emerged as "an independent creation, drawing from its environment but also struggling against American culture in an effort to realize itself." Bearing this thought in mind, I will argue that Mormonism emerged as one of a number of revitalization movements—many of them also emphasizing egalitarian and communitarian ideals—that appeared during the first half of the nineteenth century as responses to social strain and social dislocation among Americans.

The proposition that Mormonism emerged as a revitalization movement must address itself to two major questions. First of all, what segments of society did it appeal to, and second, why did it appeal to these segments? Whitney R. Cross (1950), Thomas F. O'Dea (1957), and others have stressed the birth of the Mormon Church in the Burned-over District while at the same time deemphasizing the importance of the Ohio period in its early development. The religious activities and the social conditions of western New York had an important impact on the emergence of the Latter-Day Saints religion. Yet, the new church had only some seventy members in that area when Joseph Smith decided to move its headquarters to Kirtland, Ohio in late 1830. Within a few weeks of its move to the Western Reserve, the church added 150 converts, more than twice the number that had followed Joseph from New York; the church membership in Kirtland increased to more than one thousand by the spring of 1831 (Cannon 1950, 16). Kirtland served as the church's headquarters and the primary center for missionary activities during the 1830s; a secondary center was established also in 1831 in Jackson County, Missouri.

Orson Spencer, one of the few relatively well-educated early Mormons, remarked that "our people were mostly the working class of the community, from the United States and Great Britain and her provinces . . . Our elders . . . accustomed to fatigue, privation, and opposition" (quoted from Flanders 1965, 2). Other sources confirm Spencer's observation that the early Mormons were derived primarily from humble social origins. M. Hamblin Cannon (1950, 16–19) notes that because most of the early converts were poor, church leaders stationed in Missouri had to request in July, 1832, that further migration to the area be halted until those who had already arrived could be taken care of. In commenting on the socioeconomic status of 28 converts to Mormonism during the period 1830–1840, Laurence M. Yorgason notes the following:

> Mormonism did not attract the highly urbanized, those sophisticated in business, politics or religion. The wealthy did not flock to its message, neither did the very poor nor the transients of society. In short, the Mormon converts from the period under consideration seldom came from society's highest or lowest levels, neither economically, socially, religiously nor geographically. They were, since becoming Mormons, often called extremists, but the items in their background considered here seem to suggest that Mormonism had its roots in the average and unobstrusive segment of society (Yorgason 1970, 282).

Another historian, Mario S. DePillis, notes that early Mormon converts came from the "low but not the lowest classes, whether rural or urban in their origin" (DePillis 1968, 63).

Rank and file Mormons of the 1830s and early 1840s came primarily from the Methodists, the Presbyterians, the Baptists, and other less established religious groups, such as the Disciples of Christ and the Millerites (Yorgason 1970). Few Congregationalists, Lutherans, Anglicans or Roman Catholics converted to Mormonism. The Mormon mission to Britain found its greatest appeal among working class members of the Primitive Methodist Church and other nonconformist sects (Cannon 1950, 48–52).

Most initial converts prior to the relocation of the church's headquarters in Ohio resided in southwestern New York rather than in the Palmyra area. Many converts both in western New York and Ohio originally came from the remoter parts of New England, particularly Vermont, Massachusetts and Connecticut, as well as from Pennsylvania. Mormon missionaries often proselytized in their "home" areas of New York and New England. While the concept of the 'gathering' drew many converts to large Mormon centers in the Midwest, church branches were established in many other parts of the country. George S. Ellsworth (1951) presents some demographic data on the location of Mormon communities during the 1830s. Among his observations are the following:

1. Seventeen Mormon centers located on the densely populated coast between Philadelphia and Portsmouth, Maine, were for the most part short-lived ventures. On the other hand, there were more than one hundred Mormon branches in the sparsely populated areas of northern Missouri, Illinois, Ohio, New York, Vermont, New Hampshire and Maine which were relatively long-lasting and stable.
2. Seventy-one percent of the Mormon missionary locales were located in areas with a population density of 18–45 inhabitants per square mile, 25 percent were in those with a population density of 2–18 inhabitants per square mile, and only 3 percent were in those with a population density of over 90 inhabitants per square mile.

3. The Mormon centers that were not in sparsely populated areas like Chester and Delaware Counties in southeastern Pennsylvania often were located in environments that were still basically agrarian.

An examination of the 1860 census figures of the birthplaces of Utahns indicates that substantial numbers of converts were made in both the East and the Midwest, but that few were made in the South (DePillis 1966, 63). While the total number of American-born Mormons in Utah was 27,490 in 1860, the total number of foreign-born stood at 40,244. Mormon missionary activity in Britain began as early as 1837, but impressive gains in converts commenced with the mission of the church's Twelve Apostles during 1840 and 1841. The establishment of a transatlantic emigration program resulted in the move to America of more than 88,000 Mormons, including some 55,000 from Britain (Allen and Thorp 1975, 501). Extensive missionary activities in other parts of Europe, especially Scandinavia, were established after the assassination of Joseph Smith in 1844.

In attempting to understand the origin of Mormonism, various scholars tend to view it as either basically a continuation of the New England Puritan tradition or as a frontier religion which appealed to the national and democratic spirit of the times. Although both of these perspectives offer valuable insights for understanding the origin of Mormonism, the new sect had a more universal appeal, which is demonstrated by its ability to make substantial converts in eastern and midwestern America and the urban areas of Britain. On the one hand, Mormonism reflected Puritanism in its theology, as was mentioned earlier, and in its social organization, described as "an orderly, hierarchic commonwealth in which both economic enterprise and social institutions were communally regulated for the sake of spiritual values" (Berthoff 1971, 194). On the other hand, Mormonism created a lay priesthood that enabled men of humble social origins to preach the gospel and to become members of what they believed to be the most important religious councils ever to have been established. Religious leadership was based upon talent and religious fervor rather than upon education and social position.

Numerous sociological studies of religious groups indicate that social strain and dislocation are among the most important factors contributing to the emergence of religious sects. According to Rowland Berthoff (1971), the social structure of American society underwent serious strain during the first half of the nineteenth century—a period of rapid economic and population growth, migration and rising expectations. In contrast to those who enjoyed the fruits of an expanding economy, others did not share in them, at least to the extent that they believed they should have. In other words, their deprivation was often relative, a phenomenon which occurred within the Smith family itself. During the 1820s the area around Palmyra had grown 412 percent in population and, with the opening of the Erie Canal in 1825, had become a trade market center (Cross 1950, 55–59). Palmyra itself, being located on the Erie Canal, became an important local market center. Despite these improvements, Joseph and his father's family remained very poor as he stated more than once. Some parts of northern and western New England and western New York had begun to decline in competition with the still new and much richer areas in the Midwest. Mormonism also made converts in some of the eastern backwater areas (such as Monmouth County, New Jersey and the Fox Island off the coast of Maine), which had been left behind by agricultural, commercial, and industrial expansion.

In addition to relative deprivation, the fluidity of migration from the more established areas of the East created social disorientation in the newer settlements of the Midwest. DePillis provides the following description of rural environments of western New York, western Pennsylvania, Ohio, Missouri, and Illinois:

> Such areas were marked by primitive schooling, isolation of families, breakdown or disappearance of orthodox religion, perfervid evangelical religion (with its revivals, sects, and prophets, many coming from varied eastern backgrounds), the lack of any stable political power structure, and the extreme spatial mobility of individuals (especially young men). This was the psycho-social environment of Mormonism between 1827 and 1844 when it germinated and flourished (DePillis 1968, 79).

Mormonism also appealed to certain people in Britain who were experiencing social tensions. In 1837 English industry came to a near standstill, and produced high unemployment among the working classes in the urban manufacturing districts (Allen and Thorp 1975). By this time, the Methodist Church had achieved middle class respectability and no longer actively proselytized working class people. The Mormon Church provided the opportunity to immigrate to America and promised a better future in its theocratic kingdom. The church also often lent converts their Atlantic fare and chartered ships to bring them across the ocean.

## *Mormon Communitarianism*

Nineteenth century Mormonism emphasized cooperation, egalitarianism, and provisions for the needy. According to Mark P.

Leone (1979, 1), "during much of the nineteenth century its goals were common ownership of property and classlessness, both of which were based on a vocal criticism of industrial capitalism as it then existed in Europe and the United States." Nineteenth century Mormonism stressed cooperation first in the development of communities in the Midwest, in the crossing of the plains, and later in the colonization and settlement of the Intermountain West and other areas in western United States, southern Canada, and northern Mexico. J. Kenneth Davies makes the following comments about nineteenth century Mormon economic philosophy:

> Mormon economy was not based on private ownership and direction but on a combination of private, state, and Church ownership—with Church direction. The distribution of the goods produced was to be more or less on the basis of equality and need. Church funds were to be used, among other things for the "poor and needy." Profits, if any, were to be used to build up the Kingdom, not to enhance personal wealth. Mormon economic contact with the outside world was limited by preachment and if necessary even excommunication. There was to be no accommodation to the economic system of the world (Davies 1968, 44).

Many other groups which developed out of early Mormonism, including the Strangities, the Cutlerites, and the nineteenth century Reorganized Church of Jesus Christ of Latter-Day Saints of Josephites, also practiced some form of communalism (O'Dea 1957, 188–189).

In 1831 while the Mormons were residing in the vicinity of Kirtland, Ohio, Joseph Smith proclaimed a new revelation referred to as the "Law of Consecration," the "United Order," and the "Order of Stewardship" (O'Dea 1957, 188). The Law of Consecration attempted to combine communalism and private enterprise. Individuals or families transferred or "consecrated" their property to the church but retained use of it under a "stewardship" (Gardner 1922, 142–143). The bishop of the ward held the title of possessions as "common property of the church" but returned to members in the form of stewardship what he felt they required for their livelihood. The "surplus," defined as the amount earned over and above that required for the support of a member or his dependents, was to be returned to the bishop. This surplus was to be used "first, in supplying the deficiency where stewardships fail to yield sufficient income for the necessities of those who possess them; second, to form or purchase new stewardships for such as have not received any; third, to supply those with means who may need it for the improvement or enlargement of their respective stewardships; fourth, the purchase of lands for the public benefit, to establish new enterprises, develop resources, build houses of worship, temples, send abroad the Gospel or anything else that looks to the general welfare and founding of the Kingdom of God on earth" (B.H. Roberts, as quoted in Gardner 1924, 144).

It was not long before this plan faced opposition and encountered serious problems (O'Dea 1957, 192–193). In June 1834 Joseph Smith received a revelation calling for the withdrawal of the United Order on the grounds that the Mormons were not yet prepared for it (Doctrine and Covenants, Sec. 105, 188–190). In 1838 Joseph Smith received a revelation, often referred to as "the lesser law," requiring that the Mormons tithe or "pay one-tenth of all their interest annually" to the church (Doctrine and Covenants, Sec. 119, 212).

Although the practice of United Order was suspended until after the main contingent of Mormons settled in Utah, a spirit of communitarianism pervaded the establishment of Mormon communities in other parts of the Midwest. In the summer of 1831, Joseph Smith designated the town of Independence in Jackson County, Missouri, as the location for the New Jerusalem over which Jesus Christ would rule during the millennium. Due to the antagonism of the Gentiles, those Mormons who had settled in Jackson County later moved to the Missouri counties of Clay and Caldwell. By 1836 most of the Mormons in Clay County had resettled in Caldwell, which had been designated by the Missouri legislature as a special place for the followers of Joseph Smith. Two years later, most of the Kirtland Mormons joined their Missouri brethren after the collapse of the Kirtland Safety Society Bank in 1837. Far West in Clay County had been barely established as the new Zion when hostility expelled the Mormons from Missouri altogether, forcing them to resettle in Illinois during the winter of 1839–1840.

This time Joseph Smith must have thought, at least for a brief time, that his followers had finally arrived at a place of refuge. A liberal charter from the Illinois legislature allowed Nauvoo to become a virtual city-state with wide powers of self-rule. By 1844 Nauvoo had a population of over 12,000 making it, next to Chicago, the largest city in the state of Illinois. The city council could enact any ordinance as long as it did not conflict with federal and state laws, while the municipal court system ensured the Mormons that they could administer justice within their community without external interference. Furthermore, Nauvoo had its own municipal militia, the Nauvoo Legion, which was subject only to the authority of the governor. As its commander, Joseph Smith became the only Lieutenant General in the United States. Unfortunately, various external and internal factors acting upon the Mormon city-state culminated in the assassination of the Mormon prophet on June 27, 1844 at the jailhouse in Carthage, Illinois.

The Mormon social experiments and the antagonisms that hounded the followers of Joseph Smith from place to place in the Midwest had important implications for the subsequent development of their culture. Mark Leone summarizes the dynamic interplay between Mormonism and the larger American society:

> The economic and missionary success that followed Mormon social and ideological innovation at every stage of its development brought inevitable pressure from the outside community, which in turn pushed Mormons into increasingly marginal areas. Each new area permitted and required progressively more dramatic innovations, many of which led to even greater economic growth. This in turn provoked suspicion, which again resulted in expulsion and movement further West, where experimentation and growth were once more both required for survival and permitted by the increasing closeness of the frontier with its absence of developed institutions. The final move, to Utah, passed beyond the frontier into an institutional vacuum, where a totally new social order had to be established for survival, but where it could at the same time enjoy uninhibited growth (Leone 1979, 16).

The story of the Mormon emigration to and colonization of the Intermountain West has been told many times and does not need to be repeated here. Nevertheless, it is important in order to understand the nature of nineteenth century Mormonism to present a brief description of the cooperative and communal endeavors among those Mormons who settled, under the leadership of Brigham Young, in Utah. When the Mormons first arrived in the Salt Lake Valley, the area was still part of Mexico but became United States territory in 1849 following the Mexican War. Nevertheless, Utah remained relatively independent between 1847 and the later 1880s. In 1849 the Mormons established the provisional state of Deseret, a large region comprising all of present-day Utah and Nevada; small sections of Oregon, Idaho, Wyoming, Colorado and New Mexico; over two-thirds of what is now Arizona; and a small section of California, including the San Bernardino Valley and the port of San Diego. The federal government rejected this territorial concept and instead created the Utah Territory (an area of still substantially greater size than the present state of Utah). Despite this, much of what the Mormons designated as the state of Deseret is still commonly referred to as "Mormon country." In essentially this area the Mormons continued the social experiments that they had started in the Midwest.

Much of the early distribution of land in the Salt Lake Valley and elsewhere in Utah followed the "law of stewardship; equal according to circumstances, wants, and needs" (Arrington 1958, 51). The extraction of natural resources, such as water, pastureland, timber, and minerals, functioned as public works projects so as not only to build up the

Kingdom of God on earth, but also to provide gainful employment for the thousands of new immigrants from the East and also from Europe. Whereas settlements on the Gentile frontier in the West had tended to be scattered, specialized, individualistic and fiercely competitive, Mormon economic institutions were marked by social planning, joint action, and communitarianism. According to Leonard J. Arrington (1958, 63), "Isolated as they were from American thought-currents after 1847, and under the necessity of continued group action to solve the many problems which plagued them, the Mormons were not affected by the growing accommodation to the private corporation, rugged individualism, Social Darwinism, and other concepts which account for the rise of laissez-faire after 1850."

Mormon economic enterprises were primarily of a "mixed type," combining principles of cooperative and private ownership, rather than of a communal form per se during the nineteenth century. Perhaps the most important cooperative arrangement that the Mormons instituted was an elaborate irrigation system (O'Dea 1957, 198–205). Other cooperative institutions developed by the Mormons during the nineteenth century included a system of cooperative stores and industries, established largely to boycott Gentile commerce in the Intermountain West; the Perpetual Emigrating Fund Company, which helped many Mormon converts from eastern United States and Europe migrate to Zion; the Zion's Board of Trade, a cooperative for Mormon businessmen; the Women's Relief Society, and various cattle and sheep cooperatives.

The Mormon Church delegated a large share of the responsibility for the organization and management of resources to private interests. This pattern contained one of the seeds for the stratification that emerged among the Mormons in the latter part of the nineteenth century and that became especially pronounced during the twentieth century. While the cooperative pattern was the norm, the communal ideal emerged at different times during the nineteenth century. Even though the Law of Consecration was originally announced in 1831 and had been "the higher law," it became an ideal to be implemented at a more opportune time. In 1854 the church attempted to revive the Law of Consecration, asking its members to comply by deeding over all their properties to its trustee-in-trust, namely their President-Prophet, Brigham Young. Due to the failure of Congress to legalize such a system and widespread reaction in the national press to what was seen by many Gentiles as another extension of theocratic despotism, the Mormon hierarchy dropped the plan in the summer of 1857.

Later, largely as a response to the Panic of 1873, Brigham Young initiated the Second United Order (O'Dea 1957, 206). Between 1873 and 1874 the Mormon leaders created over one hundred United Orders in communities throughout the Intermountain West. Economic enterprises such as the cattle and sheep herding and grist mills and sawmills operated on a communal basis, but generally the private ownership of land, houses, cattle and sheep, and some businesses were retained (Gardner 1922, 162–165). Seven United Order experiments, namely, those at Bunkervile, Nevada; Sunset, Arizona; Allen's Camp (St. Joseph), Arizona; Woodruff, Arizona; Orderville, Utah; Kingston, Utah; and Springdale, Utah functioned communally (Arrington 1954). The Orderville United Order in southern Utah, the most successful of these, operated for almost ten years and had a population of about 205, five years after its incorporation in 1875 (Arrington 1958, 333–337). The Second Order was more successful in the newer communities than in the older ones, and was opposed by many prosperous Mormon businessmen. By the end of 1874, most United Order experiments had been disolved.

## *Mormonism's Evolution from a Utopian Sect into a Corporate Church*

As was argued earlier, Mormonism emerged as one of many religious communitarian experiments which responded to the social strains and contradictions associated with industrialization and urbanization in nineteenth century America. While the larger society became increasingly occupied with competition and laissez-faire capitalism, Mormonism embraced a form of theocratic communitarianism. The inability of the Mormons, due to hostility from the larger society to establish their religious utopia in the Midwest, made it imperative that they pursue a policy of separatism. During much of the latter half of the nineteenth century, Mormonism was more or less independent from the United States and essentially constituted "a new state emerging on the edge of an older one" (Leone 1979, 5).

The roots of this state formation laid in Joseph Smith's establishment of the Council of Fifty as the legislative branch of the Mormon Kingdom. The Council of Fifty, a secret political body, was differentiated from the ecclesiastical structure of the Mormon Church, and was to form the basis of a world government that was to precede the second coming of Jesus Christ (Hansen 1967). The geographic isolation of the Intermountain West permitted Mormonism through its policies of imigration and colonization to establish a religious group on American soil. While other social groups, including the Puritans, had been organized in the United States on the basis of religious inspiration, none came even close to the far-flung empire that the Mormons created on the Western frontier. Leone describes the pattern of colonization that the Mormons followed in the settlement of Utah:

> They tied the whole of the kingdom together in a well-designed administrative structure in which all functions were filled by churchmen and all churchmen had to be either farmers or workers. In the trackless Great Basin, Mormons established an entire social environment, complete with schools, courts, irrigation systems, exchange networks, price controls, systems of weights and measures, a monetary system including specie, a network of roads, maps, an exploration plan, land, timber and water rights management, and printing facilities. Everything from the founding of basic agrarian industries to the invention of a new alphabet sprang into existence as much from necessity as from conscious forethought, and it all spread quickly over the vast territory which was to become Mormondom or the Mormon theocratic state (Leone 1979, 18).

Mormonism functioned as a relatively autonomous agrarian state for several decades, but its independence became increasingly threatened by the westward expansion of the political economy of the United States. The military conflict which preceded the absorption by the industrial North (or East depending upon one's geographical perspective) of the agrarian South merely delayed the fate of the Mormon theocracy. The Republicans' denunciation at their 1856 convention of slavery and polygyny as the "twin relics of barbarism" manifested the intent of the larger society to bring both the agrarian South and the Mormons under its hegemony. Leone (1979, 26) notes, "Under this double banner the Union attacked the only two regions that had achieved a degree of political and economic autonomy beyond that thought compatible with a strong federal government." Elsewhere, Arrington (1958, 63) suggests that "the well-publicized conflicts and differences between the Mormons and other westerners and Americans were not so much a matter of plural marriage and other reprehensible peculiarities and superstitions as of the conflicting economic patterns of two generations of Americans, one of which was fashioned after the communitarian concepts of the age of Jackson, and the other of which was shaped by the dream of bonanza and the individualistic sentiments of the age of laissez-faire."

The completion of the transcontinental railroad in 1869—an event which had been delayed by the Civil War—portended the eventual absorption of the Mormon state into its parent society. For one thing, the coming of the railroad made the extraction of the extensive mineral deposits in the Intermountain West profitable. In addition, both Mormon and Gentile Utahns now could more easily obtain products which were unavailable or more costly to manufacture in their region. Despite

Mormon efforts to boycott Gentile commerce by establishing cooperatives and even reinstituting the Law of Consecration or United Order in the 1870s, federal legislation attacking the practice of plural marriage made capitulation of the Mormon state inevitable. When such legislation failed to control the Mormons completely, the federal government embarked upon a program of confiscating church property, disincorporating the church, and imposing an alien government on Utah territory. These and other pressures forced the Mormon hierarchy finally to admit defeat when President Wilford Woodruff proclaimed an end to Mormon polygyny within the territorial boundaries of the United States. According to White (1978, 173), the Manifesto "legitimated the change from a posture of resistance to the nation-state to one of accommodation without repudiation of the polygamy doctrine."

Despite the emphasis on egalitarianism during the nineteenth century, we should not romanticize Mormon cooperative efforts during this period. Mormonism created a hierarchical politico-religious organization at its beginning, and a strong association between church position and socioeconomic status appeared at a fairly early date. In an exhaustive comparison of the probate records of the estates of the General Authorities (the upper echelons of the Mormon ecclesiastical structure) and those of other church members for the period of 1832–1932, Dennis Michael Quinn (1976a) offers empirical support for this contention. A disparity of wealth and income between the General Authorities and the rank and file membership appeared in Kirtland, accelerated at Nauvoo, and became even more pronounced in Utah. The personal wealth of Brigham Young at the time of his death in 1877 was in the order of one million dollars—no mean sum at that time (or even today for that matter) for a man of humble social origins, and an obvious contradiction of Mormon ideals. While the majority of new appointees already generally had assessed property values above that of the average Mormons, selection into the Mormon hierarchy eventually provided new economic opportunities, such as special land allotments, election to public office, and seats on the board of directors of church owned businesses.

According to Quinn, the Mormon hierarchy constituted throughout its history a "stratified economic elite":

> New members of the hierarchy tended to be drawn from economic levels that were above the average of the Mormon population from which they came, and once in the hierarchy, their economic status tended to remain at inertia until opportunities for economic improvement were structured by the hierarchy in such a way that they corresponded roughly to the ecclesiastical status of the echelons of the hierarchy: the greatest improvements in income and wealth came with service as the

> President of the Church, then as his counselors, then as the Presiding Bishop and Quorum of the Twelve, then as the counselors to the Presiding Bishop, and to the least degree, if at all, with service as Council of Seventy (Quinn 1976a, 155).

Kinship figured as a very important variable in the social elitism of the Mormon hierarchy. Twenty-five percent of the appointees were sons of other General Authorities and relationships as distant as sixth cousin were recognized in selection into the Mormon hierarchy. Nevertheless, despite the early appearance of patterns of elitism, the disparities between the rich and poor within the Mormon Church were not as apparent and pronounced in the nineteenth century as they became in the twentieth century.

After the proclamation of the Manifesto in 1890, Mormon cooperative efforts declined appreciably. According to Robert Gottlieb and Peter Wiley (1984, 68), "In the 1890s, Mormon leaders contacted eastern financial interests for loans and investments to keep the church and its enterprises afloat. Out of these negotiations came a series of business alliances that tied the church to a number of leading eastern financiers and businessmen and ultimately to the political party that they supported—the Republican party." As the Mormon Church entered the twentieth century, it accommodated itself more and more to the political and economic institutions of the United States. Despite some initial ambivalences about the business ethic, church leaders became staunch advocates of individualism, laissez-faire capitalism and social stratification and critics of federal welfare programs and of unionism. Furthermore, church leaders castigated secular utopian and Marxian visions of cooperation. As Thomas G. Alexander (1986, 184) observes, "those in the church who accepted the increasing pluralism and wished to extend it to their vision to embrace the left wing of American political and economic society experienced increasing difficulty." Nonetheless, Mormons constituted more than 40 percent of the members of Utah's Socialist Party during the early twentieth century, and various Mormons, including ward officers, ran and occasionally won election on the Socialist ticket (Sillito and McCormick 1985, 123).

As the twentieth century progressed, the Mormon Church expanded its financial investments or created new ones in the sugar beet industry, mercantile establishments, publishing houses, communications, ranching and farming, real estate, insurance, mining and many other economic enterprises (Alexander 1986). The church rationalized many of its financial investments on the premise that they provided income and employment for the poor. Mormon leaders often sat on the board of directors of church-owned businesses or ones in which the church had large investments. Several years after the onset of the Depression, the cooperative approach of an earlier era reemerged in a muted form with the establishment of welfare farms and industries. The transition of the Mormon hierarchy from the trustees of a theocratic state to corporate managers dedicated to a capitalistic economy was completed well before the onset of the Great Depression of the 1930s.

Since 1959 Mormon leaders have refused to divulge publicly the total financial holdings of the church. Yet, evidence demonstrates that it is the richest church in the world in proportion to its general membership. Using available public and church records, interviews with General Authorities, statistical data and other business information, Bill Beecham and David Briscoe (1976) estimate that the income in contributions and sales by church-controlled corporations exceeds $3 million a day. Their estimate of a gross annual income of over $1 billion for the church does not include rents from its commercial buildings and apartments (which include a 36-story apartment building in New York City), undisclosed real estate transactions, interest and dividends from stock investments, or large individual donations. Based upon more recent data, John Heinerman and Anson Shupe (1985, 76) maintain that "The Church runs a virtual business empire, with assets close to $8 billion by conservative estimates." They estimate that the church had about one-hundred and nineteen million dollars invested in stocks and bonds, about one-hundred and nineteen million dollars invested in insurance portfolios, and earned an annual income of two billion dollars in 1983 (Heinerman and Shupe 1985, 76–127). The Mormon Church is the sole owner of three insurance companies (Beneficial Life, Utah Home and Fire, and Deseret Mutual); it has controlling interest in several corporations (such as Utah-Idaho, Inc. and a chain of Utah department stores), and owns the largest cattle ranch in the state of Florida. Other church holdings include television stations in Salt Lake City and Seattle, eleven radio stations, one of the two Salt Lake newspapers as well as considerable stock in the Times-Mirror Corporation (publisher of the Los Angeles Times), a computer firm, a shopping mall in downtown Salt Lake City, and dozens of commercial buildings (Gottlieb and Wiley 1984, 95–128; Heinerman and Shupe 1985).

As twentieth century Mormonism developed, positions of leadership in the church hierarchy became progressively more difficult for the "common man" to acquire, particularly in the urban areas, and tended to be granted to the successful businessman or professional. In the 1930s, Wesley P. Lloyd (1937, 151–153) examined the occupations of upper echelon Mormon officers at the time of their appointments. Table 1-1 below lists the occupational areas of the General Authorities.

Table 1-1
Occupational Areas of the General Authorities of the Mormon Church at the Time of Their Appointments

| Church Position | Number of Members | Occupational Area at Time of Appointment (Number of Individuals Holding Position) |
|---|---|---|
| First Presidency | 3 | Business (1)<br>Law (1)<br>Education (1) |
| Apostles | 12 | Education (5)<br>Business (4)<br>Law (2)<br>Farming (1) |
| Presidents of the Seventy | 7 | Business (4)<br>Education (1)<br>Livestock (1)<br>Mission President (1) |
| Presiding Bishopric | 3 | Engineering (1)<br>Farming (1)<br>Bookkeeping (1) |

*Source:* Adapted from data present in Lloyd (1937, 152).
*Note:* Presiding Patriarch unoccupied at time of study.

J. Kenneth Davies (1963) conducted an exhaustive study of the socioeconomic structure of 1,160 Mormon family units derived from a random sample of thirty-seven stakes located in Arizona, California, Colorado, Idaho, New Mexico, New York, Texas, Utah, Washington, and Wyoming. Table 1-2 below summarizes some of the data compiled by Davies in a much more abbreviated form than he presents in his article. Seven categories of church members were presented, but only category 1 (members most active) and category 7 (members completely inactive) are presented in Table 1-2.

Table 1-2 shows that church officers and "most active" members were more often college graduates and Republicans than "general" and "completely nonactive members." No stake presidents in the sample were skilled or unskilled laborers, whereas 16.7 percent of the bishops were in this group as compared with 37.5 percent of the general membership. The greater the church inactivity, the more were members found to be skilled or unskilled laborers. It is interesting to note, and perhaps

Table 1-2
Socioeconomic and Political Characteristics of Mormon Church Officers and Members

| Category | Completed College (%) | Political Affiliation | | | Occupation | | | | |
|---|---|---|---|---|---|---|---|---|---|
| | | Rep. | Dem. | Other | A | B | C | D | E |
| Stake presidents | 42.8 | 89.3 | 10.7 | 0.0 | 60.7 | 10.7 | 7.1 | 21.5 | 0.0 |
| Bishops | 25.0 | 55.6 | 22.2 | 22.2 | 30.6 | 19.4 | 16.7 | 16.6 | 16.7 |
| General members | 13.2 | 40.8 | 38.3 | 20.9 | 26.6 | 9.0 | 13.6 | 15.3 | 37.5 |
| Class 1—most active | 23.1 | 58.4 | 24.1 | 17.6 | 28.2 | 17.2 | 23.4 | 15.8 | 14.9 |
| Class 7—completely non-active | 10.1 | 31.3 | 48.3 | 20.4 | 30.4 | 6.8 | 6.1 | 12.1 | 44.5 |

*Source*: Adapted from data present in Davies (1963, 87).
*Note*: Item A consists of supervisors and owners; item B primarily professionals (including teachers); item C farmers; item D sales and office workers; and item E skilled and unskilled laborers.

somewhat paradoxical, that a relatively high percentage of class seven members were supervisors or owners. J. Kenneth Davies (1963, 93) states that "it may possibly be true that there is something about the church which drives the working man out of activity." Davies' study of the Mormon Church's "middle-class propensities" clearly illustrates its accommodation to secular political and economic institutions during the twentieth century. Whereas nineteenth century Mormonism drew its converts from the "disinherited" and often substituted religious for social status, twentieth century Mormonism achieved middle class respectability and made religious and social status congruent.

Efforts to fit Mormonism into one or another of the categories that social scientists have devised to classify religious movements have proven to be elusive (Ahlstorm 1972, 508; Michaelsen 1977; Shipps 1985; Stark and Bainbridge 1986). In attempting to define the Mormon Church as a religious organization, it is crucial that it be placed into a temporal as well as a sociocultural context. The Mormon Church cannot be defined in the same way within the larger context of American society as it might be in the more restricted context of the Intermountain West, where it is by far the most dominant religious organization demographically, politically and economically.

Based on the distinction that Max Weber made between priest and prophet, Ernst Troeltsch makes a distinction between church and sect. According to Troeltsch (1931, vol. 1), the church recognizes the strength of the secular world and accepts the main aspects of its structure. The church is mobile and adaptive and "utilizes the state and the ruling classes, and weaves these elements into her own life; she then becomes an integral part of the existing social order; from this standpoint, then, the Church both stabilizes and determines the social order; in so doing, however, she becomes dependent upon the upper classes, and upon their development" (Troeltsch, vol. 1, 331). The sect develops when the church loses some of its ability to satisfy various group and individual needs. Troeltsch focuses primarily on lower class sects which he views as protests against the failures of the church to satisfy the lower classes emotionally, and to give them a sense of dignity. In a somewhat similar vein, Benton Johnson (1967, 127) defines a church as a "religious group that accepts the social environment in which it exists" and a sect as a "religious group that rejects the social environment in which it exists."

Without for the moment considering other typologies of religious groups, it seems apparent that the Mormon Church during the nineteenth century resembled the "sect" and that it has evolved into an approximation of the "church." As I have already noted, the Mormon Church during the nineteenth century rejected many aspects of the larger American society, including the latter's emphasis on individualism, competition, the concept of separation of church and state, and a strictly monogamous family structure. While Mormon leaders frequently lambast some of the more permissive or liberal trends in American society, they more often support more traditional American values and institutions, such as patriotism and the "free enterprise" system. Mormonism even goes so far as to regard the United States Constitution as a divinely inspired document. Mormons generally regard worldly pursuits, both in work and in recreation, as integral parts of the American way. The Mormon Church has probably accommodated itself more than any other religious organization to the political, economic, and social institutions of American society.

Roland Robertson (1970, 124) maintains that any classification of religious organizations must account for the "societal context" in which they exist. Consequently, he labels the Mormon Church in Great Britain as a "sect" but in the United States as an "institutionalized sect." In other words, the social position of Mormonism in Britain is much more marginal than in the United States where it has earned a fair degree of middle-class respectability. In a even more localized vein, Rodney Stark and William Sims Bainbridge (1985, 193) argue that whereas the Mormon Church and Mormon schismatic groups constitute "cults" in the larger society due to their drastic departure from the Judaeo-Christian tradition, "in the state of Utah, Mormonism is the dominant religious tradition. To be a Mormon in Utah is to be normal, not deviant." Following these arguments, if we consider the Mormon Church within the context of the state of Utah, it may be argued that it constitutes what Howard Becker termed an "ecclesia."

> The social structure known as the ecclesia is a predominantly conservative force, not in open conflict with the secular aspects of social life, and professedly universal in its aims . . . The fully developed ecclesia attempts to amalgamate with the state and the dominant classes, and strives to exercise control over every person in the population. Members are born into the ecclesia; they do not have to join it . . . The ecclesia naturally attaches a high importance to the means of grace which it administers, to the system of doctrine which it has formulated, and to the official administration of sacraments and teachings by official clergy . . . The ecclesia as an inclusive social structure is closely allied with national and economic interests; as a plurality pattern its very nature commits it to adjustment of its ethics to the secular world; it must represent the morality of the respectable majority (Becker 1932, 624–628).

The ecclesia includes people at all levels of society but is particularly well adapted to the needs of the dominant classes. Consequently, as I will show to be the case for the Mormon Church, some of its adherents have been and continue to be prone to seek out sectarian groups that much more adequately fulfill social, psychological, and cognitive functions of religious affiliation.

The notion that the Mormon Church may be viewed as an ecclesia with the context of the state of Utah is supported by the facts that about 70 percent of Utah's population is at least nominally Mormon, that about 90 percent of Utah's state legislators are Mormon, and that the resounding defeat of a proposal to ratify the Equal Rights Amendment in 1975 occurred after an editorial in the Mormon-operated newpaper, the *Deseret News*, opposed this measure. Furthermore, although the Mormon Church includes members from diversity of socioeconomic backgrounds, we have already noted its bourgeois tendencies.

H. Richard Niebuhr elaborated upon the church-sect typology by introducing the concept of "denomination." The denomination results when the sect loses its charismatic elements and institutionalization begins. Sectarian ideology promotes a puritanical ethic in its adherents, stressing self-discipline, frugality, thrift, and industry, which ultimately raises some of them to middle class status. Unlike the universalistic church, the denomination restricts its appeal to the middle classes and minimizes its critique of the larger society. The denomination claims: "While there are doubtless many keys to many mansions, it is at least in possession of one of them, and anyone who thinks he has the sole means to open the heavenly door is plainly mistaken," (Martin 1962, 5).

Despite its institutionalization and bourgeoisification, the Mormon Church cannot easily be marshaled into the category of denomination because of its nonacceptance of the legitimacy of other religious groups. Evidence of this is provided by former church president David O. McKay's statement on ecumenism in 1962: "I'm all for unity provided everyone joins the Mormon Church" (Whalen 1964, 292).

Another trait of the denomination as described by various scholars is the presence of a professional clergy—an indication that the religious organization has begun to accommodate to the larger society. In this regard, Mormonism retains a sectarian nature because of its emphasis on a lay clergy. Mormon bishops and stake presidents, for example, are always part-time clergymen, generally having relatively little formal training in theology. Even specialized and full-time church leaders, like members of the Presidency and the Twelve Apostles, generally lack formal training in theology and are largely self-educated in the intricacies of Mormon theology.

O'Dea (1954) maintains that the Mormon Church is a mixture of pure categories of types. Within the context of American society, it exhibits both sectarian and denominational features. Nevertheless, its hierarchical structure and conservative theological orientation give it a strikingly ecclesiastical quality. In fact, O'Dea (1954, 227) argues that the Mormons evolved from "near sect to near nation" in that they "had become a people, with their own subculture within larger American culture and their own homeland as part of the American homeland."

While the various categories associated with the church-sect continuum provide us with important heuristic devices for recognizing the accommodation of the Mormon Church to the larger society, they fail to consider the dynamic relationship between them. Categories such as 'church,' 'ecclesia,' and 'denomination' imply a passive acceptance of capitalist society on the part of the Mormon hierarchy. It may be argued that not only has the Mormon Church come to accept capitalism, but that it also has in essence become a full-fledged participant in it. In addition to being one of the fastest growing religious organizations in the world, the Mormon Church is also the richest church per capita. According to Leone (1979, 28), "The business and social practices of the modern church—the use of tithing as investment capital, the presence of church officials on boards of large corporations, opposition to labor, church patronage of favored businesses . . . and church investment in large enterprises like sugar refining—have combined with other practices to regenerate its wealth and sustain its growth."

Twentieth century Mormonism created an elaborate and complex bureaucracy to administer its financial, educational, missionary, building, welfare, and genealogical research programs (Alexander 1986). The church headquarters are now housed in a modern twenty-five story skyscraper adjacent to the Salt Lake Temple, towering over it and downtown commercial buildings. Pictures of the First Presidency and the Quorum of Twelve Apostles depict elderly and some middle-aged men in conservative business suits who give the viewer the distinct impression that he is looking at the board of directors of a thriving corporation instead of the leaders of a religious organization per se. Indeed, considering that these same men sit on the boards of church-owned and church-controlled businesses as well as those in which the church has substantial investment, this impression is not far off the mark.

Although other large religious bodies own large amounts of stock in and even occasionally may have representatives on the boards of national and multinational corporations, the Mormon Church appears best to exemplify a merger of entrepreneurial and ecclesiastical goals and objectives. Despite the fact that the Roman Catholic Church is the richest religious body both in the United States and in the world (keeping in mind that it has the largest church membership in these respective settings), it does not as general policy recruit individuals into its clergy on the basis of their business acumen, although there is no denying that it may promote individuals within the hierarchy for this reason. The Mormon Church, on the congregational level and particularly on the level of the General Authorities, actively selects leaders who have proven themselves competent in business affairs.

In that the Mormon Church in many ways operates like a business corporation, it may be argued that the church constitutes an excellent example of what might be termed a "theocratic corporation" or "corporate church." Like the modern business corporation, the Mormon Church closely resembles the classical pyramidal bureaucracy in which all major decision-making processes and power are centralized at the apex. In the case of the church, policies of corporate investment and expansion are intricately intertwined with more explicitly religious undertakings, such as proselytism, the construction of chapels of worship services, and religious instruction. While, for example, a substantial share of the church's income is set aside for missionary activities, the tithes and other financial contributions from the ever-swelling numbers of new converts, not only in the United States but also in other parts of the world, undoubtedly more than offset this expenditure. In fact a significant portion of this expense is provided by the families of young missionaries who the church sends out to recruit new members.

The argument that the modern Mormon Church constitutes a corporate church is buttressed by data demonstrating that its assets rank it among the fifty largest corporations in the country (Beecham and Briscoe 1976). Elsewhere, in his discussion of the economic transition of Mormonism, White (1980, 107) observes: "While it is extremely difficult . . . to determine the extent of Mormon capitalism, there can be no doubt the contemporary church is a multinational corporation in the most profound sense." In a similar vein, Heinerman and Shupe (1985, 253) assert: "The LDS Church is a corporate religion which administers theologically determined decisions in the same manner as it does investment portfolios—and often mixes the two."

The Mormon Church still theoretically espouses the Law of Consecration or United Order and the concept of stewardship as ideals to be followed, but maintains that these are not followed because its members are generally not yet worthy and ready to do so. Joseph Smith maintained that United Order would have to be established before the Second Coming of Christ (Anderson 1942, 374). In actuality, there exists little serious discussion among Mormons about the establishment of communal living in the near future. As Gordon Shepherd and Gary Shepherd observe:

> Mormon accommodation not only meant renouncing the practice of plural marriage, it also meant—more essentially—greatly modifying the

> religion's fundamental objective of a temporal Zion or theocratic social order. The church relinquished its role as planner, financier, and regulator of the region's economic development. The ideal of the self-sufficient Mormon commonwealth was abandoned and Utah's material welfare was not subject to the outside domination of the national corporate economy. The church itself began making large-scale investments in various private commercial enterprises, which entangled church interests with capitalist business interests (Shepherd and Shepherd 1984, 35).

The Mormon hierarchy and most active Mormons are firm believers in the "free enterprise" system and often outspoken critics of unionism and the welfare state. The current church president, Ezra Taft Benson, is an ultraconservative who in the past has addressed and participated in John Birch Society activities. Considering these facts and the extensive involvement of the church in corporate capitalism, Mormon leaders are unlikely to reactivate nineteenth century Mormon collective ideals for some time to come.

Mormonism evolved first from a utopian sect in the Midwest into a near-independent theocratic state on the periphery of its parent society, and finally into a corporate church which is now an integral part of the very same society it once so vehemently rejected. It is important, however, to point out that Mormonism did not accommodate itself to the environment of the larger society simply because its leaders became corrupted by the trappings of capitalism. Quite in contrast, the Mormon hierarchy made vigorous efforts, particularly during the 1870s and 1880s, to resist the expansion of the outside world into Utah Territory. Ultimately, with the federal government threatening to dismantle the entire structure of the church, its leaders were forced to capitulate in order to ensure its survival.

Ironically, the compromises which ensured the survival of Mormonism resulted in various contradictions, such as class and profitmaking, that, when combined with the expansion of the Eastern political economy, led to the subordination of the Mormon populace by its own leaders as well as by the encroaching larger society. Thus, as Leone notes, we see a fulfillment of Marx's prediction that utopian movements, which emerge as responses to the evils of capitalism, are doomed to become "reactionary sects" if somehow they manage to survive:

> The last century was full of utopias in this country and abroad. All died out or were, like Mormonism, transformed. The members of most utopias were reabsorbed into society after having populated some frontier or performed some social experiment that the society was later willing to undertake itself in an altered form . . . Mormonism underwent the

> very transformation that Marx feared. Spawned, along with a large number of other utopian and religious movements, by major changes in human affairs in the nineteenth century, Mormonism rejected, though not completely, its parent and then was reabsorbed by the parent as a useful, even productive, and supportive component. The modern period of late capitalism has thus been presented with an effective set of supports which adjust themselves to absorb the most ferocious aspects of change while not seeing some of its upsetting effects (Leone 1979, 214–215).

In the next section, I will discuss the schismatic tendencies that have been a part of Mormonism since almost its very beginning. The accommodation of the Mormon Church to the political and economic institutions of American society resulted in the loss of many of its egalitarian and cooperative features. In response to this accommodation or routinization, various sects that appealed to the "disinherited" of Mormon culture emerged during the post-Manifesto era. The Aaronic Order, the focus of this book, will serve as a case study of the consequences of the transformation that Mormonism underwent during the nineteenth century.

## *Mormon Schisms*

Social scientists often note the abundance of religious bodies found in the United States. Like other religious movements, Mormonism has spawned a large number of sects that emerged directly or indirectly out of its mainstream. And like Joseph Smith, the leaders of Mormon schismatic groups have claimed that they received revelations. Some groups claimed that Joseph Smith had become a "fallen prophet" and/or rejected the doctrine of plural marriage.

Due to their nature as protest movement, sects show "fission rather than fusion processes" (Scharf 1970, 110). Yonina Talmon makes the following remarks concerning the "strong fissiparous tendencies" of millenarian movements:

> Millenarian movements suffer from frequent cessation and fission partly because they base their recruitment of their leaders on inspiration. A revelatory basis of recruitment facilitates the emergence of numerous leaders and prophets since many may claim divine inspiration. That is only a partial explanation as suggested by the fact that millenarian movements seem to suffer from fissiparous tendencies more than religious movements with equally inspirational leadership. It seems that because they teach rebellion against authority and probably attract

> rebellious and non-conformist and contentious people. The denial of authority seems to be a factor in perpetuating internecine strife (Talmon 1965, 528–529).

Given the importance of revelation as a basis for religious doctrine in Mormonism, it should be no surprise that it has spawned schisms of its own. While such spin-offs may occur at almost any time, it is more likely that they will appear during periods of cultural crisis. In the case of Mormonism, despite the fact that it has undergone a long series of minor crises, one may pinpoint three major crises that were especially significant in creating the conditions that were conducive to the formation of schismatic groups: (1) the assassination of the prophet Joseph Smith in 1844; (2) the Manifesto in 1890 which theoretically brought an end to plural marriage among the Mormons residing within the United States; and (3) the Great Depression of the 1930s which adversely affected Utah as it did other parts of the country. In the following section, I will review some of the schisms that have occurred in Mormonism.

### Period of 1830–1844

Nine groups broke directly away from the early Mormon Church prior to the killing of Joseph Smith by a mob in 1844. All of these schisms were small and quickly passed into obscurity. Nevertheless, they demonstrate that internal conflicts have been a part of Mormonism since its beginning. The first of these was established by Wycam Clark who, claiming to be a prophet, attracted five followers to his short-lived Pure Church of Christ in Kirtland, Ohio, in 1831 (Rich 1959, 1). A more significant offshoot, known as the Church of Christ, appeared during the Panic of 1837. Warren Parrish, treasurer of the Kirtland Safety Company, and his followers claimed that Joseph Smith was not a true prophet of God, confiscated funds from the bank, and temporarily gained control of the Kirtland temple and the church periodical, the LDS Messenger and Advocate (Morgan 1953, 256; Rich 1959, 2). This schism also came to a quick demise after the Kirtland Mormons joined their brethern in northern Missouri.

The most significant schism during this period involved a series of events which culminated in the assassination of Joseph Smith. Of particular importance in its formation was William Law, a wealthy entrepreneur who settled in Nauvoo, invested heavily in the city's real estate, construction and steam mills and quickly became Joseph's second counselor. According to Fawn Brodie (1971, 368), because William Law and Robert Foster, the other chief contractor in the city, "paid wages, while the prophet paid the workmen on the temple and the Nauvoo House in goods and city scrip, a nasty labor crisis resulted." Apparently this fundamental difference of economic philosophies came to a head when Joseph Smith, having had a revelation sanctioning the practice of plural marriage and busily enlarging his circle of wives, approached Law's wife. The friction that ensued resulted in Law and several of his compatriots establishing a church of their own and publishing a newspaper, the *Nauvoo Expositor*, which they used as a mouthpiece for demanding the repeal of the city charter, renouncing the secret practice of polygyny by certain members of the Mormon hierarchy, and severely criticizing Joseph Smith. Upon Joseph Smith's urging, the city council declared that the press was libelous and ordered it to be destroyed by the Nauvoo Legion. Upon an appeal of Law's group, Governor Thomas Ford demanded that Joseph Smith and everyone else implicated in the destruction of the *Expositor* submit themselves for trial in Warsaw, Illinois. After an unsuccessful attempt to escape across the Mississippi River to Iowa, Joseph Smith's brother Hyrum, convinced the prophet that they should give themselves up. During the wait for the trial, a mob assaulted the jail, shot and killed Joseph and Hyrum and wounded several others in the late afternoon of June 27, 1844. While Gentile antagonism toward the Mormons resulted in the killing of Joseph Smith, ironically, internal conflicts at Nauvoo were also instrumental in bringing about this event.

## Mormon Sects Resulting from the Succession Crisis Following the Assassination of Joseph Smith

Largely as a result of Joseph Smith's failure to present a clear plan of succession in the event of his death to the general membership of the church, his assassination was followed by a major crisis that divided the Mormons into several factions. Furthermore, the situation was even more complicated by the fact that "between 1834 and 1844 Joseph Smith had by word and action established precedents or authority for eight possible methods of succession: (1) by a counselor in the First Presidency, (2) by a special appointment, (3) through the office of Associate President, (4) by the Presiding Patriarch, (5) by the Council of Fifty, (6) by the Quorum of the Twelve Apostles, (7) by three priesthood councils, (8) by a descendant of Joseph Smith, Jr." (Quinn 1976b, 187). Brigham Young, the leader of the faction that favored succession by a member of the Quorum of Twelve Apostles, emerged as prophet-president of the largest contingent of Mormons—the one destined to transport the Mormon social experiment to the Intermountain West. Nevertheless, many other individuals appeared as claimants to Joseph Smith's mantle of leadership.

Perhaps the most colorful of the Mormon sects that emerged as a result of the succession crisis was the Church of Christ of Latter-Day Saints (Strangite) led by James J. Strang. According to Strang, Joseph

Smith had selected him to be the next Mormon leader and commissioned him to establish a new city in Wisconsin to be known as "Vorhee" or "Garden of Peace" (Webber 1959, 246–248). He also claimed to have found ancient metal records called the "Plates of Laban," which were translated into the Book of the Law of the Lord and presented the details of the organization of the Kingdom of God (Hansen 1967, 100–101). After a short stay in Wisconsin, the Strangites migrated to Beaver Island on Lake Michigan and established the Halycon Order of Illuminati with their leader as its "Imperial Primate." Strang later received a revelation condoning the practice of polygyny which he confirmed by taking five wives. The Strangites were besieged with internal conflicts, and on June 15, 1856, their leader was assassinated by two followers (O'Dea 1957, 71). Nevertheless, three small remnant groups continue to acknowledge James Strang as the legitimate successor of Joseph Smith (Shields 1982). The members of the largest of these, a group led by Vernon Swift, is centered in the Burlington (or Vorhee) area of Wisconsin and "worship on Saturday, try to observe the Law of Moses, and offer animal sacrifices to God" (Whalen 1964, 282).

Earlier in this chapter, we noted the important impetus that the infant Mormon Church received when Sidney Rigdon attached his congregation in the Western Reserve to it. While Rigdon played an extremely significant role in the development of Mormonism during its first decade, in time he encountered irreconcilable differences with Joseph Smith which resulted in the loss of his favored status. Despite the fact that he had not been deposed as First Counselor to the prophet, in 1841 Joseph Smith appointed John C. Bennett his assistant in the church presidency (Arrington and Bitton 1979, 72–73). In his position as second in command to Joseph Smith, Bennett became mayor of Nauvoo, the chancellor of the University of Nauvoo, and Brigadier General of the Nauvoo Legion.

Apparently this was too much for Rigdon, who removed himself to Pittsburgh, Pennsylvania. After Joseph Smith's assassination, Rigdon returned to Nauvoo, claiming that he was to lead the church as its "guardian" since he was still First Counselor. When the Quorum of Twelve Apostles rejected his offer, he was sustained as president at a conference of his followers in Pittsburgh on October 12, 1844, which was followed by the establishment on April 6, 1845 of yet another Mormon sect with the name of the Church of Christ (Quinn 1976b, 191). Although Rigdon attempted to gather a community at Greencastle, Pennsylvania, his social experiment disintegrated by the spring of 1847 (Morgan 1953, 258). Nevertheless, despite Rigdon's withdrawal into a life of seclusion in Friendship, New York, scattered groups, particularly in Iowa, remained loyal to him until his death in 1876.

In contrast to Rigdon, one of his converts, William Bickerton, was somewhat more successful in creating a permanent religious organization. Bickerton, the presiding elder of Rigdon's followers in West Elizabeth, Pennsylvania, became dissatisfied with Rigdon's claims and associated himself briefly with a branch of the Utah church in West Elizabeth. Bickerton organized his own group, the Church of Jesus Christ, in 1856. Despite the emergence of a number of sects out of this organization, the Church of Christ (Bickertonite) continues to survive, with its strongholds being in Pennsylvania, Ohio, New York, New Jersey, and Michigan (Morgan 1949, 50).

Of all the groups that have developed from the religion started by Joseph Smith, the only one that is relatively large and maintains a fairly strong rivalry with the Utah-based church is the Reorganized Church of Jesus Christ of Latter Day Saints headquartered in Independence, Missouri. During the 1970s the Reorganized Church claimed some 220,000 members, including those in foreign countries (Arrington and Bitton 1979, 93). It developed out of the merger in 1852 of former members of earlier Mormon schisms and other scattered Mormons (including Emma Smith, Joseph Smith's first wife) who had stayed behind in the Midwest after the assassination of Joseph Smith. The Mormon prophet's son, Joseph Smith, III, became president of the Reorganized Church in 1860, setting a precedent for the church's principle that its leader be a patrilineal descendant of Joseph Smith, Jr. A group of these "Josephites" established an Order of Enoch community in southern Iowa in 1870 and later established the town of Lamoni, which was the headquarters of the Reorganized Church until its removal to Independence in 1921 (O'Dea 1957, 188). Unlike the Utah church, the Reorganized Church denied until recently that Joseph Smith practiced polygyny and consequently rejected the doctrine of plural marriage, and denies the concept of the plurality of gods. Somewhat to the consternation of the Utah church, the Reorganized Church owns the Kirtland Temple, the original manuscript of the Book of Mormon handwritten by Oliver Cowdery and Emma Smith, and the graves of Joseph, Emma, and Hyrum Smith in Nauvoo. In addition to the Kansas City and Independence areas, other strongholds of this group are in the Los Angeles and Detroit areas (Whalen 1964, 275). According to William J. Whalen (1964, 288), "Although the Reorganized Church would reject the suggestion, it might be said that the Reorganized Church is in a sense a reform of Mormonism and a return to more orthodox Protestantism."

### Western Schisms prior to the Manifesto

During the second half of the nineteenth century, while various remnants of early Mormonism were fissioning and, on occasion, fusing (such as in the case of the Reorganized Church), the main contingent of Mormons were busily involved in the creation of a religious commonwealth in the West. Despite the increasing pressures exerted upon them by the expansion of Eastern capitalism into the Intermountain West, the period between 1847 and 1890 was one of relative solidarity for the Mormons. Nevertheless, even during this period they were not spared schismatic tendencies.

Ironically, the earliest of these Western schisms involved a group of Eastern Mormons who planned to meet their brethren in the Great Basin. In 1846 Samuel Brannan, a Mormon elder in New York, took a group of about 230 Mormons on the ship *Brooklyn* around Cape Horn. Many of these Mormons established an agricultural settlement, called New Hope, near the California gold fields. Brannan, who apparently decided that California was a better place than Utah to make his fortune, made the "Gold Discovered" announcement, advising those under his leadership to go to the gold areas. Brannan came into possession of "a store at Sutter's Fort, a river launch, a large stock of supplies brought on the *Brooklyn*, a considerable sum of church money (tithing) with which he could obtain more supplies, and a large fenced-in farm in New Hope" (Arrington 1958, 65).

Another schismatic group was established by Joseph Morris, an Englishman who had converted to Mormonism after he immigrated to the United States. Morris spoke out several times against what he regarded to be the excessive materialism of Brigham Young (Anderson 1981, 53). In 1859 he wrote a letter to Brigham Young claiming that he was "the seventh star spoken of by John the Revelator, representing the seventh angel that has come forth" (quoted from Arbaugh 1932, 183). When Young refused to become his First Counselor, Morris established a religious group on April 6, 1861. After a short time, he managed to gather about five hundred followers in a United Order community located at the mouth of Weber Canyon near Ogden. Morris, whose revelations were eventually compiled into a six-volume (664 page) scriptural document called "the Spirit Prevails," apparently was the most prolific prophet that the Mormon tradition has ever produced (O'Dea 1957, 105).

Trouble developed for the Morrisites when its members decided to withdraw from the community in the late spring of 1862 and to take what they had consecrated to the group. When several of these dissidents were caught, sentenced to be executed in one of Morris' revelations, and imprisoned at Kingston Fort, the headquarters of the community, Justice Kinney issued writs demanding the release of the prisoners. Morris was killed in the battle that ensued when his followers refused to release the prisoners to a militia that had been called out to enforce the judge's order.

After Morris's death, the sect broke into several factions, each with a prophet of its own. In 1865 many of the Morrisites settled at Soda Springs, Idaho, but were split by dissension, with some relocating in Nevada (Arbaugh 1932, 186–187). Later some went to California and others to the Deer Lodge Valley in Montana. Of these remnants of Morris' sect, the one led by George Williams had the largest following. In July, 1876, the Church of the Firstborn was established in San Francisco with George Williams, who claimed to be "Cainan" (one of the seven angels and the reincarnation of Melchizedek), as its prophet. Williams had his largest following in the Deer Lodge Valley, which he never visited (Anderson 1981, 208–212). By the 1940s, there were less than a dozen active Morrisites left. According to Anderson (1981, 229), the "Morrisites church" ended in 1954 with the death of its last leader, George Johnson of Deer Lodge.

The most significant schism in Utah prior to the Manifesto occurred shortly after the completion of the territory. In 1869 a group of prosperous Mormon merchants, including William S. Godbe, E. L. T. Harrison, Edward W. Tullidge, W. H. Sherman, and T. B. H. Stenhouse, questioned the autocratic policies of the church's hierarchy. Opposing Young's economic boycott on trade with Gentiles, the Godbeites campaigned for cooperation with non-Mormons and the development of mining. After the leaders of what came to be called the "New Movement" were excommunicated from the Mormon Church, they established the Church of Zion (Rich 1959, 64). Irrespective of the claim that the head of the new church was yet to come forth, Godbe and Harrison were chosen as counselors to its future president, understood to be Joseph Smith III, the son of Joseph Smith, Jr. The Godbeites added a new theological twist by dabbling in spiritualism. After the anticipated leader and thousands of converts failed to come forth, the Church of Zion disintegrated while its leaders turned more to political affairs rather than religious ones. What the Godbeites were actually calling for was accommodation to the larger political economy that the Mormon hierarchy was to undertake only a few decades later. In recognizing this, Klaus J. Hansen (1967, 183) notes that "It is an ironic commentary on social change that the liberalism of the Godbeites has become the conservatism of twentieth-century Mormons."

### Schisms during the Period of 1890–1928

Although the Manifesto of 1890 theoretically prohibited plural marriage among Mormons residing in the United States, this practice continued, even among members of the church hierarchy. As Samuel W. Taylor notes, for one thing, the exact status of the Manifesto was not at all clear to many Mormons, or Gentiles for that matter.

> Ordinarily, a revelation would come to public attention when presented at conference and accepted by the congregation. Yet the Manifesto was first issued as a press release from Washington by Utah delegate in Congress, John T. Caine, September 15, 1890. As such, it was signed only by Woodruff, not by the First Presidency as an official declaration ordinarily would have been. "We cannot resist the thought that this was not promoted by President Woodruff at all," the (Salt Lake) *Tribune* commented next morning, "but that it was prompted by shrewd men in the Church, and that the object is purely political (Taylor 1978, 38).

Despite the fact that the Manifesto appears at the end of the earlier revelations in the Doctrine and Covenants, it does not have the same standing as the latter, including Section 132 which legitimized plural marriage. Unlike other revelations, the unnumbered Manifesto is entitled "Official Declaration." Furthermore, the Manifesto didn't negate the religious significance of polygyny. According to sociologist Kimball Young (1954, 146), a grandson of Brigham Young, "It must be remembered that theologically speaking, plurality of wives is still a principle of Mormonism and this at least is one way of providing for future happiness and glory."

In many cases, plural marriages entered prior to 1890 continued. Many Mormons, including members of the church hierarchy, also entered into such relationships after the Manifesto. Plural marriages continued to be performed in Mexico where the First Presidency had created a polygynous refuge in 1885. While some of their marriages were done for those living in the Mormon colonies located in the states of Chihuahua and Sonora, in other cases the parties involved crossed over into Mexico just for the marriage ceremony, then returned into the United States. Contrary to common Mormon belief, these marriages violated Mexican law, but "officials agreed to turn a blind eye" to them (Quinn 1985, 17). At a time when the total membership of the Mormon Church was between 200,000 and 250,000, O'Dea (1957, 246) estimates that the number of Mormons living in polygynous households during the years 1890–1904 was in the order of 21,000–28,000. Apparently because the Mormon Church continued to contract plural marriages between 1890 and 1904, only one schism emerged during this period. In 1895 Israel A. J. Dennis received a revelation from an angel to form the Church of the First Born. "When Dennis was arrested and tried for adultery in 1896, he and his new wife (who was still legally married to another man) denied 'having ever had criminal relations,' and they were acquitted by the jury, but by then Dennis's schismatic polygamous organization had disintegrated" (Quinn 1985, 56).

In 1904, after being forced to testify at a Senate Committee hearing that he lived with his plural wives, Joseph F. Smith issued the "Second Manifesto" declaring again that plural marriages were forbidden and adding that those entering such arrangements would be excommunicated from the church. Two active polygynists among his fellow apostles—John W. Taylor and Matthias Cowley—were dismissed from their positions shortly afterwards. When Heber J. Grant, also a former polygynist, succeeded Smith as president of the Mormon Church, he decreed in April 1921 that his office would accelerate the fight against polygynists through increasing cooperation with law enforcement agencies.

Despite these warnings, various individuals and groups continued to practice and/or advocate polygyny, an activity which still exhibits a tremendous vitality in the Intermountain West. The continuation of plural marriage served as one of several rationales for many of the Mormon sects that have appeared during the twentieth century. The precursors of the contemporary polygynist sects, commonly referred to as Fundamentalists, can be traced to men such as Josiah Hickman, Samuel Eastman, John Tanner Clark, Moses Gudmundson, and Nathanial Baldwin. Hickman reportedly established a polygynist sect sometime between 1900 and 1903 (Carter 1961, 54). Samuel Eastman, a resident of Salt Lake City, claimed in 1904 that he was the One Mighty and Strong who was prophesied in the Mormon scriptures to come forth and restore the church (Carter 1969, 54–55; Shields 1982, 108). The group that he organized apparently was active for about thirty years. Paul Feil, Eastman's former secretary, claimed that he had been chosen to continue Eastman's work. Until he was killed in an automobile accident, he published a pamphlet and distributed copies of his revelations at conferences of the Mormon church during the 1930s and early 1940s.

A more central figure in the emergence of the Fundamentalist movement was John Tanner Clark, who was excommunicated from the church in 1905 after having circulated letters condemning the Manifesto and the church leaders. Clark, who also claimed to be the One Mighty and Strong, received financial support from Nathanial Baldwin, a former professor at Brigham Young University, for the publication of religious tracts condoning plural marriage (Singer 1979, 45). Baldwin, an ingenious and successful inventor of radio equipment, incorporated the Omega Investment Company in 1922.

Singer presents evidence indicating that Baldwin's factor provided the setting that proved to be crucial to the development of the present-day Fundamentalist movement:

> A list of the directors and other individuals involved with this corporation reads like a Who's Who of the early Fundamentalist movement in Utah. This fact is historically of interest because it ties together many of the individuals who later formed the Council of Friends of God, the present organization of the larger Fundamentalist groups in existence today. Among the prominent names in the post-manifesto polygamous movement who either worked for or were in some way affiliated with Baldwin, were: John T. Clark, Josiah Hickman, Clyde Neilson, Daniel Bateman, Paul Feil, Matthias Cowley, John W. Taylor, John Y. Barlow, Israel Barlow, Ianthus Barlow, Albert Barlow, Lyman Jessop, Moroni Jessop, Margarito Bautista, Leslie Broadbent, Joseph W. Musser, and Lorin Woolley. Undoubtedly, many of the ideas and beliefs of the contemporary Fundamentalist groups were formulated in the cottage meetings and prayer gatherings dating to the Baldwin period (Singer 1979, 51).

Contrary to popular belief, Baldwin did not insist that his employees be polygynists, but generously gave of his funds to polygynists who were in need of financial assistance in order to support their large families. Unfortunately for Baldwin and the Fundamentalist movement, the Baldwin radio industry went into a serious decline beginning in 1924, from which it never recovered.

Although somewhat peripheral to the emergence of the modern Fundamentalist movement, another interesting figure responsible for the establishment of a Mormon sect during the post-Manifesto periods was Moses Gudmundson, a former music professor at Brigham Young University. According to Kimball Young (1954, 426), "The Gudmundson colony was founded in 1918 in the western part of Juab County, Utah, and at best never had more than sixty residents." Prior to forming his cooperative community, Gudmundson had been involved with a group known as the Springville "Separatists" that periodically gathered for exuberent prayer meetings, which involved criticism of the Mormon hierarchy, communication with the spirit world, speaking-in-tongues, and interpretation of tongues. Hannah Sorenson, a colorful woman who arrived in the Utah Valley shortly after the turn of the century, attracted a sizable number of Mormons to her meetings. Some of the Separatists frequently climbed up Mt. Kolob, a mountain east of Springville, to pray, fast and heal (Shields 1982, 114). One of the principal doctrines of the group, later incorporated by Gudmundson into his group, was that of the "true mates"—a notion that certain individuals were spiritually intended for each other and consequently were free to live together.

Initially the Mormon Church did not oppose the Gudmundson group. In fact, the church organized a branch in the colony in December of 1919 with Gudmundson as its presiding elder (Young 1954, 428). By

Figure 1–1
Schismatic Tendencies of the Mormon Fundamentalist Movement

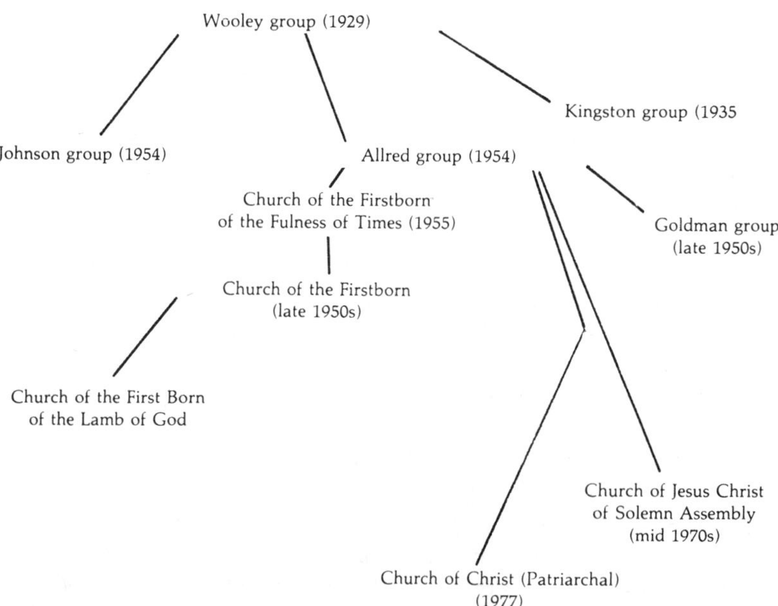


the spring of 1920, the tiny colony had become communal with a common fund, storehouse and dining hall. Apparently after Gudmundson began to claim communication with God and announced the "Principle of Wife Sacrifice," which permitted men who were not matched to their wives to take "spiritual wives," the church perceived the group as a threat to its authority.

These claims prompted the church to excommunicate Gudmundson and several of his followers in the spring of 1921. Shortly thereafter, these difficulties along with internal conflicts resulted in the temporary collapse of the colony with its leader moving to California. In August of the same year, Gudmundson suddenly reappeared and told his followers the day of destruction was upon them. The authorities immediately brought him to trial in Eureka, Utah, for adultery. After he was acquitted, he returned to Los Angeles along with a few of his followers.

## Schisms since the Great Depression

Most Fundamentalist groups point to a statement by Lorin Woolley in

September 1929 as the rationale for their practice of plural marriage (O'Dea 1957, 248–249; Wright 1963, 52–55; Carter 1969, 51–52). Woolley claimed that John Taylor, a polygynist president of the Mormon Church, called seven men together in September 1886 shortly before his death and told them that plural marriage was not to disappear from the face of the earth. Taylor was reportedly hiding from legal authorities in Centerville, Utah. He allegedly ordained Samuel Bateman, George Q. Cannon, John W. Woolley, Lorin Woolley, and Charles Wilkins (not all of whom were present at the secret meeting) as "apostles and patriarchs" to continue the practice of the plural marriage. Since Taylor was the president of the church, Fundamentalists view this purported instruction as a revelation which was to be carried out no matter what the costs.

Claiming direct authority from Taylor, Lorin Woolley ordained J. Leslie Broadbent, John Y. Barlow, Joseph W. Musser, and Charles F. Zitting to be "high priest-apostles" of the "Council of Friends"—a body designated to continue polygyny among the Mormons (Van Wagoner 1986, 209). When Woolley, the presiding officer of the organization, died on September 19, 1934, Broadbent took over his leadership. Broadbent, however, also passed away the following year, and Barlow, the senior member of the council, was designated as its presiding officer.

As is characteristic of religious sects, the Fundamentalist movement itself has exhibited more than its share of schismatic tendencies. Figure 1-1 above illustrates the linkages among the various Fundamentalist groups that have emerged either directly or indirectly from the one that Woolley started with his public statement in 1929 concerning the revelation allegedly given by President John Taylor over four decades earlier. The first schism emanating from the Woolley group occurred when upon Broadbent's death, Eldon Kingston claimed to have been the former's "second elder" and consequently his legitimate successor (Wright 1963, 58–59). When his claims were rejected by others in the organization, Kingston left and found a following among various people who were adversely affected by the Depression and were interested in practicing United Order.

After a short cooperative experiment in the vicinity of Ammon, Idaho, the Kingstonites returned to Utah. In 1943, under leadership of Charles W. Kingston, the group was incorporated as the Davis County Cooperative (Carter 1969, 55–56). John Ortel Kingston succeeded his father as the leader of the group and continued its various economic endeavors.

> By the 1970s, the co-op had successfully purchased and was operating at least thirty businesses in Utah. The Kingstons also owned several farms, including a 300-acre dairy farm in Woods Cross, a

> 1,000-acre general crop farm at Tetonia, Idaho, and a cattle ranch in Emery County. Add to that list of only the known businesses, their largest operation, a bituminous coal mine in Huntington Canyon, Utah, and a coal trucking business, and the group easily achieved the kind of self-sufficiency that Eldon had only dreamed about in 1941. In 1974 the group had about 500 members—some fifty families—who were worth, altogether, about $50 million, according to the best estimates (Bradlee and Atta 1981, 167).

While apparently the group had its roots in the Fundamentalist movement, it reportedly has attempted to sever its connections along these lines (Hilton 1965, 40).

Despite the fact that the Mormon Church stiffened its opposition to polygyny by issuing nine additional "manifestos" between 1904 and 1921 following the first two famous ones, plural marriage or "the Principle" continued to thrive during the 1920's (Taylor 1978, 99–100). On April 4, 1931, President Heber J. Grant announced that the church would offer legal assistance in the prosecution of individuals engaged in plural marriage. Following the church's "final Manifesto" in 1933, the Utah legislature passed a bill on March 14, 1935 declaring "unlawful cohabitation a felony." Apparently in response to the church's stringent position, a month later the Fundamentalists came "out of the closet" and began a monthly magazine, *Truth*, which continued to be published for the next fifteen years and was devoted to the defense of the Principle. The decision by its editor, Joseph W. Musser, to publish the speeches and writings of the nineteenth century Mormon leaders contributed to the church's concerted effort to suppress *Truth*.

> *Truth* was such a thorn in the official flesh that there was an attempt in 1944 to get rid of it. Musser was indicted on the charge of publishing an "obscene, lewd, and lascivious" magazine—which the fundamentalists considered hilarious for a periodical devoted to quotations from pioneer prophets. Evidently the judge saw the irony of the situation, for he threw the case out of the U.S. District Court (Taylor 1978, 100–101).

The following year fifteen Fundamentalist leaders, including Joseph W. Musser, Rulon Allred, John Y. Barlow, and Charles F. Zitting, were arrested, tried and convicted for practicing polygyny (Wright 1963, 60–61). After eleven of these men agreed to refrain from "advocating, teaching or countenancing" polygamy, they were paroled.

Short Creek, the well-known polygynous community on the Arizona-Utah border, affiliated with the Wooley group in the mid 1930s. A group of polygynists living at Lee's Ferry, Utah, about sixty-five miles to the east, decided that it would be safer to move into Arizona when around 1929 they heard rumors that the Mormon Church might take action against them (Young 1954, 432–435). When in 1935 the Arizona authorities prosecuted two residents for practicing polygamy, Joseph Musser and John Barlow came to assist them, and came to view Short Creek as a place where a large number of Fundamentalists could await the millennium. When Musser lost interest, the aging Barlow remained to become its spiritual leader and ordained one of its residents, LeRoy Johnson, to be his successor in the community. Short Creek was not self-supporting and was subsidized with funds from other Fundamentalists. Nevertheless, it became a showcase of the Principle (Taylor 1956, 120–130). The community operated on a quasi-communal basis called "United Effort," and since there were few local jobs and the land was harsh, many of the men worked elsewhere and contributed their wages to a common fund (Maloney 1974).

Given its status as a showcase for polygyny, it is not surprising that over the years the community experienced harassment. In July 1953, upon the order of the Arizona governor, over one hundred police officers raided Short Creek and arrested thirty-six men and women (Young 1954, 437–438). State welfare agencies initially planned to place all the children in foster homes. National outrage forced authorities to release the women and 263 children who had been taken into custody. As Richard S. Van Wagoner (1986, 204) observes: "The $600,000 'Operation Short Creek' failed to eradicate polygamy from the community. . . . Men returned from their jail sentences to their wives and children with increased resolve to 'live the principle' of polygamy." Since then, law enforcement agencies have looked the other way. The community, which renamed itself Colorado City in hopes of escaping some of its notoriety, has spilled over into Utah, and a nineteenth century Mormon practice is thriving and growing in the sparsely populated Arizona Strip.[3]

When John Barlow died in 1951, Joseph W. Musser succeeded him (Wright 1963, 61–62). Due to Musser's poor health and mental lapses, the other members of the presiding Council of the Woolley group had reservations concerning his leadership. When Musser ordained Rulon Allred and Margarito Bautista as High Priest Apostles and members of the Council, and designated Allred as his counselor, the members of the Council objected. The Council's refusal to recognize these appointments prompted Musser to form a new Council, of which Allred was second in command. Apparently the organization continued to operate with the same membership and two councils for the next few years. However, when Musser died on March 29, 1954, both councils claimed the right to determine his legitimate successor (Wright 1963, 64–65). Rulon Allred, the senior member of the new Council, became its presiding officer and continued in this capacity until he was asassinated in 1977. Allred's views were published in a newspaper called *The Star of Truth*. Charles Zitting's tenure as presiding officer of the old Council ended a few months later when he died on July 11, 1954. When the next two men in order of seniority declined leadership of the old Council, it went to LeRoy Johnson, who led the polygynous community at Short Creek until his recent death in late 1986. Guy Musser, a son of Joseph Musser, served as leader of the Johnsonite group in Salt Lake area (personal communication with Merrill Singer). Some members of this branch reside in a colony of some twenty white buildings located in Salt Lake City proper.

Much of the contention within the Fundamentalist movement has revolved around the issue of who holds the "keys" or the authority of the priesthoods and rights of succession to the Council leadership. Fundamentalists generally regard the Mormon Church as a legitimate body (Wright 1963, 73–73). Consequently, Fundamentalists tend to refer to the various factions by the names of their leaders (e.g., Johnsonites, Allredites, etc.). Most Fundamentalists apparently regard themselves to be members of the Mormon Church, even if they have been excommunicated by the latter. They often refer to themselves as "old line Mormons," "Joseph Smith Mormons," "old-fashioned Joseph Smith, Brigham Young, and John Taylor Mormons," and "Fundamentalist Mormons," while referring to regular church members as "popular Mormons." Since they are struggling to preserve the Principle, the Fundamentalists regard themselves as having achieved a higher level of sanctity than regular Mormons.

Many Fundamentalists recognize three levels of priesthood (a) the Melchizedek, (b) the Patriarchal, and (c) the Aaronic or Levitical (Wright 1963, 68–72). The highest of these is the Melchizedek priesthood, which includes the office of the President of the High Priesthood—a position that Fundamentalists claim was held by Joseph Smith entirely apart from his office as President of the Church. The High Priesthood is to consist of seventy members and is to be presided over by seven men. The "keys" to the priesthood reside within the Council of Seven. The President of the Priesthood, the Council of Seven, and Council of Seventy are regarded to be above the President of the church in authority. Since the High Priesthood organized the church, the latter cannot supercede the former's authority. Fundamentalists regard their excommunications from the Mormon Church to be invalid. Fundamentalists are not to organize a new church, but rather to preserve the integrity of the High Priesthood and to perpetuate the practice of plural marriage. Also they generally believe that the church leaders have lost the major keys and offices of the priesthood and access to divine revelation (Wright 1963, 75).

William Goldman was the leader of yet another polygynist group (personal communication with Merrill Singer). He was originally called to the old council by Joseph Musser sometime in the early 1950s. Following the 1954 split of the council, Goldman joined the Allredite faction and served on its council. He began conducting meetings and later established an Allredite branch in Farmington, a suburb located to the north of Salt Lake City. Eventually, Goldman began to claim that he held the "keys" or the authority to act as the leader of the Fundamentalists, and precipitated a major split with the Allredite group.

The most turbulent faction within the Fundamentalist movement has been connected with the LeBaron family of Mexico. Alma Dayer LeBaron, Sr., became loosely affiliated with the Fundamentalist movement during its early years in Utah. After he was excommunicated from the Mormon Church, he returned with his family to Colonia Juarez—one of the several Mormon colonies that had been established in northern Mexico during the 1880s when various polygynists were fleeing prosecution—and took a second wife (Wright 1963, 87–102). Although by this time the residents of Colonia Juarez had come to accept the church's ban on plural marriage, the LeBaron brothers attended the local Mormon school and became members of the church. Apparently they acquired the independent ways of their father, which eventually culminated in their expulsion from the Mormon Church during the 1940s. In fact, the eldest son, Benjamin T. LeBaron, began to claim during the 1930s that he was the One Mighty and Strong. In 1951 Margarito Bautista traveled to the LeBaron homestead at Galenda Springs in Chihuahua and organized a branch under the authority of Joseph W. Musser. Three of the brothers—Joel, Ervil, and Alma—joined the branch with the first two being designated elders. After about a year, the branch was briefly disbanded. In 1953 Bautista returned to the area and established a United Order community and appointed Joel LeBaron as its head. On September 21, 1955, Joel, Ross, and Floren LeBaron established their own sect, which was incorporated in Salt Lake City as the Church of the Firstborn of the Fulness of Time [sic]. The sect advocated plural marriage and claimed that its politico-religious hierarchy was of a higher status than either those of both the other Fundamentalists groups or of the Mormon Church (Wright 1963, 136–138, 147). The Mormon Church was viewed as a lower level in the LeBaron sect. Shortly after the establishment of the group, Ross split with Joel and formed his own organization which he simply called the "Church of the Firstborn."

Sometime later, another quarrel within the LeBaron family prompted Ervil to establish the Church of the First Born of the Lamb of God (Bradlee and Atta 1981). In 1972, over a power struggle for the "keys" in Mexico, Joel was murdered, and his brother, Ervil, convicted of instigating the crime. Taylor (1978, 105) notes: "Two years later Ervil was out of prison and accused of leading an attack on the Fundamentalist community of Los Molinos with firebombs and shotguns, in which two men were killed and nineteen people wounded." Still more violence within the Fundamentalist movement erupted when Rulon Allred was assassinated on May 19, 1979 in his naturopathic office by two women wearing wigs and heavy make-up. In May 1979 Mexican authorities finally apprehended Ervil LeBaron, who was convicted the following May in a U.S. courtroom for masterminding the assassination of Rulon Allred, and for conspiring the unsuccessful murder of his own brother, Verlan LeBaron (Van Wagoner 1986, 217). Ervil LeBaron died in his maximum security cell at the Utah State Prison. Owen Allred, Rulon's younger brother, became the new leader of the sect in August 1981. Considering that the various Fundamentalist sects are in common agreement on the Principle, it is indeed ironic that their history has been marked by factionalism and violence.

Probably the most colorful of the various polygynist sects is the group started by pistol-packing, ex-Marine Alex Joseph. In 1975 Joseph, some fifteen of his wives, and twenty-three other families settled on public land near Glen Canyon City in southern Utah (Davidson 1975). After joining the Mormon Church in 1965, Joseph caused a stir in his California ward by advocating plural marriage. After being excommunicated from the church in 1969, Joseph, along with his sister and twenty members of his ward, moved to the Allredite colony in Pinesdale, Montana. Differences apparently developed between Joseph and the leadership of the Allredite group, resulting in his decision to establish the Church of Christ of Solemn Assembly. In the fall of 1975, Joseph's group was evicted under a federal district court order from the Bureau of Land Management site upon which it had squatted. Nevertheless, members of the group, when not making forays for varying periods of time elsewhere, remained in the general vicinity. For awhile they settled near Highway 89 in the new town of Bac-Bone but quickly abandoned this site (*Salt Lake Tribune*, July 4, 1976). Recently, the group incorporated what was formerly called "Glen Canyon City" as the town of Big Water, and elected Alex Joseph as the community's mayor (*Salt Lake Tribune*, December 31, 1983). In 1986 Joseph ran for the Kane County Commission on the Liberitarian Party ticket, and led Big Water's four town council members into the Liberitarian fold (*Sunstone* 1986).

A fourth schism from the Allredite sect occurred in 1977 when John Brian established a "provisional church" called the "Church of Christ" (Patriarchal), which is preparing to establish a temple in which proper "sealings" can be performed (personal communication with Merrill Singer). In addition to plural marriage, the new sect advocates consecration of goods and United Order. It operates a storefront center with a "reading room" in downtown Salt Lake City and publishes various items, including a serial entitled *Voice of Zion*.

In addition to the organized Fundamentalist groups, enclaves and families of independent Fundamentalists are scattered about the Intermountain West and California. The Levites often speak of such an enclave of "independents" which reportedly is located north of Partoun in the Snake Valley. Law enforcement officers have estimated that perhaps as many as 35,000 individuals are members of Fundamentalist families (*Newsweek*, May 19, 1975). If indeed this is the case, the majority of Fundamentalists may be independents who choose to carry on the Principle in a less conspicuous manner than the organized sects. Furthermore, a fair number of these independents may continue to be active Mormons, patiently awaiting the day when the higher form of marriage will be reinstated by the Mormon leaders.

The various Fundamentalist sects as well as their precursors were not the only schisms that emerged during the twentieth century. It should be noted that the Reorganized Church of Jesus Christ Church of Latter-Day Saints, which probably may be accorded the sociological status of a denomination rather than a sect today, has also spawned a number of small sects. In addition, many of the current Mormon sects did not emerge directly from the Mormon Church but rather from earlier Mormon splinter groups.

While the Aaronic Order—the sect that constitutes the main concern in this book—does not condone plural marriage, it emerged during roughly the same time period as did the Fundamentalist movement. In fact, at least some of its early members, as well as many of those who investigated it during the 1930s and 1940s, were interested in polygyny. The fact that Maurice Glendenning was not reared a Mormon appears to have played a crucial role in the Levite rejection of plural marriage. But, as I will demonstrate in subsequent chapters, like the Fundamentalists and many other Mormon sects, the Levites were interested in revitalizing the egalitarian and communal ideals that mainstream Mormonism had lost after the Manifesto of 1890 due to its accommodation to the larger society.

# 2

# *The Aaronic Order as a Modern Revitalization Movement*

In this chapter, we will see that the Levite sect emerged as a revitalization movement which attempted to resurrect the *Gemeinschaft* ethos that its early adherents perceived twentieth century Mormonism to have lost. About one hundred years earlier, Mormonism itself had emerged as a revitalization movement that appealed to the "disinherited" in various parts of America, but also in Britain and several other European countries. Anthony F. C. Wallace's (1956a, 268) revitalization process "consists of five somewhat overlapping stages: (I) Steady State; (II) Period of Individual Stress; (III) Period of Cultural Distortion; (IV) Period of Revitalization [in which occur the functions of mazeway reformulation, communication, organization, adaptation, cultural transformation, and routinization], and finally, (V) New Steady State."

During the steady state stage, the vast majority of people in the population are able to utilize "culturally recognizable techniques for satisfying needs . . . with such efficiency that chronic stress within the system varies within tolerable limits" (Wallace 1956a, 268). Despite various threats that Mormons encountered from the westward expansion of the American political economy, the period between the 1850s and the late 1880s was one of relative stability—the vertible Golden Age of a new theocratic kingdom—dedicated, at least in theory, to ideals of cooperation and egalitarianism.

Following the Manifesto of 1890, however, Mormonism entered into a period of increased individual stress. During this phase, "the culture may remain essentially unchanged or it may undergo considerable changes [as was the case in Mormonism], but in either case there is continuous diminution in its efficiency in satisfying needs" (Wallace 1956a, 269). Essentially, as the twentieth century progressed, mainstream Mormonism increasingly lost many of its sectarian and utopian features, accommodated itself to the political economy of the United States and developed many bourgeois or middle class tendencies.

By the Roaring Twenties, Mormonism was well on its way to becoming fully integrated into the larger American political economy which it had initially shunned. The 1920s are generally depicted as a time of economic prosperity and frivolity. As Howard Zinn (1980, 373) observes, however, "prosperity was concentrated at the top" and widespread misery was the general lot for both black and white tenant farmers in the South, and European immigrants in the big cities "either without work or not making enough to get the basic necessities." In the Intermountain West, the Mormon Church was evolving into an organization in which the place of the "common man"—the type of man or woman who played an instrumental role in the colonization of the area—lost much relevancy and significance. While, as a result of the process of class struggle, the powers-to-be were forced to grant greater recognition to the common man. In their reluctant acceptance of labor unions, and the passage of various forms of social legislation, the Mormon hierarchy shifted from a radical and utopian philosophy to a conservative and capitalist one. Ephraim E. Ericksen a professor of philosophy at the University of Utah, captured the growing mood of many rank and file Mormons toward their church during the Jazz Age:

> This pecuniary point of view which has developed among the authorities of the church is criticized not only by some of the younger members of the church who find it out of harmony with their growing democratic ideals, but also by the older members of the church, who live in rural districts and have not kept pace with this developing business spirit, holding still to the old co-operative and communistic notion of the pioneers. The latter especially are inclined to question some of the business attitudes of their leaders. (Ericksen 1922, 71).

The period of cultural distortion began with the stock market crash of 1929. Mormons, like many other Americans, were adversely affected by the Great Depression. People react to internal distortions of the sociocultural system in different ways. According to Wallace (1956a, 269), "rigid persons apparently prefer to tolerate high levels of chronic stress rather than make systematic adaptive changes in the mazeway (or worldview). More flexible persons try out various limited mazeway changes in their personal lives, attempting to reduce stress by addition or substitution of mazeway elements with more or less concern for the *Gestalt* of the system."

Consequently, it is probably not a mere coincidence that what later became the Aaronic Order began to emerge shortly after the onset of the Depression. The dire events that a population or even a segment of a population faces as a result of deteriorating conditions are often forestalled or ameliorated by a revitalization movement, or, in the case of a complex society, a series of revitalization movements. For Americans during the Depression, the revitalization process took on various forms, including increased membership in labor unions, heightened political activism and radicalism, and religious innovation. Indeed, Anton T. Boisen (1939) notes that there was a great proliferation of new sects in American society during the 1930s. Some Mormons, particularly those of a working-class background, wanted to revitalize their church. As noted in the previous chapter, the Mormon Fundamentalist movement really began to accelerate during this time. While the Levite sect was not formally organized as a religious organization until the early 1940s, its beginnings go back to the early years of the Great Depression.

A religious revitalization movement is generally initiated by a charismatic individual who on the basis of a psychic experience provides a reformulated mazeway or "guide to action" which explains "his own and his society's troubles as being entirely or partly a result of the violation of certain rules" (Wallace 1956a, 270).

Maurice Glendenning was a prototypical prophet in that his messages from the Angel Elias served as the basis of a new religion. In addition to sharing his revelations with members of his Mormon ward, his disciples spread word about the firstborn son of Aaron who was ordained to put the House of Israel back in order throughout northern Utah.

The impetus for transforming the new movement into a formal organization came from Glendenning's most ardent disciples. In adapting to the opposition of the Mormon Church, the Levite prophet stressed that his revelations merely complemented those received earlier by Joseph Smith and the other Mormon prophet-presidents. While the intent of Glendenning's de-emphasis of a program of active prosleytism is not clear, it assured Mormon leaders that mass defections to the new "apostate" group were unlikely. The Levite prophet's rejection of plural marriage and incorporation of many aspects of evangelical Protestantism may have also deterred some disaffected Mormons from investigating the Order. Indeed, following the formative decades of the sect, new membership came more from biological reproduction than recruitment. Successful revitalization from Wallace's perspective occurs "as the whole or a controlling portion of the population comes to accept the new religion with its injunctions" (Wallace 1956a, 275). In this sense, the Aaronic Order is an abortive movement—one which had its development arrested at some intermediate stage. For the Levites, however, cultural transformation was exemplified in the establishment of a series of cooperative and communal ventures which were seen as reenactments of the nineteenth century ideal of United Order. However, not only has the Aaronic Order failed to halt the transformation of Mormonism from a religious utopia into a theocratic corporation, the Order itself as we will see in greater detail later in this book, also underwent a routinization and arrived at a steady state of its own. These developments in turn contributed to the emergence of a "revitalization movement within a revitalization movement" in the mid-1970s.

## *Glendenning and the Early Levites*

Max Weber (1963), Anthony Wallace (1956a, 1956b), Weston LaBarre (1962), Kenelm Burridge (1969) and others have stressed the importance of "prophets," "messiahs," and "culture heroes" in the establishment of revitalization movements. The Levites regard Glendenning to have been a "mediator" or "recorder" who transcribed the words of the Angel Elias, but he closely fits Wallace's characterization of the prophet in that he heard a voice, had visions, and formulated a new code for living. Just as Joseph Smith and his successor, Brigham Young, exerted strong and permanent influences on Mormonism, the same can be said of the effect that Glendenning had on the Levites. The relationship between Glendenning and his followers was not unilateral, but rather dialectical. According to Peter Worsley (1968, xiv), "A more valid model for the analysis of charismatic authority has to be interactionist: One in which followers with possibly utopian or at least diffuse and unrealized aspirations cleave to an appropriate leader because he articulates and consolidates their aspirations. He then specifies and narrows these aspirations, converting them both into more concrete and visible goals towards whose achievement collective action can be oriented and organized, and into *beliefs* which can be validated by reference to experience." In the case of concern to us, this relationship involved a congruence between the personal needs of Glendenning and the yearning of the Levites for the communitarian spirit that they found wanting in modern Mormonism. At the same time, however, a constant tension existed between Glendenning, whose roots were in Protestant evangelicalism, and the sons and daughters of the American Zion.

Most of the Levites as well as their prophet were people of humble social origins. Despite limited financial means, they had given generously to their church. As Mormons they had had to be satisfied with the vicarious experience of being members of what was rapidly becoming the richest church for its size in the world. The closest that they came to the wealth of the Mormon Church was their occasional, and in some cases frequent, pilgrimages to the inner chambers of the temple in Salt Lake City, or to one of the more modest temples in the outlying regions of Utah.

## Glendenning as a Charismatic Prophet

Since we still know relatively little about the psychic make-up of prophets and other religious founders, in my view a close examination of Maurice Glendenning constitutes one of the significant contributions of this study of the Levite sect. While I was able to obtain much information about the history of the Aaronic Order, unfortunately very little is known about the childhood and youth of its founder. Furthermore, because he was often away from his family for extended periods, gaps in information about his later life also exist. Even individuals who appear to have been the most intimate with Glendenning have only a superficial knowledge of major portions of his life. This paucity in important details about Glendenning's life supports Jacob A. Arlow's (1951, 378) contention that prophets generally reveal little about their personal lives. They often speak of the events in their lives in allegorical rhetoric—a pattern particularly true of Glendenning.

Prophets generally are described as possessing an elusive trait called "charisma." Max Weber (1947, 358–359) defined charisma as "a certain quality of an individual by virtue of which he is set apart from ordinary men and treated as endowed with supernatural, superhuman, or at least specifically exceptional powers or qualities." Charisma largely lies in the eyes of the beholder. Whereas some may regard an individual to be a divinely-inspired prophet or even a saint, others may view him as an imposter, a deluded megalomaniac, or an amusing but harmless eccentric. As Worsley (1968, xii) observes, charisma "sociologically viewed, is a social relationship, not an attribute of individual personality or a mystical quality."

The perceptions of Glendenning held by elderly and middle-aged Levites strongly indicate that indeed Glendenning was a prototype of the prophet. Many Levites noted that Maurice L. Glendenning was a striking figure to see and hear. He was only about five feet seven inches in height and fairly heavy (perhaps weighing two hundred pounds), but is described as a handsome man with a well-groomed beard (although at times he did not wear one) and, in later years, silver-colored hair. Some Levites commented that when Glendenning walked into a public place, people responded to his impressive appearance. Glendenning reportedly had the ability to read people's minds, to identify individuals whom he had never met by name, and to travel in the spirit to the inner sanctums of the Salt Lake temple as well as faraway places such as China. According to a Partoun resident who was involved in mining work with Glendenning, the Levite prophet had a "fourth dimension," which enabled him to go underground in the spirit in order to locate precious metals.

Many Levites perceive Glendenning as having been an interesting conversationalist and an extremely well-informed individual who could comment on almost every subject. A large number of diplomas and certificates (perhaps ten or more), including ones in chiropratic and naturopathy, adorned the walls of his office. Ralph D. Erickson (1969, 35) learned in a personal interview with Glendenning in 1966 that he held a Doctor of Chiropractic, Doctor of Electrical Therapeutics, and Doctor of Divinity degrees. Robert Conrod told me that although Glendenning did not hold a degree in geology, he could speak knowledgeably about the subject with geologists and petroleum engineers. Glendenning instituted the practice in the Aaronic Order of granting certificates to individuals who achieved various positions, such as discipleship, within it.

The Levites often spoke of the winning and charming personality which Glendenning had but readily admitted that he was "human" and had faults. He was warm, friendly, had a good sense of humor, rarely if ever was discouraged, made decisions quickly, and was very affectionate with children. A male informant stated that Glendenning "made people feel like they were something special." Two other informants noted that Glendenning told some people, including themselves, that he had known them in their earlier existences. A now deceased Second High Priest of the Order stated that Glendenning also told him this. Apparently Glendenning granted positions of leadership to individuals with whom he was impressed shortly after they joined the Order. A man now deceased was made the director of the Christian Aid Service of America and the chairman of the Supreme Council shortly after he joined the Order. Glendenning called Robert Conrad, who had lived at Eskdale for about a year before he actually joined the Order, to become the First High Priest shortly after his conversion. Some members maintained that Section 155 of the Book of Elias prophesized the coming of Conrad to the Order.

Members of the Aaronic Order were also impressed with Glendenning's willingness to help with the mundane work necessary for the establishment of the desert communities and his humble life style. Some remarked upon how Glendenning worked with a pick and shovel on the erection of a building or on the drilling of a well, even though he had more important tasks to perform. Others commented on the time when Glendenning lived in a building which had been designed as a chicken coop at the Springville branch farm. Many Levites spoke of the poverty, the poor and demeaning working conditions, and suffering which Glendenning experienced as a result of the curse for his failure to record the revelations given to him by the Angel Elias.

Glendenning received revelations from the Angel Elias at almost any time or place, although he was usually alone when he received them. He generally carried a pencil or a pen and a note pad with him so that he could record the revelations. Sometimes Glendenning received revelations while driving an automobile and would have to pull over to the side of the road to record a revelation. Glendenning received one of the revelations while he was studying in the Salt Lake City Library. He wrote the revelations down in a shorthand, called the Adamic language, which no one has been able to decipher. The Angel Elias taught him this shorthand in the "twinkling of an eye." In a somewhat similar vein, Joseph Smith claimed that the Book of Mormon was written in "Reformed Egyptian" and that he needed magic spectacles called the Urim and Thummin to translate it into English (Brodie 1971, 39–40). Robert Conrad is responsible for preserving the untranslated Writings which Glendenning had received. Glendenning publicly promulgated some of the revelations shortly after he had received them, but released others only years later when an appropriate occasion arose.

The Levitical Writings can be classified into the following categories: (1) those outlining the politico-religious organization of the Aaronic Order; (2) those establishing various rituals and ordinances; (3) those prescribing various rules and regulations (such as tithing, dietary proscriptions, etc.); (4) those defining specific theological or cosmological points; (5) those defining the lineage and work of Glendenning and the Levites; (6) those urging the Levites to gather and work together; (7) those warning of internal opposition to the work of the Levites; and (8) those describing visions which Glendenning had. In reality a single Writing may include a number of the categories outlined above. Some of the Levitical Writings are letters, referred to as "epistles," from Glendenning to the Levites. Most of the Writings are, however, the recordings of the revelations that Glendenning received from the Angel Elias. Glendenning is referred to as "Aubrey," his spirit name, in many of the Writings.

Although Glendenning's lineage was revealed in a number of Writings, he also discovered other evidence indicating that he was a lineal descendant of Aaron. In 1945 and 1946 Glendenning and his wife began genealogical work to prove that he was an Aaronite and traveled throughout the Midwest and eastern United States (Beeston 1957, 142–157). He reportedly found two important items, which are now relics of the Order, establishing his lineage—the Catskin and Marble Tablet. The Catskin, which was found in the spring of 1946 at a farm in an old trunk (Beeston 1957, 145–148), contained a blessing written in A.D. 1799 from Glendenning's great-great-grandfather to his son noting that the Glendennings were Aaronites. Shortly thereafter, Glendenning had a vision that directed him to the discovery of the Marble Tablet at his grandfather's abandoned homestead in Missouri (Beeston 1957, 148–151). The Marble Tablet contained a blessing written in A.D. 1863 from Maurice Glendenning's grandfather to his son, again noting that the Glendennings were lineal descendants of Aaron.

**Glendenning among the Mormons**

On the surface, Glendenning lived an ordinary, perhaps some may even say a pathetic and tragic life. It is highly doubtful that he and the Levites will ever receive the place in the annals of American history that Joseph Smith, Brigham Young, and the Mormons have won. At one level, Glendenning is probably closer to the average religious founder than were men like John Wesley and Joseph Smith or women such as Mary Baker Eddy and Ellen G. White. The latter were great prophets, for the religious groups that they started became relatively well-known and in some cases large denominations. Glendenning was one of the countless number of minor prophets who at best receive a footnote here and there or, perhaps more often, are quickly forgotten after they and their religions pass into obscurity. On another level, however, there is a bit of all of us in Glendenning and his followers. Perhaps anyone given the proper time and circumstances might choose to seek truth in a manner not too different from the Levites. Members of the Aaronic Order represent one example of the "search of the primitive," which Stanley Diamond (1974) so cogently describes, that humanity embarked upon following its attainment of civilization and its accompanying alienation and solitude. It is only when viewed in this light than an account of the history of the Levite sect has any real significance.

Glendenning, often involuntarily, moved from place to place throughout the entire course of his life. While his wanderings became less frequent in his later years, even after the Aaronic Order was well established, he continued to move frequently, spending perhaps several months at the Eskdale commune, several months during the winter in Arizona, and varying periods in other locations. Glendenning was born on February 15, 1891, in Randolph, Kansas, a community that was later to be eliminated by the construction of a reservoir. Because his father was a traveling Methodist minister and photographer, during his early years Maurice lived in Oregon, Montana, and Nebraska.

The Levite prophet claimed that at the age of seven years he began to hear "faint sounds of music" and the singing of a choir which no one else could hear (Beeston 1966, 17–19). About this time, Glendenning's father told him about his descent from Aaron and that this knowledge had been transmitted in the Glendenning lineage for many generations. Several years later the young Glendenning began to hear one voice in the choir especially, and by fourteen years of age he began receiving poems from this voice. When Glendenning was sixteen years old, the voice began to give him messages, many of which he did not understand (Beeston 1966, 20).

Glendenning met his wife, Helen, who was a member of one of the churches on his father's ministerial circuit. When they married in 1915, Maurice was twenty-four years old and his wife eighteen. The Glendennings lived on Maurice's homestead near Gordon, Nebraska, for about a year and then moved to Davenport, Iowa, where he studied chiropractic. Glendenning's involvement in what Wardwell (1952) termed a "marginal profession" is symbolic of the Levite prophet's marginality in the larger society. In his choice of a professional career, his marginality is further illustrated by his attendance at a now defunct chiropractic rival of the Palmer College of Chiropractic, the Mecca of American chiropractic. It is not clear whether Glendenning chose to attend the former institution because he could not afford to attend, or was not accepted at the latter, or for some other reason. Over the course of the next several years, Glendenning acquired additional training in various other forms of heterodox medicine, including naturopathy and electrical therapeutics. As in his religious views, the Levite prophet exhibited a predilection for eclecticism in his healing endeavors.

Over the years, the voice periodically spoke to Glendenning about his mission. Due to ridicule and lack of comprehension of the messages, Glendenning ceased writing them down (Beeston, 22). In fact, he did not admit to his wife until years after they had married that he had received mysterious messages from a supernatural source. As punishment for disregarding the voice, a curse was placed on Glendenning in 1923. As the following passages from the message indicate, the voice informed him that he would not prosper, would be poor and hungry, and be forced to roam the earth for seven years:

> Because of your disobedience and because that you have offended me and grieved me, by giving no heed unto my saying unto you, and that you have not written the things which have been given unto you to write, you have brought upon your head a curse and you shall not prosper nor your household.
>
> You shall become poor and hungry and your house shall suffer and for seven years shall poverty reign over you and your house.
>
> You shall be known upon the records of man and they shall talk of you among themselves and you shall not know their words but they shall be powerful against you and you shall not be able to buy, and because of this curse, they shall say evil things against you. . . .
>
> You shall be a roamer on the earth, but there shall be found no place for you until I shall plant you in a place by a water to finish your work (Book of Elias 1944, Sect. 137).

The message, however, promised Glendenning that in time the curse would be lifted and that he would be able to fulfill his preordained mission. As the message predicted, the next several years were ones of personal failure, trial and wandering. When Glendenning's chiropractic practice in Kansas began to dwindle, he closed it and moved his family to Bartlesville, Oklahoma, for a short time (Beeston 1966, 25–26). In 1925 the Glendennings moved to Colorado Springs, Colorado, where they still experienced financial difficulties. Glendenning did not tell his wife about his curse until 1926, at which time he took the Writing with the curse out of a trunk to explain to her the reason for their economic hardships. Glendenning received four more Writings in 1926, but did not receive another Writing until August 1929, after he and his family had moved to Provo, Utah.

In 1928, Glendenning moved to Salt Lake City. After his wife and daughter joined him in Utah, the Glendennings settled down in Provo, a staunch Mormon community forty-five miles south of Salt Lake City. On April 14, 1929, the Glendennings decided to join the Mormon Church after they had witnessed the baptism of their only child into that religious body, thinking that it was improper for them not to share the religion of their daughter. They became active in church activities and looked forward to the day when they would receive a temple recommend, allowing them to perform various religious rituals which only "worthy" Mormons may engage in. Glendenning found certain concepts in Mormonism similar to those in the Writings that he had received (Beeston, 35–36). On July 16, 1930, he received a Writing in which the voice identified itself as the "Elias who should come in the last days" (Book of Elias 1944, Sec. 166, 37). In a later Writing the voice identified itself as a forerunner and messenger for God, prophesying the Second Coming of Christ (Book of Elias 1944, Sec. 185, 62–63).

It was not long before the Mormon Church's hierarchy opposed Glendenning's claims. Mormonism teaches that the only individual who may receive revelations that are relevant to all members of the church is the president or "prophet" of the church. The Mormon Church formally condemned the claims of various religious groups at the annual church conference in April 1931 (Beeston 1966, 38). On the same day that the Mormon Church made its condemnation, Glendenning received a revelation instructing "you of the house of Ephraim (referring to members of the Mormon Church), who shall go before Levi, prepare yourselves to be received with Levi" (Book of Elias 1944, Sec. 189, 67). In other words, the Writing informed the Mormons that they were to accept the Levites as the priesthood tribe of Israel. Between the early 1930s and 1942 discussion meetings dealing with the Writings, which Glendenning periodically received, were held in the homes of interested people in the Salt Lake and Utah Valleys. Apparently during this period, a fair number of people investigated Glendenning's claims but gradually lost interest. Nevertheless, Glendenning gained a small but devoted following during the 1930s which formed the nucleus of the Aaronic Order when it was formally established in 1942.

Although Glendenning found a small number of Mormons who were sympathetic to his Writings in northern Utah, the Great Depression continued to be a period of wandering for Glendenning and his family. According to a knowledgeable informant, Glendenning held a series of jobs in the Provo area before embarking for seemingly greener pastures, but lost them as employers learned about his Writings. For example, after working in the furniture department of a well-known chain store for about two months, his boss told him that he would have to be laid off to prevent any potential loss of Mormon customers. The same reason was given for dismissing Glendenning from his next job at a gasoline station. After an unsuccessful communal venture (which will be discussed in greater detail in chapter 4) with some of his followers near Alton, a village in southwestern Utah, Glendenning moved his family to LaVerkin in Washington County, Utah, in 1934. Part of the reason for this move was to provide the Glendenning girl, who had by now graduated from grade school, an opportunity to attend high school in Hurricane, a community a few miles from LaVerkin. Glendenning obtained a construction job in Zion National Park for several months. After this, he purchased a gasoline station. Since he hired an operator for his gasoline station, he was still free to engage in various other business endeavors. For awhile he was involved in a mining enterprise with several other men in Las Vegas, resulting in frequent absences from home. After their daughter graduated from Hurricane High School in 1938, the Glendennings moved to Los Angeles where both Maurice and Helen acquired chiropractic licenses.

Glendenning maintained sporadic contact with the dissident Mormons in northern Utah who were attracted to his teachings during the 1930s and the early 1940s. Some of them occasionally visited him in Los Angeles, not only for spiritual guidance but also for health care. One Levite woman recalled "that he had a curious machine in his office which permitted heavenly music to be heard emanating from one's own body. Some were able to hear even strange languages through that instrument" (*Aaron' Star*, July-August 1968, p. 11). This woman told me that Glendenning also invented a "gold ray" instrument with healing powers.

Glendenning provided the basic theological framework for a new religion, but his followers took the initiative in bringing about the formal establishment of the Aaronic Order as an incorporated religious organization. As Worsley (1968, xiv) argues, in many instances "The followers, then, in a dialectical way, create, by selecting them out, the leaders, who in turn *command* on the basis of this newly-accorded *legitimacy*." While Glendenning lived in southern Utah and in Los Angeles, small groups still regularly met in the Salt Lake City and Provo areas to discuss the Writings. Some of Glendenning's followers expressed concern that an organization based on the Writings had not yet been established (Beeston 1957, 90–93). A married couple visited Glendenning in Los Angeles in September 1942 and asked him whether the time was ripe to begin "the work of Levi." When the couple returned to Utah with an affirmative answer, a party of two married couples and two women arranged to visit Glendenning. In late November of 1942 they consecrated their belongings for the establishment of the Aaronic Order. Glendenning gave the group various instructions for the establishment of the Aaronic Order, including the details of a weekly sacrament ritual. In 1943 articles of incorporation were filed with the state of Utah under the name "Aaronic Order" or "Order of Aaron" as a nonprofit, religious organization listing Maurice L. Glendenning as its president. The Aaronic Order also was referred to as the "House of Aaron," the "House of Levi," the "True Church of God," the "Church of the Firstborn," the "Church of Christ," and the "Church in the Wilderness."

At first Glendenning intended to direct the activities of the Aaronic Order from California. Since he had recently reestablished his chiropractic practice, he was somewhat reluctant to return to Utah. Glendenning was able to build a relatively successful practice, but it was not long before the rent on his office was raised to a prohibitively high rate. When he was unable to find a suitable office, Glendenning and his wife returned to Utah in the spring of 1944. Despite his return to Zion, Glendenning continued to live the life of a wanderer. After living in Salt Lake City for a short period of time, he became involved in various mining ventures with some of the Levites. During the summer of 1945, Glendenning visited cemeteries in Missouri in order to confirm his lineage as a firstborn son of Aaron. During the course of this research, he met a Mormon woman who was also conducting genealogical work. Glendenning's failure to return the car that he had borrowed from the women to visit the cemeteries at the expected time prompted her to contact the police. Glendenning had been unable to return the car because it had gotten stuck on a muddy back road. The Levite prophet was cleared of the charge of having stolen the car, but was arrested for impersonating a military officer. During World War II Glendenning wore a military uniform to designate his membership in a voluntary chiropractic association dedicated to assisting the war effort. One elderly Levite, however, suggested to me that perhaps another reason that Glendenning wore the uniform was because he was "trying to be big." On March 19, 1946, the *Deseret News*, the Mormon-owned Salt Lake City daily newspaper, reported the following concerning the incident in Missouri and its alleged consequences:

> Glendenning was recently sentenced to sixty days in prison in Kansas City, Missouri, following conviction in the federal courts there to charges of illegally wearing a soldier's uniform carrying the insignia of a captain in the U.S. Medical Corps. He pleaded guilty to the charges and was committed to the Medical Center for federal prisoners at Springfield, Missouri, on August 31, 1945. He was released October 29, 1945. He is now displaced from the presidency of the cult after less than three years control.

The article goes on to note that new and amended articles of incorporation were "signed by Edwin W. Lee of Layton, as the new president and member of the 'supreme council' of the cult." Although the article strongly suggests that Glendenning was deposed for a period of time as the leader of the Aaronic Order, it is somewhat difficult to determine whether or not this was indeed the case. According to one elderly man who was a member of the Order at the time, Lee served as the President for only several months. Robert Conrad told me that there have been times in the history of the Order when the offices of Chief High Priest and President were occupied by different individuals. Partly because he was often away from Utah for extended periods, Glendenning sometimes did not desire to serve as President.

Peter Worsley (1968, xvi–xvii) and others argue that the leadership of a revitalization or millenarian movements may be divided among several people or separately embodied in two distinct persons, one of whom functions as the prophet or dreamer and the other who functions as the organizer or doer. As Bernard Devoto (1936, 106–107) observes, "Whatever else Smith was, he was primarily a prophet, a religious leader, a man drunk on God and glory . . . Young was primarily an organizer of the kingdom on this earth, an administrative and executive genius of the first order, the greatest colonizer in American history." While it is true that Mormonism enjoyed relative growth and prosperity under the mantle of Joseph Smith's leadership, it was not until Brigham Young became the prophet-president of the church and took it to the safety of the Intermountain West that it became an ecclesiastical dynamo.

To a large extent, the distinction of leadership roles also existed in the Aaronic Order, at least until the death of Glendenning in 1969. During the early years of the Order, since Glendenning was absent much of the time, the actual construction of the Order was a collective endeavor carried out under the leadership of his disciples. Glendenning provided the inspiration for the group, but it is not clear as to what degree he contributed to its actual development on a day-to-day basis. As we will see in chapter 4, a formal distinction between the spiritual leadership and the temporal leadership of the Aaronic Order was institutionalized later in the offices of the Chief High Priest and the First High Priest, respectively. Glendenning appointed Robert Conrad, a man with highly-developed administrative skills in business and education, to serve as the First High Priest. The Levites believe that upon the death of Glendenning, the Angel Elias ceased speaking directly to them, a matter which was dealt with in a revelation that their prophet received entitled "No Other to Receive My Voice" (Book of New Revelations 1948, Chap. 24, 65–66). While the Levites hold the opinions of Robert Conrad, the present Chief High Priest, in high regard, it is maintained that he is guided by "inspiration" on religious matters but does not hear a voice per se.

## *The Need of the Early Levites to Revitalize Mormonism*

We have seen thus far that Glendenning and his followers were involved in a dialectical relationship with one another that culminated in the establishment of the Aaronic Order. In his discussion of the "culture hero" or "prophet," Weston LaBarre (1972, 342) notes that "In one sense he is an exponent of his generation." Maurice Glendenning found an appeal among a certain segment of the disinherited of Mormonism because he was able to convince them that the *Gemeinschaft* of a former golden age could be restored. In this section, I will attempt to identify the types of people who were attracted to Glendenning's message during the 1930s and 1940s as well as to explain why they so ardently desired to revitalize modern Mormonism. My conversations with longtime members of the Aaronic Order suggested to me at an early point in my research that the people who showed a strong interest in the Levitical Writings during the 1930s and the 1940s were often adversely affected by the Depression. Some of these people exhibited an avid interest in polygyny and "dream mines." Both of these matters appealed to certain working class Mormons, and may be viewed as an attempt on their part to breathe new life into their religion. In a sense, the movements that emanated from these concerns were predecessors of the Aaronic Order and the Fundamentalist movement in that they addressed the same basic issues, namely, the accommodation of the Mormon Church to the larger society and its relaxation of egalitarian and communitarian ideals.

Since most of those who showed interest in the Writings during the 1930s sooner or later lost interest in them, perhaps due to the condemnation by the Mormon Church, I only have been able to reconstruct a partial glimpse of the impact of the Depression on the early Levites. Nevertheless, the following two vignettes do not appear to be atypical depictions of the conditions faced by many of Glendenning's followers during the Depression.

Henry, whose conversion experience will be described in detail in chapter 3, noted that he and many of Glendenning's followers were often unemployed during the early years of the depression. When he lost his job as a "lead man" in the electric shop of the Rio Grande and Denver Railroad in 1929, he went to work at the Koyle Dream Mine for eighteen months at a nominal wage of several dollars per week, and still later worked at the Brigham Dream Mine. Later, Henry obtained temporary employment as a carpenter on a work project at the Hotel Utah. According to Henry, his employment history during the Depression alternated between "good work" and "bad work," interspersed with periods of no work. During his periods of unemployment he did a "lot of temple work." During one of these periods he learned about the firstborn son of Aaron in Provo.

Helen and her husband, Paul, attempted to pull themselves through the early years of the Depression by leaving Utah to work in the Star Valley of western Wyoming. At first they raised carrots, lettuce, and some pigs on a leased lot. Later Paul ran a butcher shop with his brother-in-law, while Helen sold cinnamon rolls in the shop. Because they were "barely making a living" and had recently heard about Glendenning, they decided to return to the Utah Valley. Paul purchased a truck, which he initially used to haul cattle to Salt Lake City, and later fruit which he sold in the Star Valley. As the Great Depression worsened, they could no longer make the payments on their truck. Paul eventually was able to improve their financial situation after he obtained mining leases in the Great Basin.

Data that I collected on the background of individuals who joined the Levite sect during its formative years indicate that they were primarily individuals of low socioeconomic status. Tables A-1 and A-2 in the appendix list the occupational and the religious background of most of the males and females who showed a strong interest in the Levitical Writings and the Aaronic Order during the 1930s and 1940s. Because many of these individuals were deceased or had left the Order, I had to obtain this information from other members. In the case of several individuals, data was too vague to include them in the sample, but it appears that their socioeconomic background fits the general pattern for those listed in tables A-1 and A-2. Table A-1 shows that the majority of the males in the sample can be classified as skilled, semiskilled, and unskilled workers. The sample includes only one office worker, one shop owner, and two teachers. I was able to gather reliable data on the educational background of only seventeen of the thirty-five males in the sample. Of these, none had earned a college degree, five had attended college, four had only graduated from high school, four had attended but not graduated from high school, and four had only graduated or attended grade school at the time they became interested in the Levitical Writings and the Aaronic Order. All of the males had been members of the Mormon Church at one time, and at least three had converted to Mormonism.

Most of the females in the sample were primarily homemakers married to working class men. If they were involved in another occupation for a few years before they showed interest in the Levitical Writings or the Aaronic Order, this is indicated in table A-2. Again, as is the case with the males, almost all of these females were skilled, semiskilled, or unskilled workers. I found evidence that only one of the females had earned a bachelor's degree before 1950. All of the females, except one, had been members of the Mormon Church at one time, and seven had converted to Mormonism.

A perusal of tables A-1 and A-2 indicates that nearly all early Levites were members of the working class and, when employed, held jobs in the competitive sector of the economy. While in later years a fair number of Levites became members of the "labor aristocracy" (for instance, employed at the United States Steel plant in Orem, Utah), relatively prosperous building contractors, and even professionals, this was far from their general occupational profile during the early years of the sect. In other words, the Levite pioneers were drawn almost exclusively from the lowest strata of the Mormon society. This raises the questions as to how similar or different the early Levites were from the general Mormon populace of the 1930s and 1940s. Unfortunately, limited comparative data on this question are not readily available. In a listing of the class profiles of major American religious groups, Herbert Schneider (1952, 229) shows the Mormons as having the lowest overall socioeconomic status, which was determined by instructing interviewers, based upon occupation, residence area, and various lifestyle indicators, to "classify respondents 'in relation to their own community, and not in relation to the country as a whole'." He categorizes 5.1 percent of the 175 Mormon respondents as upper class, 28.6 percent as middle class, and 66.3 percent as lower class (Schneider, 228). While slightly high percentages of Catholics (66.6 percent) and Baptists (68.0 percent) were lower class, 8.7 percent of the Catholics and 8.0 percent of the Baptists were upper class. As table 2-1 below reveals, recent data compiled by Wade Clark and William McKinney (1987) Roof suggest Mormons have undergone considerable "embourgeoisement" or increased representation in the higher social strata since World War II.

Table 2-1
Socioeconomic Status of Selected Religious Bodies*

| | | % Family Income | | |
|---|---|---|---|---|
| Religious Body | Mean Years of Education | Under 10,000 ($) | 10,000-20,000 ($) | Over 20,000 ($) |
| Episcopalians | 13.8 | 25 | 31 | 44 |
| Presbyterians | 13.0 | 27 | 31 | 42 |
| Mormons | 13.3 | 23 | 39 | 38 |
| Catholics | 11.9 | 31 | 35 | 34 |
| Methodists | 12.2 | 34 | 34 | 32 |
| Northern Baptists | 11.4 | 36 | 36 | 28 |
| Southern Baptists | 10.9 | 41 | 37 | 23 |
| Churches of God | 9.7 | 53 | 31 | 17 |

*Adapted from Roof and McKinney (1937, 319).

The leadership of the Mormon Church was and continues to be drawn disproportionately from the upper and middle classes, but prior to World War II it appears that the socioeconomic profile of the Levite sect was not appreciably different from that of most rank and file Mormons. In dealing with their marginal position within the church, we can infer at least these basic responses on the part of working class Mormons: (1) acceptance, (2) passive withdrawal, or (3) conversion to another religious group. While acceptance of marginality involves a certain degree of self-effacement, it also may be the safest strategy in that it does not result in certain reprisals, such as social ostracism or loss of employment. A common form of withdrawal in Mormon culture is the process of becoming an inactive, but still nominal, member or a "Jack Mormon." Based upon his empirical research, J. Kenneth Davies (1963, 88) observes that "generally speaking, the greater inactivity, the more were members found to be skilled or unskilled members." The final response, especially conversion to a Mormon schismatic group, is of particular concern in this book.

As my discussion thus far implies, marginal socioeconomic status was an important factor predisposing some working class Mormons to seek out religious alternatives, such as the various Fundamentalist sects, the Koyle Relief Mine project, and the Levite sect. Obviously most working class Mormons chose one of the other two strategies discussed. In chapter 3, in addition to presenting more evidence of feelings of deprivation that predisposed various individuals to leave the Mormon Church and convert to the Levite sect, I will attempt to delineate factors that ultimately facilitated their conversion and distinguished them from other alienated working-class Mormons. While more evidence is needed, based upon conversations with two other anthropologists who have studied various dimensions of Mormon polygynist groups, I suspect that the socioeconomic background of individuals who are drawn to them is not appreciably different from that of Levite converts. In other words, both sets of converts tend to be recruited from the Mormon working class—a social category that is more marginal in the politico-religious organization of the church than those of higher socioeconomic status.

A significant indication of the desire of some early Levites as well as members of various Mormon Fundamentalist sects to revitalize Mormonism is a strong belief in the principle of plural marriage. In reality only a small percentage of males in the nineteenth century practiced polygyny, and generally these were the more affluent members of the Mormon Church (Arrington and Bitton 1979, 199–204). Plural marriage is not so much an egalitarian practice but serves as a symbol of an earlier period when egalitarianism and cooperation received greater emphasis. As Jan Shipps (1985, 126) argues, "The development of a fundamentalist movement having as its implicit purpose the re-creation of the nineteenth-century Mormon experience is, *ipso facto*, an indication that Mormonism has been radically changed . . ."The practice of polygyny is a means of substituting high religious status for low social status. According to Mormon theology, the more wives and children a man has, the greater will be his "exaltation" and his ability to achieve divinity in the next life. Furthermore, it is possible that Mormon polygynists subconsciously view themselves as an elect because of the opposition they have encountered from the Mormon Church and law enforcement agencies.

Although Glendenning expressed strong hostility toward polygyny or plural marriage, a fair number of early followers, at least those who were male, expressed sympathy for this principle. In fact, the practice of plural marriage was a major theological issue in the early history of the Aaronic Order. Out of the thirty-five male pioneers listed in table A-1, at least eight advocated and/or investigated the practice of plural marriage, but there exists no evidence that any of them practiced it. A middle-aged male, who is not included in the sample on table A-2, admitted to me that he also investigated polygyny before he joined the Aaronic Order. According to a Levite widow, the majority of the early Levites had polygamy "sticking to them like clay." Another elderly Levite also stated that "most of the old-timers" in the Order believed in plural marriage. Robert Conrad and the former Second High Priest, who died in May of 1975, both admitted that "many" of the early Levites advocated plural marriage, but most of them later repudiated it. Although polygyny was of special interest primarily for male Levites, some Levite women also advocated the practice at one time. One woman told me that prior to her joining the Order, she had encouraged her husband to find a second wife.

According to one Eskdale resident, the only form of polygyny that Glendenning approved of was the type that involved a rooster and a hundred hens or a bull and a corral filled with cows. Glendenning dealt with the issue of polygamy in a number of revelations and letters. Section 206 (undated) of the Book of Elias, which was published in 1944, states that "a Levite shall be husband of one wife in the flesh." Later in 1947 Glendenning received a revelation which declared that "those of the House of Aaron shall have but one wife in the flesh and so long as she liveth in the flesh, there shall be no other" (Book of New Revelations 1948, Chap. 4, 18–19). Glendenning sent a letter, dated November 6, 1953, to his "cousins" condemning polygyny. Still later on April 28, 1960, Glendenning issued another letter entitled, "To Whom It May Concern," which also condemned polygyny. Some Levites stated that Joseph Smith did not practice polygyny and that it later was first espoused by Brigham Young. There exists, however, nearly conclusive evidence that Joseph Smith advocated and practiced polygyny—a fact which the Mormon Church itself has maintained (Foster 1981, 130–159).

A fair number of individuals who investigated the Aaronic Order were interested in polygyny, but lost interest in the Order when they realized that it did not condone it. When Glendenning publicly presented a revelation opposing polygyny for the Levites, one member of the Order insisted that he retract this revelation. When Glendenning did not comply, this individual left the Order. A Levite told me that his father and uncle lost interest in the Order because of its "official" opposition to polygyny; a Levite woman stated that the same situation applied in the case of her father. Some advocates of polygyny remained in the Order. According to an Eskdale widow, Glendenning had a vision which showed a Levite, who is deceased, holding a bottle with the word "polygamy" written on it. She said that this man "shelved" his belief in polygyny but never really discarded it. An elderly Levite man told me that Glendenning's revelations on polygyny apply only to the Levites and that he would not "preach" against plural marriage. Various Mormon Fundamentalist groups attempted to proselytize among the Levites earlier in their history, but little of this has occurred in recent years. The LeBarons, the leaders of a polygynist group, visited Glendenning in Springville at one time, and one of the LeBarons visited the Colorado Springs mission home, although its residents did not realize who he was until after he had left.

We can at best speculate as to why various Levites sympathetic to polygyny did not leave the Order and become Mormon Fundamentalists. They apparently felt deep ambivalence about carrying out their belief for various reasons. While one deceased Levite was widely reputed for his interest in polygyny, he generally did not express this to his fellow Levites. Another elderly Levite stressed the importance of obeying the "law of the land," but added that plural marriage is essential for achieving exaltation as a god in the afterlife. The wife of another polygynist sympathesizer told me that, although she was born in Colonia Dublan (one of several communities established by the Mormons in northern Mexico during the late nineteenth century in order to evade United States federal prosecution of polygynists), and was the granddaughter of a polygynist who believed in plural marriage, she did not want to become personally involved in it. Some Levite pioneers believed that the Writing limiting a Levite man to only one wife was only a temporary policy.

Many Mormons and Gentiles in Utah believe that the Aaronic Order is a polygynist group—a view which is extremely annoying to the Levites. Some Levites maintain that many people believe that the Aaronic Order is a polygynist group because Partoun is close to Trout Creek which allegedly has polygynist residents and is confused with Short Creek (now called Colorado City), a polygynous community in the Arizona Strip. One Levite woman stated that the Mormons generally call the Aaronic Order a "polygamous group" because this is the label that they give to Mormon "offshoot" groups.

An incident that annoys many Levites is the one in which Harold B. Lee, a Mormon Apostle and later president of the church, told a "fireside group" in Logan, Utah, that the Aaronic Order is a polygynist group. A young Mormon woman, who had attended Eskdale High School, attempted to correct Lee, but he would not believe that the Aaronic Order is a monogamist group. The Chief High Priest noted that the Mormon Church distributes literature that lists the Aaronic Order as a polygynist group. He has written the Mormon Church about the matter, but said that nothing has been done to correct it.

In addition to polygyny, another social phenomenon that attracted some early Levites because of its emphasis on United Order and a strong sense of *Gemeinschaft* was the Koyle Relief Mine. The Koyle Relief Mine as well as several other "dream mines" constitute one of the most fascinating but overlooked chapters in Mormon history. The Dream Miners were individuals who had come to believe that the discovery of the rich ores in the mountains of the Intermountain West would be intimately connected with the establishment of the Mormon Kingdom of God on earth. Although apparently there were several dream mine projects, the most famous of these, the account of which is more a part of Mormon oral tradition than of scholarship, is the one started by a bishop named John D. Koyle. While many have viewed those who have shown an interest in Koyle's dreams and project as a conglomeration of misguided mystics and malcontents, Samuel W. Taylor comes closer to capturing the spirit of this movement by contending that the Dream Miners are very much in the Mormon pattern of doing things:

> The Dream Mine story would be incredible, except for factors peculiar to Mormon country. There is the belief in dreams, visions, inspiration, visitations—guidance from the spirit world. The church itself was founded on such manifestations. There is the folklore regarding the Three Nephites, immortal beings from Book of Mormon times who appear from nowhere to perform good deeds and miracles to worthy Saints, then vanish. To scoffers, Dreamers could always point to Jesse Knight, a Mormon who was guided by a voice from beyond to discover fabulous wealth in an area which geologists had declared worthless—in fact, he named his big strike the Humbug in recognition of expert opinion. And last was the belief that the Dream Mine was destined to strike it rich just in time to rescue Zion by saving the church in its hour of dire need, while at the same time making the stock holders wealthy and honored as redeemers of Israel (Taylor 1978, 210).

People who are captivated by dreams like this are generally not the mighty and the rich. Instead the promise of hidden treasures and a glorious future constitutes the basis by which the powerless hope to transcend their misery. The Koyle Relief Mine is of relevance in an account of the Levites because some of them had a keen interest in it.

Bishop Koyle had a dream in 1894 in which a personage took him in the spirit to a mountain in the Wasatch Range about two miles east of Salem in the southern portion of the Utah Valley (Christianson 1962,

12–15). The personage told Koyle that a mine should be constructed on the side of this mountain and that at a time when the national economy would collapse, its rich ores would provide "relief" to those sympathetic to the mining project. Excavation work began in 1894; however, it was not until 1909 that the Koyle Mining Company was incorporated (Christianson, 18–20).

The Koyle Relief Company was supported primarily by Mormons, despite the frequent opposition of the Mormon hierarchy to it. Stock in the project could be purchased directly or acquired by working at the Dream Mine which appealed to some early members of the Aaronic Order. Even today a few active Levites own stock in the Dream Mine operation and feel that some day it may prosper. Of the thirty-five male Levite pioneers listed in table A-1, six worked for a time at the Dream Mine and another four owned stock in it. Several Levite women also shared the enthusiasm of their husbands for the Dream Mine or purchased shares in it for themselves. A middle-aged Levite priest, who first moved to Eskdale in the 1960s with his family, also worked at the Dream Mine for several years, owns Dream Mine stock, and feels that eventually it may yield rich ore.

Some tensions developed between the Glendenning's followers and the Dream Mine administration. Glendenning visited the Koyle Relief Mine in 1932 upon the invitation of some of his followers, but was ordered to leave the premises by Bishop Koyle who stated that he did not wish to be part of an "apostate group" (Christianson 1962, 110). The Levites who worked at the Dream Mine encountered opposition from Koyle and at one point were asked to leave because of their connections with Glendenning. After Koyle died in 1949, some Levites worked at the Dream Mine, but again encountered opposition because of their membership in the Aaronic Order. One Levite man, who worked on and off at the Dream Mine beginning in 1921, was told to leave it on three different occasions, but he never rejected his faith in Koyle's visions. A middle-aged priest at Eskdale was also asked to leave the Dream Mine operation in the 1960s because he was investigating the Aaronic Order.

Four members of the Order also worked at the Brigham Dream Mine located in Brigham City, Utah, which was based on the revelations of Frederick J. Holton, a district judge. One Levite, who worked at the Koyle Relief Mine, also worked at the Brigham Dream Mine and facilitated the conversion of three of its miners to the Aaronic Order during the 1940s.

An emphasis on egalitarianism and communitarianism attracted some Levites both before and after the establishment of the Aaronic Order to the Koyle Relief Mine. According to Norman C. Pierce (1958, 69), the Dream Miners believed that they must deny themselves all material objects, except those necessary for basic subsistence needs, as a response to the "maldistribution of the past." The Dream Miners hope to establish a United Order community, called "White City," at the base of the Wasatch Range which would serve as a place of refuge from the United States army which will allegedly attempt to destroy the Mormons (Pierce 1958, 37–38). A middle-aged Levite man stated that it was not the promise of the discovery of rich ores that motivated him to work at the Dream Mine but the feeling of community which its workers shared. Despite the fact that the Dream Mine had been established prior to the Great Depression, individuals who were already followers of Glendenning as well as individuals who were to become his followers were among the thousands that were attracted to Koyle's prophecies. Although most Dream Miners remain within the Mormon Church, their participation in a movement that church leaders strongly frown upon clearly demonstrates their intense desire to recapture something that modern Mormonism had lost.

The search by many early Levites for the "One Mighty and Strong" who would come and set the Mormon Church "in order" again also demonstrates their initial desire to revitalize modern Mormonism. The Doctrine and Covenants (1963, Sec. 85, 143) states, "it shall come to pass that I, the Lord God, will send one mighty and strong . . . to set in order the house of God." Since the Manifesto, many Mormons have awaited the fulfillment of this prophecy, although there appears to be little concern about this matter at the present time. One of the early Levitical Writings proclaims that Elias is the One Mighty and Strong and warns the Levites to "Tarry not for another, for behold, I am he for whom you would tarry" (Book of Elias 1944, Sec. 178, 54).

According to a statement signed in 1905 by the First Presidency of the Mormon Church, which consists of the President and his two Counselors, the "one mighty and strong will be a future bishop of the church who will be with the Saints in Zion, Jackson County, when the Lord will establish them in that country" (*Deseret News*, November 13, 1905). Whether or not Mormons were aware of this "official" stance of the first Presidency, many still looked elsewhere for the One Mighty and Strong. Some believed that the prophecy referred to the second coming of Joseph Smith. A common theme in Fundamentalist discussions and literature is the prospect of the coming of the One Mighty and Strong (Wright 1963, 81–89). Some people claimed that the great reformer of the Mormon Church was an Indian whose headquarters were in the jungles of southern Yucatan and northern Guatemala (Darter 1954). A fair number of individuals, some of whom managed to attract followings, claimed to have been the One Mighty and Strong. According to an elderly Levite man, three or four individuals claiming to be the One Mighty and Strong attended meetings of the Aaronic Order, apparently searching for prospective adherents to their cause. This search among various people, including those who joined or at least investigated the Order, for someone to set the Mormon Church in order expresses their desire to revitalize an organization which by the twentieth century had alienated a large segment of its membership.

Apparently the major dissatisfaction that the early Levites had with the Mormon Church was its failure to practice consecration and United Order, particularly during the Depression, but also later. Some converts, particularly men, questioned the business orientation of the Mormon Church and/or felt discriminated against because they were not as affluent or educated as the prominent members of their wards. Although some men had achieved positions in the Mormon Church at the ward level, most Levites had held only minor office, if any. Except for the present Chief High Priest, who was in a ward bishopric and a stake mission presidency in California, it appears that no other members of the Order had a position in a ward bishopric or one of higher status.

Many elderly Levites stated that they thought that the Mormon Church should be living the Law of Consecration and United Order and that these practices should not be delayed until an indefinite time in the future. Some form of communal or cooperative living has been the goal of the Levites or Glendenning's early followers since the early 1930s. In this regard, the early Levites followed a pattern exhibited by a large number of other Mormon sects, including the Colorado City community, the Church of the Firstborn in the Fulness of Times (sic), and other Fundamentalist groups. A short-lived cooperative community led by Moses Gudmundson in eastern Juab County preceded by forty years the establishment of Partoun in the western section of the same county (Hilton 1965, 36–38). It is difficult to determine to what extent the early Levites were affiliated with or at least demonstrated an interest in some of these cooperative and communal groups.

A Levite widow and her husband, who were among the more prominent members of the Aaronic Order in its early years, belonged to the Davis County Cooperative before they joined the Order. The Davis County Cooperative, which was established in the 1930s by Eldon Kingston, also advocated a communal philosophy and operated several businesses in Davis County and other areas of Utah (Turner 1966, 216–217). The Levite woman who belonged to the Cooperative stated that she and her husband were disillusioned with several aspects of the Mormon Church, including its failure to promote United Order. Consequently, they were attracted to the Cooperative and later the Aaronic Order.

It is important to emphasize that initially the Levites were primarily interested in reforming Mormonism from within rather than establishing an independent religion, regardless of what Glendenning's intentions may have been. The belief by many early Levites that the Levitical Writings and the Aaronic priesthood (Aaronic Order version) eventually would be accepted by the Mormon Church exemplifies this intent. According to Joachim Wach (1944, 186), "protest against conditions in an ecclestiastical body usually begins from within as a reform movement, not necessarily with the intentions of causing a schism." It is only after failure that the reformer becomes a separatist and the reform group a sect. During the 1930s those sympathetic toward Glendenning's claims often continued to be active in Mormon religious and social activities. A longtime female member of the Aaronic Order stated that in the 1930s she and other interested individuals attended Mormon religious activities on Sunday mornings and afternoons and convened for discussions of the Levitical Writings in the evenings, even while Glendenning was not residing in northern Utah. After the formal establishment of the Order, particularly during the 1940s, Levites still continued to attend Mormon meetings, often using these as a vehicle to express their belief in the messages of Elias. It was not until the 1950s, with the beginning of the Aaronic Order's contact with evangelical Protestants, that it started to make a definite break with Mormonism. What began as an attempt to revitalize Mormonism from within resulted in a independent religious movement that emerged because it failed to accomplish its original objectives.

With the abandonment of certain aspects of early Mormonism, a certain segment of its adherents became alienated, and began to look elsewhere to revitalize traditional ideals and forms of social organization. As a Mormon historian, Klaus J. Hansen observes:

> From a cultural perspective modern Mormonism differs fundamentally from the Mormonism of the nineteenth century though little official change in theology has occurred. Yet the sectarian aspects of Mormonism have vanished into a forgotten past. Thus, while providing "cognitive distance" through its theology, Mormonism has in fact become a mainline religion (at least in Utah) that is socially acceptable nearly everywhere in the western world. Mainline religions, as Martin Marty has observed, often produce "very worldly looking cultures," perhaps symbolized in Mormonism by the popularity of Donny and Marie Osmond among the middlebrow Saints and Gentiles alike (Hansen 1981, 212–213).

The Aaronic Order and other organizations, such as the Fundamentalist sects, the Koyle Relief Mine, and the Davis County Cooperative, attempted to revitalize the doctrines and practices which have been held in abeyance by mainstream Mormonism during the twentieth century. The attempts by members of the Order and these other groups to reestablish cooperative and egalitarian ideals, United Order, and polygyny provide strong support that these groups fit Wallace's concept of a revitalization movement.

## *The Levite Ideological Position Relative to Mormonism*

The Aaronic Order exhibits a large number of ideological features which indicate that it emerged as an attempt to revitalize modern Mormonism. Glendenning quickly became acquainted with Mormonism and incorporated many of its elements into the Levite religious system. Furthermore, as we have already seen, his followers during the 1930s and 1940s believed that eventually the Order and Mormon Church would merge. The continuity between Mormonism and the Levite religious system is perhaps most concretely exemplified by the practice of numbering revelations in the Book of Elias. Just as 135 of Joseph Smith's revelations and one of Brigham Young's revelations are printed in the Doctrine and Covenants, the Levitical Writings or the revelations that Glendenning received from the Angel Elias were transcribed in three separate books—the Book of Elias, the Book of New Revelations, and the Disciple Book. Despite the denial by the Levites that the Book of Elias is a continuation of the Doctrine and Covenants, it seems more than coincidental that the latter ended prior to 1981 with Section 136 while the former began with Section 137. When asked to explain this apparent continuity in the numbering of revelations, the Levites appeal to a revelation instructing them to "all the Levitical Writings as they have been received from 137, to the end of all things which have been received and which are yet to come" (Book of Elias 1944, Sec. 175, 50). The revelations received by Glendenning are considered to be a restoration of the "Record of John" spoken of in Section 93 of the Doctrine and Covenants (Aaronic Order, "Tract No. 1 of the Aaronic Order," n.d.). The *Aaron's Star*, a newsletter that is periodically printed, always notes on its first page that the Order is not affiliated with the Mormon Church. Nevertheless, many Levites, particularly elderly and middle-aged ones, acknowledge a certain theological connection between the Order and Mormonism. Many elderly and middle-aged Levites maintain that the Mormon Church was theologically valid (and perhaps still is in some respects) until about the time of the formal establishment of the Aaronic Order. Some Levites even feel that eventually the two organizations will merge and that perhaps at the present time they have separate but complementary functions.

The diversity of religious viewpoints among members makes a formal definition of the Levite religious belief system extremely difficult, if not impossible. Levite theology is not explicitly stated in a formal creed or in one or two documents. Therefore, the definition of the "official" Levite belief system presented in this book is derived from the following sources:

1. Statements made by the current Chief High Priest, who appears to be the final arbiter determining what constitutes ideological orthodoxy
2. Statements made by other Levites who are well acquainted with the ideology of the Aaronic order and
3. Levite "in-house" documents and scriptures

## Concepts of Restoration, Israel, the Gathering, and the Millennium

The notion of "restoration" is an explicit claim on the part of both the Mormon Church and the Aaronic Order that they began as revitalization movements. Mormons view their church as a restoration of primitive Christianity which they believe went into apostasy. Like the Catholic Church, the Mormon Church maintains that it is the "one true" church and that all other churches are in a state of heresy or apostasy. Mormons generally hold a greater respect for various Protestant denominations because they believe that the Protestant reformers at least attempted to undo the error and confusion that the Catholic Church had created. Mormons also assert that Jesus Christ came to the Americas to establish his church, but that it also lost its orthodoxy and vitality, degenerating into the many American Indian religions. In the early nineteenth century Joseph Smith restored the Church of Jesus Christ during the "latter days." The Mormon Church claims that all the ordinances and priestly orders of both the Old and New Testaments were restored to it.

While the Levites do not claim that their organization is a revitalization of Mormonism per se, they imply this indirectly by claiming that a second "restoration" must occur before the Second Coming of the Christ—that of the House of Israel; however, this first necessitates the restoration of the Order of Aaron (Childs, n.d., 13). The Levites, the priesthood tribe of the House of Israel, will build the Kingdom of God on earth and prepare for the Second Coming of Christ.

The Aaronic Order maintains that there have been "seven dispensations of the gospels given to man," those of Adam, Enoch, Noah, Abraham, Moses, Jesus, and Joseph Smith (Weight, "The Aaronic Order," n.d., 2). The seventh or "last dispensation of the fulness of times" (sic) consists of two periods—the first given to the "Gentiles through Joseph Smith" and the second given to the Levites. The "Gentile Mormon generation" ended in 1940 and the Lord took the gospel "from the Gentiles unto the house of Israel."

Both Mormons and Levites believe that they are Israelites—either by direct patrilineal descent or by "adoption." According to Thomas F. O'Dea (1954, 291), "the Mormon restoration was not only a Christian renewal; it was a Hebrew revival. Mormondom conceived of itself as a modern Israel." Mormonism teaches that Mormons are literal patrilineal descendants of Ephraim, a son of Joseph of Old Testament times, or at least have become descendants of Ephraim by adoption.

The Book of Mormon states that Hebrews came to the New World prior to the Christian era in several migrations. Mormonism teaches that American Indians and Polynesians are the descendants of the Lamanites, an "apostate" group. They and the more virtuous Nephites built the great Mesoamerican and South American civilizations. The Lamanites annihilated the Nephites in a massive battle in upper state New York during the fifth century. Because of the belief that the American Indians and Polynesians are Israelites, the Mormon Church has strongly emphasized missionary work among them.

Mormons regard themselves to be a "chosen people" who have a covenant with God. Just as the ancient Hebrews wandered in the desert for forty years after leaving Egypt, so the Mormons had to wander from place to place to escape persecution—from New York to Ohio, from Ohio to Missouri, from Missouri to Illinois, and finally from Illinois to the Intermountain West. Both Brigham Young and Moses led their people out of bondage and into the "promised land." The Mormons refer to nonmembers of their faith as "Gentiles." Mormonism also partially rationalizes its nineteenth century practice of polygyny and its construction of temples by noting that these were Hebrew customs.

Mormons believe in the "literal gathering of Israel and in the restoration of the Ten Tribes; that Zion will be built upon this American continent" (Article 10 of the Articles of Faith of the Church of Jesus Christ of Latter-Day Saints). In the nineteenth century the Mormon concept of the "gathering" implied "both a withdrawal of the elect from the gentile world and a separate community of the Saints" (O'Dea 1957, 165). The concept of the gathering was a factor in prompting the immigration of many European converts to the Intermountain West.

The Levites also believe in a literal restoration and gathering of the tribes of Israel in the "latter days." Many Levites point to the creation of the state of Israel as the beginning of the fulfillment of this prophesy. According to Robert Conrad, Israel will be brought together as an "identifiable body," although it may not be totally located in one place. Each tribe of Israel will have Aaronite and Levite priests officiating for it.

Like Jews, the Levites observe Saturday as their Sabbath, but rather than defining the Sabbath as the period from sundown on Friday to sundown on Saturday, it is defined as "from the beginning of the light of a new day, and shall end in the light of the disappearing of sun of that day" (Disciple Book 1955, 32). Glendenning received a revelation on this matter in a canyon about ten miles east of Eskdale, now called "Sabbath Canyon," and instructed the Levites to initiate this practice on September 27, 1958 (*Aaron's Star*, June–July 1971). The members of the Aaronic Order also observe the Judaic dietary laws as prescribed in the Book of Leviticus, which prohibits the consumption of foods such as pork, shrimp, crab, lobster, or any other animal which creeps, crawls, or swims. Like the Jews and the Mormons, whose histories are marked by persecutions, many elderly Levites feel that they have been persecuted by the Mormons. Levites generally believe that they will experience much persecution shortly before the Second Coming of Christ. Like the Mormons, the Levites make a distinction between "Israelites" and "Gentiles," although they sometimes also refer to Latter-Day Saints as "Gentiles."

Both Mormons and Levites subscribe to a millenarian ideology, although among the former it has been considerably relaxed since the nineteenth century. Early Mormons were certain that they were living in the "latter days," would live to establish Zion and would see Jesus Christ return and take charge of his millennial kindgom on earth. Before Jesus Christ comes, the tribe of Judah will be gathered at Jerusalem and Zion in the Americas (McConkie 1966, 306). Jesus Christ will reign from the New Jerusalem, which will be situated in the vicinity of Independence, Missouri. He will supervise the construction of a countless number of temples where, just as is the case today, ordinances for the dead will be performed. The Mormon Church will establish the Kingdom of God on earth and will function both as an ecclesiastical and political government—a theocracy in a complete sense (McConkie 1966, 500).

The Levites, like the early Mormons, believe that the Second Coming of Christ is imminent. They generally believe that it will occur before the year A.D. 2000, and some older Levites pinpoint the date A.D. 1990 as the time when Christ will return. This view is based on the following passage from one of the Levitical Writings:

> Now therefore, O Israel, that the third day does draw near, and that the temples are being prepared according to the promise, and that restoration of all things is drawing near, I do cry unto you with a loud voice to prepare the way for yet sixty years, and the third day shall be and then shall the temple be built for Judah and Ephraim (Book of Elias 1944, Sec. 149, 18).

Since this Writing was received by Glendenning in 1930, and many of his early followers adhered to the Mormon belief that the construction of the Great Temple of the New Jerusalem will occur after the Second

Coming, they concluded that the Second Coming will occur in A.D. 1990. Many Levites believe that the prophecies in the Book of Revelations in the Bible are now being fulfilled, as is evidenced by events such as the state of the economy and the beginning of the "death of the dollar," the existence of nuclear weapons, the liberalization of sexual norms, and the widespread practice of abortion.

## Cosmology

Mormon and Levite conceptions of the godhead share some striking similarities and yet are quite different from those found in Catholicism and Protestantism. Both groups maintain that the "God of this world" is Jesus Christ but that other worlds have their own gods. Concerning the doctrine on a plurality of gods, the Mormon Apostle Orson Pratt stated, "If we should take a million worlds like this and number their particles, we should find that there are more gods than there are particles of matter in those worlds (Journal of Discourses 1955, Vol. 2, 345). The following passage from the Levitical Writings indicates the "official" Levite belief in the doctrine of the plurality of gods: "Behold, God is of Gods before Him; a Lord of Lords before Him: and a King of Kings before Him; as He is a God before those who shall come after Him, and there shall be Gods after Him who are of Him" (Book of Elias 1944, Sec. 213, 91).

Both Mormons and Levites maintain that Jesus Christ is the Son of God and is also the Jehovah of the Old Testament, whereas traditional Christianity defines Jehovah as God the Father (Whalen 1964, 93). The Mormon God is an anthropomorphic being who has a "tangibile body of flesh and bones" and is not a spirit as is believed by traditional Christians and also by the Levites (McConkie 1966, 250). Whereas traditional Christians and the Levites believe that the godhead consists of three "persons" in one God, Mormonism claims that the godhead consists of three distinct and separate gods. In Mormonism God the Father and God the Son are separate entities. God the Son is the firstborn son of God the Father in a spiritual preexistence and was ordained by the latter to create the earth; the Holy Ghost is a spirit without a body (McConkie 1966, 129).

Unlike traditional Christians, the Mormons and the Levites adhere to the concept of the 'pre-existence.' The pre-existence refers to the state in which billions of spirits dwell prior to their entrance into this earthly or mortal existence. Mormons and Levites both believe that one's place of birth and status in this life are related to one's performance in the pre-existence. According to Robert Conrad, those spirits who are born in families dwelling in the slums of Calcutta, for example, probably did not perform as valiantly in the pre-existence as did those who are born into middle class American families. Many Mormons and Levites use the concept of the pre-existence to explain, at least partially, the existence of social inequality. Mormonism teaches that one-third of the heavenly host sided with Satan and rebelled against God, for which they were denied the possibility of obtaining a human body and progressing to higher status. The Aaronic Order maintains that human beings are the one-third of the "heavenly host which was cast out of heaven" for disobedience and for participating in a war against God. According to one Levite woman, human beings are the "tail end of Satan's following." Mormonism teaches that God the Father procreated the billions of spirit creatures which came to this planet (Whalen 1964, 93–94). Conversely, the Aaronic Order argues that God the Father created God the Son (Jesus Christ) who in turn created the sons of Aaron. In other words, Aaron was the first born son of Jesus Christ in the spirit, and the Aaronites are the "literal descendants of Jesus Christ in the spirit" (Book of Elias 1944, Sec. 213, 92).

Both Mormons and some Levites adhere to the doctrine of the progression of gods as is expressed in the maxim, "As man is, God once was; as God is, man may become." During a study class Robert Conrad stated that some persons in the room might at sometime in the future on another planet have to perform the same things which Christ did on the earth. Mormonism teaches that in order for a spirit in the pre-existence to progress to the status of godhood, it must first come to this earth where all of its memory of the pre-existence is extinguished. The Levites maintain that spirits come into this world because they fell in the pre-existence and must be "redeemed" (in the case of the Israelites) or must be "saved" (in the case of others). In Mormonism a god is married to one or more female deities; the greater the number of wives a god has, the greater will be his "exaltation" (Whalen 1964, 92). This view served as the rationale for the Mormon polygyny in the nineteenth century.

Both Mormons and Levites believe that the afterlife consists of "three degrees of glory"—the celestial, the terrestrial, and the telestial. All faithful Mormons will enter the celestial kingdom, but the two highest levels within the celestial are reserved for those Mormons who have undergone temple endowments and those who have been married in the temple, respectively. Individuals who died with a clear chance to "hear the gospel" will be given a chance between their death and their resurrection upon Christ's return. Individuals who died as children will enter the celestial kingdom automatically. Lukewarm Mormons and other religious people who did not take the opportunity to accept Mormonism will enter the terrestrial kingdom where they will be in the presence of God the Son (Jesus Christ) but not God the Father (McConkie 1966, 784). Most people who have "lived after the manner of the world" will enter the telestial kingdom, which is a sort of earthly paradise, but will be denied the presence of God the Father and God the

Son (McConkie 1966, 784). Mormonism teaches that the "sons of perdition" will consist of all who "deny the Holy Ghost" (meaning not clear and/or would have assented to the crucifixion of Jesus Christ. On the other hand, the Levites appear to de-emphasize the "three degrees of glory"concept and the achievement of godhood, although these are official beliefs of the Aaronic Order. The Levites deny the practical universalism of Mormonism and accept the concepts of heaven and hell as found traditionally in Christianity.

## Race

The racial attitudes of some Levites, particularly the older ones, must be considered within the context of certain racist doctrines found in Mormonism. Until the momentous decision during the summer of 1978 of the Mormon hierarchy to reverse the policy on the matter, the denial of the priesthood to males of African ancestry stood as the most controversial Mormon doctrine during the 1960s and 1970s. While there did not appear to be a consensus among Mormons as to why blacks were not permitted to hold the priesthood or visit a temple, the notion that blacks had been cursed in pre-existence often buttressed these restrictions. According to the popularly held "fence-sitter" theory, certain "less valiant" spirits, who did not actually side with Satan but were not totally committed to God, were sent to this earth with black skin as a punishment for their ambivalence. As interpreted by one Mormon apologist, such spirits were sent to the earth through the lineage of Cain and Ham, who married Egyptus, a descendant of Cain (McConkie 1966, 527). Needless to say, many liberal Mormons found themselves highly embarrassed by such beliefs. Some Mormon intellectuals argued that the church's policy on blacks was based on historic circumstances rather than on any explicitly theological "truths" (Bush 1973). In an overview of much of the earlier literature on the black priesthood ban, Newell B. Bringhurst (1981) interprets the emergence of this policy as an attempt by an initially besieged people to balance anti-abolitionist and abolitionist sentiments both within and outside of the church.

O. Kendall White, Jr., and Daryl White (1980, 243) explain the Mormon Church's decision to reverse its policy on blacks in 1978 as "an adaptation to environmental pressures, the logical outcome of established organizational practices, and the resolution of internal contradiction." Among the factors forcing the church to alter its policy, they note the relentless pressures from the black American community, the fear of litigation charging the church of denying blacks their civil rights, the organizational growth of the church in Latin America where many converts are individuals who clearly exhibit some degree of African ancestry, a concern with middle-class respectibility, challenges from Mormon intellectuals, and dissatisfaction on the part of black Mormons with second-class citizenship within their church. In a critique of the Whites' position, Armand L. Mauss (1981a, 278) contends that the revelation of 1978 is primarily a product of internal developments within the Mormon Church, including: (1) "a trimming of the scope of the ban on priesthood access, begun already in the mid-1950s"; (2) "deliberate sponsorship by the Mormon leadership (beginning late in the 1960s) of greatly increased *visibility for blacks themselves* in the media of the Mormon heartland"; and (3) "the gradual dismantling of the array of non-canonical theological folklore that had traditionally been used in support of the priesthood ban in official and unofficial statements on the subject." Bearing in mind the complex dialectic between external and internal developments, it is important to add that the revelation of 1978 affected policy rather than doctrine (Mauss 1981b, 32).

While the racist views of the Mormon Church toward blacks became well-publicized during the 1960s and 1970s, far less attention has been given to those on American Indians and Polynesians. Despite the fact that these groups have neither been categorically denied the priesthood nor participation in temple ordinances, according to Mormon doctrine, these peoples are descendants of Israelites, namely, "Lamanites," who came to the Americas before the time of Jesus Christ, but later fell into "apostasy" and were consequently cursed with dark skin. Despite these views, Mormons view the American Indians and Polynesians as "chosen people" because their ancestors were Israelites.

Given the racist teaching of Mormonism, it should not be surprising that some Levites hold explicitly racist attitudes toward blacks and possibly other peoples. The Order has never maintained an official position on the status of blacks, American Indians, or Polynesians other than the view that all races are fallen spirits from different planets. The Levite position closest to an official one on the status of the blacks is based on a letter that Glendenning wrote to a Levite who inquired about this matter. Some of Glendenning's comments in this letter are as follows:

> He [God] told the Levites that the priesthood should be their inheritance forever; He just did not include any of the Gentiles. Whether they be black, or white, green, brown or yellow does not enter into the subject at all.
>
> The Negro is not excluded any more than any of the other eleven tribes of Israel.
>
> In regards to his salvation, yes; every soul is entitled to his salvation whether he be black or white . . . and we have no right to refuse him a seat in the congregation. As for his equal, it is not for me to judge; God alone can know.

> . . . If a Negro can prove that he is a son of Zadok, a son of Aaron, who is a son of Levi, we would, according to the word of God, have no right to reject him [for the priesthood], providing he is otherwise qualified, if there is a need in the True Church of God for his officiation.
>
> . . . God alone can answer this question [as to whether blacks are cursed]. If the Negro is cursed, God will in the last days lift the curse from all who love and obey the commandments. I am not the judge (Letter dated August 7, 1963; reprinted in *Aaron's Star*, September 1963).

It is interesting to note that Glendenning claimed that a black can obtain the Aaronic priesthood if he "can prove that he is a son of Zadok, a son of Aaron, who is a son of Levi." No other priests in the Aaronic Order have been able to prove this to the Chief High Priest nor have been required to do so. The Chief High Priest determines whether an individual is a lineal descendant of Aaron. Several Levites told me that Glendenning held some antiblack sentiments. A woman, who has been a member of the Aaronic Order since the late 1940s, stated that Glendenning did not encourage interracial marriages, especially between whites and blacks, and that he had an "allergy to blacks."

A fair number of elderly Levites subscribe to the traditional Mormon doctrines concerning the degraded status of blacks. It appears that most middle-aged and young Levites do not subscribe to this view. Some Levites in particular are bothered by racism within and outside the Aaronic Order and by the discrimination which blacks have experienced in American society. One young Levite man was extremely disturbed by comments that were made about blacks and the use of the term "nigger" at a Partoun meeting. He said that if the Aaronic Order ever made an "official" statement opposing interracial marriage, he would seriously consider leaving it. Another young Levite man was impressed with the great diversity of racial and ethnic groups that were represented at a Pentecostalist convention that he attended in California.

An interesting case illustrating racial attitudes of various Levites involved the contact by correspondence in mid-1974 of a small Nigerian religious group which was interested in learning about communal living. The Nigerian group desired to send one or two representatives to visit Eskdale for about six weeks. Some Levites seemed unsure if the members of this Nigerian group were black. One Levite felt that God would not permit a situation to occur in which blacks would be interested in the Aaronic Order. During one Tuesday evening study class, discussion turned to the subject of Nigerians. I told the group about some Nigerians that I had taught and some general information about Nigeria. One Levite woman asked if these Nigerian students were black; I replied that almost all Nigerians are black—an answer that surprised her. One of Conrad's daughters told me that her father was concerned that some

Levites might react negatively toward the Nigerians' visit. A few delays in the plans of the Nigerians to visit Eskdale occurred, and finally in May 1975 a representative visited Eskdale for about a week. I did not witness any open opposition to the visit of the Nigerian representative, either prior to or during his stay at Eskdale. Despite the Nigerian visitor's reserved mannerisms, people were cordial toward him, and attempted to include him in activities. Members spoke fondly about him afterwards and said group prayers for the success of the Nigerian group, which renamed itself the "True Church of God," one of the names that the Levites use for their church. Partial credit for the cordial reception that the Levites extended to the Nigerian visitor must be given to the Chief High Priest who tactfully and diplomatically prepared them for this event.

Although the official ideology of the Aaronic Order maintains that Israelites came to the Americas before the Christian era and that Jesus Christ preached to these peoples, I heard little reference to the racial status of the American Indians by the Levites. Although it is likely that many elderly Levites subscribe to the Mormon concept about the status of Indians, it is likely that most young and perhaps even many middle-aged Levites are unfamiliar with this view. Despite the fact that many Levites feel a strong attachment to the Jewish people and the state of Israel, which is viewed as one of the signs that the millennium is imminent, one elderly Levite man did not share this enthusiasm. While he was still a Mormon, he wrote pamphlet, entitled "Is God a Jew?" which he sent to every Mormon bishop in Utah. This man claimed that the Jews are a "mongrel race" and that Jesus Christ was "of Judah."[2] For awhile he subscribed to an anti-Semitic magazine, *the Cross and the Flag,* which was published by the Christian Nationalist Crusade. Also, a Levite widow stated that B'nai B'rith is an "anti-Christ" organization.

## *The Levite Religious System as a Defense Mechanism for a Troubled Soul*[3]

Like many other revitalization movements, the Aaronic Order was started by a charismatic leader who experienced religious inspiration and formulated a new code for living. As O'Dea (1966, 37) observes

> In the study of a religion, however, it is also important to know the specific content of the religious experience involved, or of what theologians would call the "revelation." For the kinds of stable forms which evolve in the development of religious organization will bear a significant relationship to the content of the religious experience of the founder or founders.

Various behavioral scientists have viewed religion as a "projective system" which ventilates and more or less resolves tensions which members of a particular culture or subculture experience (Kardiner 1945; Spiro 1965; Waelder 1951). As I will illustrate, the Levite religious system to a large extent evolved as a projective system that served to resolve or at least alleviate various tensions and conflicts experienced both by Glendenning and his followers. In the next chapter, I will examine the factors that predisposed and led certain persons to convert to the Aaronic Order. In this section, I will employ a psychocultural approach in explaining how the Levite religious system provided Maurice Glendenning with a sense of community, a source of economic and moral support in the event of illness, compensation for feelings of low esteem, and a prophet-like status that he could never have attained in the larger society.

Since psychohistorical or psychobiographical interpretations have come under severe and often valid criticism, it is imperative that I justify use of such an approach in analyzing the role of the Levite prophet in the development of a Mormon schismatic group. William McKinley Runyan (1982, 202–209) recognizes three sets of questions concerning psychobiography, namely, those about inadequate evidence, reconstruction and reductionism. Following Runyan (1982), I will address how I intend to overcome some of the pitfalls of psychobiography and mention some of the advantages that this approach may have over conventional psychotherapy.

One of the most common criticisms of psychobiography is the paucity of information on the subject's early childhood years. As noted earlier, I was unable to find out much about Glendenning's childhood. While this problem may in part have been overcome by interviewing his siblings and even playmates and schoolmates, financial constraints made it difficult for me to undertake such an endeavor. From a psychoanalytic perspective, spotty data about Glendenning's early years is indeed unfortunate. Conversely, insistence that such information always be available in order to conduct psychocultural studies of prophets and religious leaders would prevent obtaining penetrating insights into their lives.

Barzun (1974, 46) argues that the techniques which psychohistorians use are indirect and scant:

> . . . the patient is absent, and the clues he may have left to his once living psyche are the product of change. Diaries, letters, literary work form a random record, in which expressions of mood are more frequent than evidence of actions. "Dream material" is extremely rare. Compared to the volume of data elicited under therapy and consciously directed at relevance and completeness by the analyst, this trickle from written remains seems almost negligible.

Despite an element of truth to these observations, they overlook the limitations of the analyst's techniques. The psychobiographer has information about a person whose life is complete and from others who knew the subject. Several of my informants had been in contact with Glendenning over several decades, as opposed to a few months or years as is generally the case for the analyst. Furthermore, whereas the analyst generally listens to the subject relate what he did, my informants directly observed Glendenning's actions.

As Runyan (1982, 205) observes, "if the subject is a literary or creative person, the psychobiographer has a wealth of creative material, perhaps expressing inner psychological states and conflicts, which may, with caution, be drawn upon in interpretation of the subject's personality . . . Some creative individuals have been more articulately expressive of their inner states and experiences than the typical therapy patient." In the case of Glendenning, many of his innermost thoughts and conflicts were revealed in three published volumes of his revelations—the Book of Elias, the Book of New Revelations, and the Disciple Book. In addition, he related many aspects of his life to a member who authored two books about the Order.

Regardless of its advantages or flaws, reconstruction or retrodiction, particularly of events in the subject's childhood, is a technique that I have avoided.

Psychobiographies also have been criticized for their reductionism, particularly in overemphasizing psychological factors at the expense of external social and historical factors, focusing excessively on psychopathological processes and giving insufficient attention to normality and creativity, and explaining adult character and behavior exclusively in terms of early childhood experience while neglecting later formative processes and influences (Barzum 1974; Coles 1975; Stannard 1984; Stone 1981). As I have indicated, the last of these areas is one that I automatically avoid as a consequence of the lack of information that I have about Glendenning's early years. As for the first of these areas, I prefer to term my approach a "psychocultural" one in that I attempt to view the Levite prophet within the larger sociocultural and historical content in which his life occurred.[4] Indeed, it may be argued that most conventional psychoanalysts, whose work is often used as the standard bearer for psychohistory, tend to be quite reductionist in their interpretation of human behavior, largely due to their limited understanding of sociocultural processes and differences. Finally, while some of Glendenning's weaker psychological states will be discussed, in many ways I see Glendenning as a rather ordinary person who was subjected to many of the types of hardships that countless numbers of working class people experience every day.

As we have seen, Glendenning belonged to that stratum of the American populace that is particularly subject to the swings of a capitalist economy. Even during good times, lower-class people barely eke out a living, largely because they are relegated to the competitive sector of the economy as opposed to the monopoly sector. Whereas the monopoly sector is characterized by large-scale, capital-intensive production, "in the competitive sector the physical capital-to-labor ratio and output per worker, or productivity, are low" (O'Connor 1973, 13). According to Douglas F. Dowd (1977, 103), "the monopolistic sector, and those benefitting from it, moved dynamically through the 1920s; the competitive sector lagged behind, afflicting those dependent on it." The 1920s was the period during which Glendenning came under the curse—the curse of being on the periphery of an otherwise booming economy. Hoping once more to find gainful employment, this time in the West where so many others before had sought their fortune, Glendenning moved to Salt Lake City in 1928, and settled his wife and daughter there the following year in Provo where he worked as a sales agent for a coffee company. The manifest reason that Maurice and his wife joined the Mormon Church was their daughter's involvement in it. Perhaps a latent reason for their conversion was the realization that Provo was a Mormon town and that membership in the dominant religion might insure permanent employment.

In many ways, the stresses emanating from Glendenning's structural position in the larger society fit Wallace's (1956b, 635) description of many individuals who experience religious inspiration:

> They display, prior to their revitalization experience, such symptoms as depression, extreme sense of guilt, inactivity, alcoholic addiction, and various somatic illnesses. They may complain of the pressures of bereavement, of failure in careers, of uncongenial social demands, although their personal difficulties seem no different from those of others who are not ill. They are people to whom it can be fairly said that they suffer severe stress and that they show evidence of mazeway disorder. . . .

Prolonged stress and the biochemical products of stress induce in the prophet a psychic experience, such as a vision, which may in turn result in a statement of religious inspiration or a revelation. Prior to a psychic experience, the mazeway or total view that the individual holds of himself and his environment is distorted. The psychic experience results in mazeway resynthesis which restores biopsychic equilibrium and "reduced ambivalence and conflict, but necessarily involves a change in the individual's perception not only of himself but also of the environment, and it may involve his taking action to insure correspondence between the new mazeway and reality" (Wallace 1956b, 637).

Mazeway resynthesis creates in the prophet a new view of self, society, culture, and nature which in turn motivates him to rework his sociocultural milieu. The prophet feels a need to tell others of his experiences and the revelations which he has received. He may actively seek recruits to his message and may encourage others to spread it. Based on the perceptions which the prophet acquires in mazeway resynthesis, he formulates a new code for living which constructs a utopian image of society and attempts to revitalize the existing culture. In other words, the reformulated code acts as a "transfer culture" between the "existing culture" and the "goal culture" (Wallace 1966, 158–161). The prophet derives his authority largely from his own charismatic powers, partly acquired during the process of mazeway resynthesis, but often ascribed to supernatural sources.

Some anthropologists have interpreted the behavior of prophets as evidence of mental derangement. Weston LaBarre (1972, 315) maintains that "in naive common-sense terms, crisis cults have often enough had prophets showing evidence of mental instability, or of abnormality even in their specific culture context, for the question of their mental status to be raised." George Devereux (1955, 148–150) argues that charismatic leaders have been "neurotic" and were "actually elevated to social leadership because their behavior fitted the childish expectations of their potential followers." Wallace (1956a, 273), however, contends "that the religious vision experience per se is not psychopathological but rather the reverse, being a synthesizing and often therapeutic process performed under extreme stress by individuals already sick."

Prophets develop not only a vehicle for dealing with their own problems but also those of others who became their followers. In addition to having spent their youth generally in poverty or obscurity, Stephen Fuchs (1965, 5) states that prophets are sometimes "outsiders" who completely identify with the plight and aims of their followers. This observation is particularly noteworthy in light of the fact that Glendenning was a Gentile (non-Mormon) newcomer to Utah who joined the Mormon Church and almost immediately perceived the social and ideological strains that some of its members were experiencing.

We can only speculate as to what prompted Glendenning to share his Writings with his fellow Mormons even before he had been granted a temple recommend. Given that revelations were commonplace among Mormons, did he believe that the words of the voice might strike a responsive chord? The church hierarchy was not at all sympathetic toward this man who claimed to be a firstborn son of Aaron, but some working class Mormons were moved by Glendenning's revelations. As Anthony Oberschall (1973, 158) observes, "leaders cannot create a substantial following and a social movement if there are not already widespread shared grievances experienced by a collectivity or groups in the population." The opposition of the Mormon Church to his claims undoubtedly added yet another stress upon Glendenning's psyche. In the remainder of this section, I will suggest how the Levite religious system, which Glendenning developed as he made new contacts and encountered additional problems, served to ease his troubled soul.

It has been noted that Glendenning's childhood and early adulthood were periods of seemingly constant migration and social dislocation. He apparently enjoyed traveling, but many of his moves were involuntary and probably contributed to a desire for some sense of permanence and community. When Glendenning came in contact with the Mormons, he found a people who had developed, at least theoretically, a strong concept of *Gemeinschaft.* Glendenning also probably observed this trait among his Hutterite patients in South Dakota. A strong sense of community is an integral part of Mormonism, and although he initially failed in implementing it, Glendenning incorporated it into his own cognitive framework at a very early stage of his divine calling. After the Aaronic Order took on a semblance of structural stability, the Levite prophet established a series of cooperative and communal ventures over a period of several years. These included the Alpha Colony (established in the beginning of 1949) located at the Springville branch, the Partoun cooperative (established in the spring of 1949), the Eskdale commune, (established in 1955), and a mission home for young Levites who attended a Bible college in Colorado Springs, Colorado (which existed between 1954 and 1966). Glendenning spent the winters near Phoenix, Arizona, but during his later years he had a permanent homesite at the Eskdale commune and was particularly fond of visiting the young Levites at the Colorado branch. Glendenning had succeeded in creating a string of communities of which he was the ordained representative or "Servant," as he was often called, of the gods. After years of what may have seemed like aimless wandering, Glendenning not merely joined but provided the inspiration for the type of community that provided him with a sense of belonging.

Glendenning experienced many physical illnesses throughout his adult life and underwent major surgery several times. He had a ruptured appendix as a young man and intestinal and heart problems during much of his life. According to one Levite informant, Glendenning referred to many of his physical ailments as his "unknown illnesses." In 1962 Glendenning was struck by an affliction which he referred to as the "onslaught of Satan upon his body using the stings of wasps, the stings of scorpions, the venomous poison of centipedes." The religious order that Glendenning instituted gave him the security in the event of illness that the larger society failed to provide. For example, he often spent the winters in Arizona because the climate there was better for his health than that in Utah. Members of the Aaronic Order were a major source of moral and financial assistance during Glendenning's assorted somatic illnesses.

Some of Glendenning's actions indicate that he was attempting to compensate for feelings of inferiority which undoubtedly were related to his marginal socioeconomic status and unsuccessful endeavors. Unfortunately, I was unable to inspect the various diplomas and certificates that Glendenning held, but it seems that most, if not all of them, were not conventional measures of academic achievement. Keeping in mind that chiropractic is generally considered to be a fringe form of medicine, it is interesting to note that Glendenning obtained part of his training at the less prestigious neighbor of the Palmer College of Chiropractic. Further evidence of Glendenning's efforts to compensate for feelings of low status was his wearing of an incomplete military officer's uniform and his membership in a voluntary military organization of chiropractors during World War II.

Apparently Glendenning felt a need to validate his divine mission in ways which were compatible with Mormon beliefs. Whether or not the Catskin and the Marble Tablet were fraudulent, his use of these alleged discoveries provided convincing evidence for a group of people whose religious heritage places a high value on genealogical research. One Levite woman told me that the Catskin and the Marble Tablet served to reinforce her "testimony" of the teachings of the Levite prophet. Glendenning, based on a revelation that he received from the Angel Elias, claimed that his ancestors moved into the area of Scotland named "Glen Dan" and were descendants of Christian Israelites (Book of Elias 1944, Sec. 139, 4–5). Sometime during the 1950s, Glendenning traveled to Scotland, claiming to uncover even more evidence that his ancestors were Aaronites.

Despite the unconventional nature of his own educational endeavors, Glendenning encouraged many young Levites to attend state and private colleges and universities. Consequently, whereas the older Levites were, or are, primarily members of the working class, the younger Levites have considerably more formal education, and have often gravitated toward professional occupations, including law, medicine, engineering, and particularly teaching. Glendenning was not solely responsible for the achievements of the Eskdale educational system, but he certainly was a major factor in its establishment and was able vicariously to enjoy the conventional respectability that his followers had achieved.

Glendenning perceived a considerable amount of opposition to his mission from external sources, especially on the part of the Mormon Church, and within the Aaronic Order. The curse, which Glendenning claimed had been placed on him in 1923, appears to have been related to disturbed interpersonal relationships and feelings of persecution resulting from his claims of receiving the writings. The opposition of the Mormon Church to Glendenning's mission and to those of other schismatic groups was countered by a revelation that again served to deflect the idea of personal failure. Glendenning claimed that an attempt was made upon his life while he was confined at a federal prison hospital in Missouri during 1945. He claimed that a physician, however, discovered that he had been poisoned and revived him from a three day coma. The physician asked the Levite prophet if he had any enemies in Utah. When Glendenning admitted that he might, the physician allegedly stated that some people had offered him a large sum of money if he would make sure that Glendenning would be killed. According to one knowledgeable informant, the physician implied that Mormons were behind the unsuccessful assassination plot.

Included among those who challenged Glendenning's authority were Kenneth Farnsworth and Sherman Lloyd. According to a middle-aged Levite man, during the late 1940s Farnsworth and some of his admirers frequently quoted a particular passage in the Book of Elias in making their claim that Glendenning was merely a "channel' who received messages from the Angel Elias. The interpretation of these messages was to be the responsibility of more enlightened souls. An elderly Levite woman stated that Farnsworth and Lloyd claimed that their "great Elijah work" superceded Glendenning's mission. A few people apparently left the Order in order to follow Farnsworth and Lloyd. In the 1960s Sherman Lloyd founded the Believe God Society or the Angel Elias Study Class, which claimed that "Joseph Smith, Jr., had returned to earth and Elias had been on the earth for some forty years preparing for the second phase of the Dispensation of the Fullness of Times" (Shields 1982, 170). In addition to using standard Mormon scriptures, the group relied upon the Book of Elias and the revelations given in 1916–1917 to Harry Edgar Baker of Chicago, Illinois.

During the 1950s, one man, whose descendants are now prominent members of the Order, felt that Glendenning was procrastinating on the planned transition of Partoun from a cooperative to a communal community. For awhile he established a separate United Order community with members of his family and a few other people. Later this individual and his family were rebaptized into the Order, although the incident continues to be a topic of gossip and conjecture.

Like Joseph Smith, when Glendenning faced opposition in his group, he often received a revelation on the matter. Section 202 of the Book of Elias, chapter 16 in the Book of New Revelations, and nineteen Writings in the Disciple Book warn the faithful Levites that there are "deceivers" or "imposters" within the Order who are attempting to lead its members astray and claim authority for themselves. Generally the Writings do not specify who the deceivers and imposters are; however, some Levites are willing to speculate as to whom is being referred to in these Writings.

At least three of the Writings make reference to specific individuals or groups who have challenged Glendenning's authority. Probably the most serious threat to Glendenning was a charismatic individual named Marl V. Kilgore. Around 1950 Kilgore stopped at the Order's Alpha Colony in Springvile, having noticed a number of tents situated there, and asked if he could also set up a tent on the community's land for his family. He learned that the tents were only a temporary housing arrangement. The Levites did not hear from Kilgore for several months or longer. After he set up a tent at the mouth of a canyon near Springville and established a chiropractic practice, he joined the Aaronic Order. The Levites who knew Kilgore describe him as a tall, handsome man with a "beautiful" family. According to an Eskdale priest, Kilgore was a "friendly and outgoing" man who had "a sort of hypnotic power over people."

Shortly after his conversion to the Order, Kilgore claimed that he was receiving revelations. These revelations interested some Levites who began to attend meetings that Kilgore was conducting. He eventually received a revelation instructing him to move south, so his family and some other Levites moved to the property of a member of the Aaronic Order near Bicknell (Wayne County) in south central Utah. When I repeatedly attempted to determine the content of these revelations, Levite informants had no or, at most, a vague idea of their subject matter. Some informants stated that Kilgore claimed that he had a "mission" or was "the man to come." One Levite woman stated tht Kilgore attempted to "step over" Glendenning. Another Levite woman said that Kilgore claimed that Glendenning's leadership role in the Order had been fulfilled and he was to become the new leader. Glendenning received a revelation, entitled "Kilgore Group," on May 29, 1951, warning the Levites about the "deception" of "thy brethren in the South" (Disciple Book 1955, 53). Perhaps a year or so after the Kilgore group had moved to Bicknell, they moved to the Southwest (probably New Mexico) and later to Missouri. One of Kilgore's followers was an Aaronite priest who left his wife and children and married one of Kilgore's daughters. Rumors circulate among the Levites stating that Kilgore killed one of his followers by applying pressure to a vital area in the neck because the latter would not marry one of his daughters and that perhaps he had killed others in his group.

I had the opportunity to visit the Kilgore group briefly in December 1976. For many years, the group referred to itself as Zions Order of the

Sons of Levi, but now is known as Zion Order Incorporated. Its community is located at the edge of the Ozark Mountains near Mansfield, Missouri. Only a handful of families, some of which are related to Kilgore, resided there at the time of my visit. Although the group had perhaps as many as 100 residents at its zenith, its numbers had been greatly diminished due to internal conflicts.

Kilgore may have posed a threat to Glendenning for several reasons. His claims of being inspired by the Holy Spirit and being a patrilineal descendant of Levi (by way of the Scottish clans) were ideas which attracted several Levites. When I visited Kilgore, he stated that he was "excommunicated" from the Order for disobeying Glendenning. He claimed to be completely unfamiliar with the revelation on his group and stated that he did not realize that Glendenning perceived him as such a strong threat that it warranted a revelation.

Various other writings indicate also that Glendenning perceived opposition to his mission. One Writing entitled "The White Horse Experience" tells of an incident which was experienced by Glendenning in 1932 at Alton, Utah, but was not written about until 1962. In this Writing, Glendenning related the following about the suffering and persecution which he had experienced in his search for truth:

> I have been declared a robber and a thief; I have been declared a drunkard, and criminal, a scoundrel, and a devil straight from hell, worthy of death if I did not follow their instruction.
>
> Now with this picture in your mind I would like to relate to you the following experience:
>
> It was about thirty years ago, while persecution was very heavy and condemnation severe. Starvation and hunger were at the door. Sick and crippled for a very severe attack of sciatic, I was judged to be in error by four innocent and sincere souls who took the reins in their own hands that they might, according to their thinking, guide the ship into the harbor (Disciple Book 1955, 93).

Two Writings concerning Glendenning's visions discuss the presence of "deceivers" in the Order. The following is the first verse from one of these Writings.

> About a week ago, for two nights in succession I had a very vivid dream. There was a secret meeting of some kind being held, and copies of all records of the Order were there in possession of these holding the secret meeting. They were making definite plans to overthrow the Order and establish it in their own way (Disciple Book 1955, 92).

The following excerpt from another revelation warns the Levites about deceivers within their midst:

> Remember these things, my servant, for time is now come that those who declare that they are of the House of Aaron who are not obedient unto the commandment of the Lord and they who are offenders in the House of Aaron shall be judged of their iniquity.
> They are they who have crept in, perverting the word of the Lord to their own glory and selfish ambitions; and I declare unto you that they shall be cast out, for they are not those of the House of Aaron (Disciple Book 1955, 49).

Glendenning feared what others might do to him after he died. Although Glendenning was buried somewhere in Arizona, the Levites, including his wife, are not aware of the exact site of his grave. Years before he died, the Levite prophet requested that he not be given a funeral and that his grave not be marked. Glendenning reportedly stated that he did not want his enemies to descrate his body or his followers to memoralize him.

How are we to interpret Glendenning's perceptions of persecution, opposition, an attempted assassination, and even possible desecretion of his body after his death? Oberschall suggests one possible explanation for the "sometimes seemingly erratic, irrational, or even authoritarian behavior" of leaders of social movements:

> The behavior of leaders is very much a result of the context of their situation as leaders of movements. Leaders in social movements do not have a firmly established, institutionally sanctioned position as do leaders in other walks of life. They do not draw a regular salary as elected politicians or administrative elites do: hence, they are often in precarious economic position. Their positions are continuously open to challenge by lesser leaders who seek to replace them. They are often persecuted, arrested, jailed, or have to spend a good part of their life in exile or in hiding, making it difficult for them to conduct an orderly personal and family life. If they are successful, they may be the subject of adulation and cult of personality, surrounded by sycophants and hangers-on, who wish to derive personal gain from the movement's success. Often their best friends and early associates later turn against them over questions of strategy and ideology. Put any ordinary, stable individual into a similar position, and he, too, would probably exhibit what some observers consider confused or arbitrary behavior as a result of the pressures and dilemmas that one is continually faced with as a leader in an unstitutionalized and emergent organizational setting (Oberschall 1973, 148–149).

Much of the persecution and opposition which Glendenning perceived was real, even though its significance was perhaps sometimes exaggerated. The Mormon Church disapproved of Glendenning's claims and excommunicated him and many of his early followers. The Mormon hierarchy has over the years tended to lump the Aaronic Order together with various Fundamentalist sects in the Intermountain West and northern Mexico—a pattern which is extremely annoying to the Levites. Several parties indeed challenged and sometimes even attempted to usurp Glendenning's authority, particularly during the formative years of the Aaronic Order.

Real opposition, however, may have in turn contributed in the Levite prophet to a certain degree of paranoid ideation, or what David Shapiro (1955, 54–107) terms a "paranoid style with cognitive aspects." Shapiro (1955, 55) maintains tht individuals exhibiting a paranoid style are "essentially nonpsychotic people, although frequently with borderline psychotic features, in whom such paranoid traits as suspiciousness are both pervasive and longstanding." Suspiciousness, which becomes a mode of thinking and cognition, may indeed have some basis in fact, and these grains of truth are twisted in such a way as to confirm the individual's perceptions. Despite their overzealous apprehensions, suspicious people often are, as was certainly true of Glendenning, extremely penetrating observers.

While the religious system which Glendenning essentially created relieved many of his problems, it apparently did not completely resolve them. Even after the formal establishment of the Aaronic Order in 1943, and later the desert communities of Partoun and Eskdale, Glendenning continued to experience feelings of low self-esteem, rejection, and persecution. Added to these were a long series of physiological complications which progressively worsened as he aged. Many Levites perceive Glendenning to have been a confident and self-possessed individual, but some realize that he experienced moments of great uncertainty. According to one Levite man, Glendenning confessed to him in his last year of life that he had been a failure. Perhaps this is a fear that many prophets live and die with. The role of prophet is a very "heady" one, but also a very lonely one. The Mormon prophet, Joseph Smith, suggested this when he made this statement in a funeral sermon on April 7, 1844, a short time before he was assassinated:

> You don't know me; you never knew my heart. No man knows my history. I cannot tell it; I shall never undertake it. I don't blame anyone for not believing me. If I had not experienced what I have, I could not have believed it myself (quoted in Brodie 1971, vii).

Regardless of whether or not Glendenning perceived his life to have been in vain, his followers today continue to be inspired by his message. Whereas the larger society may have viewed Glendenning as a "charlatan," "quack," or simply a "kook," the Levites elevated him to a prophet-like status. The charisma of Glendenning lives on in the memory of many members of the Aaronic Order, who affectionately refer to him as "Bishop" and frequently quote statements that he purportedly made. The latter pattern has prompted many Levites to argue that their prophet was one of the most misquoted persons the world has ever encountered.

The Levite religious system that Glendenning created did more than simply provide a mechanism by which a tortured soul could cope with reality. It also provided the framework for a revitalization movement among certain disaffected Mormons who wished to rejuvenate the egalitarian and communitarian ideals that they believed had stagnated in their church. There was cultural and structural readiness for the teachings of Glendenning to take hold among a segment of the Mormon populace during the 1930s and 1940s, and it is very likely that another charismatic leader with somewhat different doctrines would have been equally appealing.

# 3

# *The Levite Conversion Experience*

In primitive or tribal societies, revitalization movements may appeal to a large proportion of the population as a result of culture contact with a more complex society. Conversely, in class or state societies, they frequently attract a small segment of the population—generally one that feels exploited and oppressed. The Levite sect appealed primarily to certain working class Mormons who felt that their church had lost its earlier communitarian and egalitarian goals and practices. At the same time, of course, we must recognize that many working class Mormons, even if they experience a sense of marginality, choose to remain within the Mormon Church. Furthermore, other disaffected Mormons may either become religiously inactive or join one of several other Mormon sects. In this chapter, I focus on the process of religious conversion in an attempt to delineate the specific factors that not only predisposed certain individuals to demonstrate an interest in the Aaronic Order, but also those that ultimately resulted in the decision to join it.[1]

Conversion has been a central concern of many studies on religion, drawing upon the interests not only of behavioral and social scientists, including psychologists, psychiatrists, sociologists, and anthropologists, but also theologians and pastoral counselors. In fact, much of the early literature on the topic of religious conversion is written with a theological bias, frequently only defining and describing various types of conversion. In recent years, with the rise of a wide variety of new religions, such as the Jesus People movement, the Unification Church, the Divine Light Mission, the Hare Krishna Movement, Scientology as well as many lesser known occult and Eastern mystical groups, there has been a renewed interest in religious conversion.

As James T. Richardson et. al. (1979, 232) noted, the literature on conversion tends to address two major issues: (1) the process of conversion and (2) types of converts and conversion. Although my examination of the Levite conversion experience will consider the second issue somewhat, I will focus mainly upon the first. In reviewing much of the literature on religious conversion, Max Heirich (1977, 677) argues that while converts are often treated by social scientists "as deviants, to be explained in terms of variations from the status quo, we might learn more about both their experience and social processes generally if we approach them as offering a unique vantage point for examining the establishment and disestablishment of root senses of reality." While undoubtedly recruits to the Aaronic Order and to other Mormon sects represent a small minority of the total membership of the Mormon Church, the value in studying such individuals as well as the groups that they join may lie primarily in the insights that they give us about modern Mormonism itself as well as about the larger society. One may view the Levite conversion experience, at least in part, as a reflection of the strains and contradictions that exist within twentieth century Mormonism.

My approach to the study of the Levite conversion experience is in part deductive and in part inductive. In examining the emergence of the Aaronic Order and continued recruitment to it, I found the concept of relative deprivation extremely useful. In casual conversations with converts to the Order, it quickly became apparent to me that various types of deprivation drew them to the sect. Many of these feelings of deprivation appeared to arise within the context of Mormon culture. In other cases, they seemed to arise within the larger context of American culture or from idiosyncratic factors, such as poor health, marital or family conflicts and feelings of insecurity.

A number of theorists have attempted to elaborate the concept of relative deprivation (Glock 1973; Yinger 1970; Aberle 1972). In addition, many other social scientists, including: Ernst Troeltsch (1931), Anton T. Boisen (1939), Yonina Talmon (1965), John Lofland and Rodney Stark (1965), John Lofland (1977) and Merrill Singer (1980) have recognized the role of some form of deprivation in the emergence of new religious groups. Of these various approaches, I have found the scheme delineated by Charles Y. Glock to be the most helpful in examining the Levite conversion experience. Glock (1973, 210) defines deprivation as "any and all the ways that an individual or group may be, or feel disadvantaged in comparison either to other individuals or groups or to an internalized set of standards." Five kinds of deprivation—economic, social, organismic, ethical, and psychic—are cited as contributing to the emergence of all religious organizations.

Economic deprivation occurs in societies where there exists differential distribution of income and limited access of some individuals or groups to the necessities and luxuries of life. Social deprivation results from a differential distribution of highly valued traits, such as prestige, power, status, and opportunities for social involvement and mobility. Organismic deprivation results from situations in which individuals experience physiological or mental disabilities. In cases where these individuals are stigmatized because of their deformities or illnesses, deprivation may be especially great. Ethical deprivation occurs when individuals perceive a discrepancy between the actual and the ideal values and behavioral patterns of their culture. When an individual finds his or her culture or life to be meaningless, he or she experiences psychic deprivation. This form of deprivation may result from widespread social disorganization or from idiosyncratic experiences, such as the death of a loved one, and an inability to adjust to one's peers, and so forth.

Glock points out that these forms of deprivation are not "pure" and may be interrelated. The existence of organismic deprivation may, for example, result in psychic and social deprivations. Also, an individual may experience several forms of deprivation with each form having a different cause. Although deprivation is a necessary condition for the formation of new religious organizations, it is not a sufficient condition. Additional conditions are "that the deprivation is shared, that no alternate institutional arrangements for its resolution are perceived, and that a leadership emerge with an innovating idea for building a movement out of the existing deprivation" (Glock 1973, 212).

Although much of my analysis of the Levite conversion experience depends upon the concept of relative deprivation, its mere existence does not ensure the emergence of a new religious group. As David Aberle (1972) points out, deprivation must be shared. Specific forms of ethical, economic, and social deprivation were shared by a large number of the people who joined the Order. Glendenning provided the charismatic leadership and a reformulated code for living which, at least temporarily and partially, resolved certain forms of deprivation that certain individuals had experienced. The question which is extremely difficult to answer is why certain individuals joined the Aaronic Order and others who were experiencing similar forms of deprivation did not. Consequently, we must consider a multiplicity of other factors that predisposed and facilitated conversion.

Some studies, both those with and those without empirical data to support their models, have attempted to outline the stages involved in conversion (Christiansen 1963; Lofland and Stark 1965; Lofland 1977;

Beckford 1975; Lynch 1978; Richardson et. al. 1979; Singer 1980). The best known of these studies is Lofland and Stark's (1965) examination of what was at the time a small millenarian cult on the West Coast which they call "Divine Precepts" (better known as the "Unification Church," led by Rev. Sun Myung Moon). Their analysis of conversion to the group is based on the "value added" concept in Neil J. Smelser's (1963) theory of collective behavior. According to the value-added concept, there are a number of factors or states which determine the occurrence of a particular social phenomenon. Each stage in the process "adds its value" to the final product. All the stages or factors are necessary for a particular social phenomenon to occur.

In their analysis of the process of conversion, Lofland and Stark divide the conditions for conversion into two principal categories—predisposing conditions and situational conditions. The predisposing conditions refer to those that motivate an individual to take a serious interest in a group such as Divine Precepts and are as follows:

1. The individual must experience "enduring and acutely felt tensions."
2. The individual must possess a religious problem-solving perspective. Rather than relying on medical therapy, psychoanalysis, or secular counseling, the individual turns to a religious ideology to solve his or her problems.
3. The individual defines himself or herself as a "religious seeker" in that he or she seeks solutions to philosophical and existential questions by means of a religious ideology.

If the predisposing conditions are met, the following situational conditions determine whether or not the individual makes a total commitment to the religious group:

1. The individual must encounter the religious group at a turning point in his or her life. Possible turning points include the loss of one's job, failure in love or marriage, or the death of one's partner.
2. The individual must develop an intimate relationship with one or more members of the religious group.
3. The individual must eliminate or at least neutralize "extra-cult" attachments. The individual must be exposed to intensive interaction with the members of the religious group. In essence, the religious group acts as a primary group for the individual in that his greatest source of satisfaction and fulfillment derives from it.

Drawing in part upon the work of Lofland and Stark (1965) and Lofland (1977), I will attempt to delineate factors which predisposed and led certain individuals to join the Aaronic Order. I will note that the

Levite conversion experience illustrates perhaps one type of conversion among several possibilities. For example, as David A. Snow and Cynthia L. Phillips (1980, 431) note, "we might expect the conversion process to vary according to whether a group is publicly defined as 'respectable,' 'idiosyncratic' or 'revolutionary.' " With this thought in mind, I hope that a discussion of the Levite conversion experience will contribute to a better understanding of religious conversion, particularly to small sects such as the Aaronic Order and the Mormon Fundamentalist groups.

## *The Sample of Levite Converts*

As noted in the preface, data were collected in both formal interviews and casual conversations with over thirty-five individuals who had converted to the Levite sect. A social profile of the sample of Levite converts follows below:

### Sex

Only thirteen (37 percent of the sample) out of the thirty-five converts were males. Most of the converts whom I didn't interview were also females. It is likely that in reality the ratio of male-to-female converts to the Aaronic Order is more balanced than the above figure indicates. Three of the females in the sample are widows whose husbands were also converts to the Order. I was unable to interview the Levite husbands of two other elderly converts. Nevertheless, there appears to be a somewhat greater tendency for females to join the Order than males. Some females joined the Aaronic Order after a divorce or the death of a husband. In most cases these females did not remarry a member of the Aaronic Order. The Order provides widows with opportunities for social interaction which are not often provided in the larger society. Women also are inclined to attend religious activities and study classes at the various branches more often and in greater numbers than men.

### Socioeconomic Status

Of the thirty-five converts only two had earned a college degree, eight had attended college, fourteen had only graduated from high school (and perhaps attended technical school or business school), six had attended but not graduated from high school, and four had only graduated from or attended grade school at the time they joined the Order. Most of the individuals in the sample were members of the working class and/or homemakers at the time of their conversion. Those who did not fit into these two categories included one accountant, one teacher, and one salesman.

Conversion to the Aaronic Order was followed by upward social mobility on the part of several individuals. One individual, who held a master's degree when he joined the Order, earned a doctorate and taught in a large state university for awhile. Two women earned high school diplomas which they had not obtained during adolescence. Two other women obtained bachelor degrees in education, but only one of them became an employed teacher. The other woman was unsuccessful in obtaining employment as a teacher because she insisted on wearing her Levite uniform while teaching. A man, who joined the Order during his early twenties, earned a bachelor's degree in psychology, undertook some graduate school study, and had worked at several social service positions, including one as the director of a community agency. A middle-aged man, who formerly worked with his father in an auto glass repair shop, took over his father's proprietorship after his conversion. Another middle-aged man became a cement work contractor years after he joined the Aaronic Order. The greatest degree of social mobility has occurred among Levites who were reared in the Aaronic Order or became members during adolescence.

## Circumstances of Conversions

Except for one man who joined the Aaronic Order during his early sixties, all others in the sample underwent conversion between late adolescence and the mid-forties. Individuals who joined the Aaronic Order during adolescence generally joined as a result of their parents' affiliation with it. Although in some cases parents gave adolescent children the choice to accept or reject membership in the Order, most of these people didn't make a strong commitment to it until later in their life. It appears that in most cases children who followed the lead of their parents into the Aaronic Order during childhood or adolescence became inactive members after leaving their families of orientation.

Most converts investigated the Aaronic Order from a few months to several years. A prominent Levite, whose wife joined the Aaronic Order before him, investigated it for over ten years and lived at Eskdale for about a year before he actually converted. During the period of investigation many pre-converts studied the Mormon and Levite scriptures and the Bible and often even continued to attend Mormon religious meetings. In a few cases a pre-convert's parent or parents joined the Aaronic Order years before he or she seriously initiated an investigation of it.

Only eight of the thirty-five conversions (23 percent of the sample) can be classified as "sudden." As a group, the sudden converts appear to have experienced more of the forms of deprivation discussed than the other converts. Six of the eight individuals who underwent sudden conversion were extremely active Mormons, although this was the case for most converts who also felt that the Mormon Church was in need of a restoration. These individuals accepted the Levitical Writings almost immediately after they were exposed to them. One man accepted Glendenning as a firstborn of Aaron after he heard three Writings read at a study meeting in 1930. A woman and her husband accepted the Writings "right away" because their "education in the Mormon Church made it easy" to do so. Another man noted that after he had examined the Book of Elias in the 1940s, he exclaimed, "This is the thing that we have been looking for."

The only sudden converts who were not seeking a restoration of the Mormon Church were a young couple. They were in the process of moving to California from the Midwest in the hopes of establishing a better lifestyle when they visited a friend in Provo. This friend had recently become acquainted with the Aaronic Order and told them about it. Shortly thereafter, this couple and their four children moved to Eskdale for several months during the mid-1950s.

## *The Role of Relative Deprivation in Conversion*

Converts' statements form much of the evidence on the forms of deprivation that contributed to the formation and maintenance of the Aaronic Order. Since individuals often justify their conversion with ideological rationalizations, it is necessary to search for other signs that indicate the existence of deprivation prior to their shift in religious affiliation. This was done by considering certain experiences in their lives prior to joining the Order. In most cases deprivation was experienced within one or two years of investigating the Order. In other cases a lifetime of deprivations appears to have predisposed certain individuals to undergo religious conversion.

### Ethical Deprivation

Thirty out of thirty-five converts (86 percent of the sample) noted feelings of ethical deprivation prior to joining the Aaronic Order. To a large extent, these feelings must be viewed within the context of converts' previous religious backgrounds. Bearing in mind the strong religious background and perspective of most Levite converts, this should not be surprising. Frequent reference was made to the various aspects of twentieth century Mormonism that are "out of order." Informants often claimed that the Mormon Church was failing to live the Law of Consecration and United Order and to carry out the "work of Levi and Aaron" which is discussed in the Mormon scriptures. Without any specific questioning on the matter by me, at least six converts stated that they had vowed to live the Law of Consecration during various Mormon temple ceremonies. One middle-aged man openly admitted that he left the Mormon Church because it was not practicing "early Mormonism." Several of the older converts stated that they were looking for the One Mighty and Strong who would set the Mormon Church "in order." Some converts felt that the Mormon prophet-presidents had not received a revelation since the nineteenth century and were disturbed by this.[2]

A fair number of individuals complained that Mormon activities had a strong secular and social tone rather than a sacred and religious one. Objections were raised to the great emphasis placed on dances, sports, and various forms of competition in the Mormon Church. One woman felt that it was not enough merely to obey the Word of Wisdom and to tithe in order to be a religious person. Instead, one has to make religion a "way of life." Others, particularly those who joined the Order in the last decade, maintained that the Mormon Church placed a greater emphasis on respect for the church leaders, past and present, than on a relationship with Jesus Christ.

Some converts complained about the manner in which various Mormon ordinances were conducted. A man, who had converted from Lutheranism to Mormonism, was disturbed by the lack of sacredness that surrounded the distribution of the sacrament of the Lord's Supper in the Mormon Church, especially when it was passed out by twelve year old boys. His wife, who was reared a Mormon, was disturbed by the mechanical nature of various temple ordinances, such as baptism for the dead. During this ordinance one would be baptized for a dead person, circle the baptismal font, wait one's turn to be baptized again, and repeat the same process many times. Two converts objected that the Mormon Church had substituted water for wine in the sacrament ordinance.[3]

Some converts maintained that they became disenchanted with the lack of intellectual freedom within Mormonism. They felt that they could not express openly certain beliefs. One woman was disturbed that the Mormons would not study the Book of Elias and that various passages in the Doctrine and Covenants had been altered. Another woman stated that she initially set out to disprove the claims of the Aaronic Order, which she had learned about from a Levite friend, by "correlating" the Levitical Writings with the Mormon scriptures and the Bible. When she did this, she was appalled by the discrepancy between ideal and actual Mormonism. She felt that the Mormons did not study the scriptures as intensively and were not as open about them as the Levites. A male convert was disturbed by the severe reprimand he had received from several prominent members of his Mormon stake and ward when he took a Sunday school class to observe a Catholic mass for educational purposes.

Several individuals were attracted to the Aaronic Order partly because of their objection to competitive aspects of American society versus the Levite emphasis on cooperation and de-emphasis of materialism. A prominent Levite male, who once held a prestigious and well-paying corporate position, stated that he became tired of dealing with the "profit motive" and wanted more fully to implement the religious ideals which had been instilled into him since early childhood.

Converts expressed the existence of ethical deprivation in their lives prior to conversion more than any other form of deprivation. In six of the thirty-five cases, this was the only form of deprivation that I was able to detect. To a large degree, the expression of ethical deprivation serves as a ideological or post hoc rationale for an individual's conversion. Whereas the occurrence of other feelings of deprivation may be consciously or unconsciously repressed, the admission of ethical deprivation increases the individual's self-esteem both in his eyes and those of the group. Members of the Order frequently state publicly the nature of the ethical deprivation that they experienced before they joined the Order.

### Economic Deprivation

Undoubtedly, economic deprivation played a more significant role in attracting people to the Aaronic Order during the 1930s and 1940s than in the period after these two decades. Of the thirty-five converts, only fifteen joined the Aaronic Order prior to 1950. The low socioeconomic status of individuals who showed an interest in the Levitical Writings and the Aaronic Order during the 1930s and 1940s indicates that a feeling of economic deprivation was prevalent in this group. The strong emphasis that this group placed on egalitarianism and communalism also indicates this.

Several elderly converts noted that they were adversely affected by the Great Depression. A woman claimed that in the early 1930s many Mormons began to ask why their church was not practicing consecration and United Order and providing for the basic needs of its members. She noted that although the Mormon Church eventually established the Church Welfare Plan in 1936, this program was a far cry from the practice of "full consecration." One of the initial members of the Order stated that many of the people who showed an interest in the early 1930s were unemployed. He himself was unemployed when he was told by another man while doing temple work in Salt Lake City that there was a "firstborn of Aaron" in Provo.

A fair number of converts felt that promotion of an individual within the Mormon politico-religious hierarchy was determined more by his socioeconomic or occupational status than his spirituality. A middle-aged man referred to the Mormon Church as a "rich man's church."

Other converts felt that they were discriminated against because they were not as affluent or educated as the prominent members of their respective wards. One man in his sixties stated that in one of the wards that he belonged to, only members of certain prominent families were allowed to bless the sacrament at Mormon meetings. He felt that the Mormon Church does not care about the plight of poor people.

Although only seventeen of the thirty-five converts (49 percent of the sample) indicated experiencing economic deprivation prior to joining the Aaronic Order, it is possible that some converts unconsciously repressed feelings of this type. Since Mormon culture greatly emphasizes economic self-sufficiency and the notion that economic prosperity is a sign of divine favor, admission of economic deprivation may be interpreted as personal weakness. Conversely, it appears that a fair percentage of the individuals who joined the Order in more recent times experienced little or no economic deprivation because they held relatively well-paying jobs or were married to men with substantial incomes.

### Social Deprivation

Fifteen out of thirty-five converts (43 percent of the sample) expressed feelings of social deprivation. Several individuals complained that they found people in some Mormon wards to be extremely "clannish." This perception was particularly felt by those Levites who had moved from one ward to another. Some converts felt more warmth and hospitality among the Levites, particularly during the early decades of the group, than among the Mormons. An elderly Levite woman complained that the Aaronic Order does not exhibit as much of a sense of community as it once did. She noted that the Levites often picked vegetables at the garden of a particular man and had a "great time."

Converts generally did not state that they were denied mobility within the Mormon politico-religious hierarchy. Although some men achieved a relatively high position in the Mormon Church at the local or ward level, most Levites held minor positions if any at all. Except for Robert Conrad, who was a member of a ward bishopric and of a stake mission presidency in California, it appears that no other members of the Order had held a position in a Mormon ward bishopric or one of higher status.

Some features of the elaborate Levite politico-religious organization, which will be discussed in the next chapter, suggests that it has served as a compensation for the low social status experienced within the contexts of American culture and more specifically Mormonism. Liston Pope's (1942, 137) observation that "the sects substitute religious status for social status" appears to hold true for the Aaronic Order. Whereas the Mormon Church may offer the common man only a minor position within its hierarchy, the Aaronic Order may make him a high ranking member in the priesthood and in the councils of the House of Israel. His position can be comparable to that of the cardinals and archbishops of the Catholic Church or the General Authorities of the Mormon Church. In commenting on the social-psychological significance of the Council of Fifty for its members, Klaus J. Hansen (1967, 92) notes that "It was, after all, a heady prospect for a tinsmith or farmer to be told that he would be one of the governing princes in the Kingdom of God with authority to rule the nations of the earth."[4] The councils of the Aaronic Order perform much the same social-psychological function as did the Council of Fifty.

## Psychic Deprivation

Twenty-two converts (66 percent of the sample) appear to have experienced psychic deprivation prior to their conversion. Psychic deprivation appears often to have been partly the by-product of other forms of deprivation. Five females in the sample had serious marital problems which resulted in one or more divorces for each. One of these women joined the Mormon Church after her second divorce. Her third husband was a Mormon whom she met in her ward and was married to until he died. Two or three years after the death of her third husband, she began to investigate seriously the Aaronic Order.

The following is a brief account about a woman who will be referred to as Jane and who experienced psychic conflict due to the death of her husband prior to her conversion. Jane said that the period after her husband's death was an unsettling one during which she saw "signs in the sky." She moved to a nearby community and began to attend Aaronic Order meetings which a relative had told her about. Her involvement in the Order kept her so occupied that she no longer had time to become lonely. After a short time, she began to attend meetings at the Salt Lake branch where she met the man whom she married about a year after her husband's death.

Some of the converts appear to have experienced severe psychic conflict during much of their lives. Some had unhappy childhoods and came from unstable home environments. A few apparently sought to resolve their conflicts by joining or at least investigating several religious groups. Generally their new religious affiliation didn't solve their problems, so they moved to yet another religious group. From the comments various Levites made to me, I would assume that the Aaronic Order attracts many such individuals, but apparently most of them move on.

### Organismic Deprivation

As opposed to conversions to groups emphasizing religious healing, such as Christian Science and Spiritualism, organismic deprivation was not a significant predisposing condition for Levite converts. Only two of the thirty-five converts (6 percent of the sample) experienced some kind of organismic deprivation within a few years of joining the Order.

Both individuals were cared for by members of the Aaronic Order during the period of their illness. In one of these cases some Levites visited a sick woman, who will be referred to as Catherine, several times and finally performed certain ordinances to restore her health. Catherine had learned about the Order from her sister who was one of its first members. Although she attended Levite meetings, Catherine was torn between this new religion and Mormonism and continued also to attend Mormon religious meetings. During her investigation of the Order, she was told that she had to have an operation to extract a large kidney stone and several small ones. During the first operation the doctors extracted the small kidney stones but were unable to extract the large one. After two more unsuccessful attempts Catherine was scheduled for yet another operation. The night before her operation, a Levite couple performed a healing ordinance for her. During the operation the following day Catherine could feel the presence of her deceased father beside her. He told her that she could not die yet because she had something she had to accomplish first. This time the doctors could not locate a kidney stone and declared its disappearance was a miracle. Although this miracle strengthened Catherine's belief in the Aaronic Order, she did not join the Aaronic Order until her daughter had also decided to do so.

## *Other Predisposing Factors*

### Previous Religious Affiliation

Thirty-two of the thirty-five converts (91 percent of the sample) were Mormons before they joined the Aaronic Order. Seven individuals in this group had converted to Mormonism while the remainder were reared in it. One couple, who had not been Mormon, had studied the teachings of Herbert W. Armstrong. Several aspects of Armstrong's Church of Tomorrow resemble those of the Aaronic Order, including the belief that some of the descendants of the lost tribes of Israel migrated to the British Isles, the observances of the pork taboo and Saturday as the

Sabbath, and a strong sense of millenarianism (Peterson 1973). Because of this resemblance, this couple found the Aaronic Order's ideology quite compatible with concepts that they had previously accepted.

A few converts had a long history of investigating and/or joining several religious groups before they joined the Aaronic Order. For example, a middle-aged Levite man, who was reared as a Mormon, investigated Seventh Day Adventism, Catholicism, the Jehovah's Witnesses, and the Assembly of God before he joined the Order. Another man, who was reared as a Greek Orthodox, became a "Billy Graham type of Christian" in his teens and later was baptized into a fundamentalist Protestant Church and the Mormon Church. His wife, who had been reared as a nominal Catholic, followed him in converting to Protestantism, Mormonism, and the Order.

It appears that in all cases, except that of a certain young man with a Protestant background, membership in the Mormon Church or, in the case of one couple, acquaintance with the doctrines of the Church of Tomorrow predisposed individuals to join the Order. Mormonism and the doctrines of the Church of Tomorrow provided smooth ideological transitions for converts to the Aaronic Order in which no abrupt change in one's world view was required. Individuals did not generally view their conversion to the Aaronic Order as a process whereby one set of religious beliefs was substituted for a new set, but rather as one where a new set was added to a theologically valid old set. Conversion was not regarded as a drastic change in religious affiliation but was believed to constitute a significant addition to one's earlier religious belief system. Most converts did not reject their Mormon upbringing but merely viewed it as a lower stage in their spiritual development.

### Background of Parents and Degree of Early Religious Socialization

Most converts were reared in familes in which at least one of the parents was Mormon. In almost all cases the converts' fathers were members of the working class, being either laborers, farmers, or post office employees. Only one convert had a father who was a professional, namely an electrical engineer. The primary occupation of all mothers was homemaking, except for one woman who combined this with clerical work.

Of the thirty-five converts, seven received at least a moderate degree of early religious socialization, twenty-seven a strong amount, and only one a weak amount. In most cases parents were generally very religious Mormons or Protestants who made religion an integral part of their children's lives. In the few cases in which the parents did not provide a strong religious socialization, the convert acquired it elsewhere. For example, one woman, whose parents were not religious people, lived next door to a very active Mormon family and learned much about Mormonism from them. Through their influence she started attending Mormon activities at seven years of age and became interested "in things that pertain to the Lord."

### Religious Problem-Solving Perspective

Almost all Levites in the sample exhibited a religious problem-solving perspective prior to conversion. Levite converts were not prone to seek political solutions in dealing with social structural problems. Levites, like many Mormons, tend to frown upon secular methods of solving personal problems, such as psychoanalysis and counseling. In order to solve personal problems, one must "get straight with the Lord." I found only one Levite convert who attempted to resolve some of his psychic conflicts after conversion by seeking professional guidance and therapy.

Levite converts attempted to answer philosophical and existential questions by religious means. The few individuals who attempted to utilize a secular philosophy to deal with these issues found it unsatisfactory. The Levite convert is an individual who feels that world events are directed to a large extent by the actions of benevolent and malevolent supernatural beings. The individual can rely on the help of the former in his daily struggles, but must fight off the incessant temptations of the latter.

## *Situational Factors Facilitating Conversion*

### Life Crisis Experience

Twenty-two of the thirty-five converts (63 percent of the sample) reported experiencing some sort of life crisis within a year or two before they started to investigate the Aaronic Order or during their investigation. Life crises included marital problems, loss of a job, financial problems, the death of a spouse or child, the birth of a deformed child, and so forth. What Lofland and Stark call the "turning point" in the prospective convert's life is roughly analogous to what I term the "life crisis experience." The turning point occurs for pre-converts when "each had come to a moment when old lines of action were complete, had failed, or had been or were about to be disrupted, and when they were faced with the opportunity or necessity for doing something different with their lives" (Lofland 1977, 50). In addition to my own data, several other studies indicate that turning point or life crisis is not an absolute ingredient of the conversion process. E. T. Clark (1929) found that only 33.9 percent of his sample experienced a form of conversion analogous to the type which involves a turning point. In their study of converts to Mormonism, John Seggar and Phillip Kunz (1972) report that 59.7 percent of their sample experienced a life crisis within a two year period prior to baptism.

In an reappraisal of the "world saver model," Lofland (1977, 815) concedes that the "concept of 'turning point' is troublesome because everyone can be seen as at a turning point in one or more important ways at every moment of their lives. Like concepts of tension, it is true and interesting but not very cutting." This observation may indirectly account for the fact that in my sample as well as those of others a significant proportion of converts could not isolate a specific turning point within a year or two of their decision to join the Aaronic Order. In that a certain amount of tension exists in almost everyone's life at any given time, perhaps particularly in complex societies, some people have difficulty in differentiating their low points from the general noise level in their lives. Furthermore, we must consider the truism that most people downplay the worst times in their lives.

### Significent Others Influential in Conversion

In thirty-two of thirty-five cases (91 percent of the sample), significant others, particularly parents, spouses, other relatives, and friends, introduced the potential adherent to the Levitical Writings of the Aaronic Order and exerted an important influence in determining his decision to convert. These factors were not present in only three cases. A man who was reared in the Utah Valley was vaguely familiar with the Aaronic Order but learned more about it when three Levites came into his store. A beautician learned about the Aaronic Order from a Levite customer. Another man learned about the Aaronic Order from his wife who had attended a revival meeting at which Jerry Owens and a prominent Levite had spoken. Although his wife was not especially interested at first in joining the Aaronic Order, he immediately investigated it.

### Influence of Parents

In six cases (17 percent of the sample) parents were influential in introducing converts to the Aaronic order. Two sets of sisters joined the Aaronic Order only after they were married, despite the fact that their parents had been members for years. In both cases, even though the women had been exposed to the beliefs of the Aaronic Order since childhood or adolescence, they remained Mormons until a later date. The deceased father of these two women was an early follower of Glendenning and a leader in the Aronic Order who had often told his children about the need of restoration in the Mormon Church and the imminence of the millennium. Because these two women were residing outside Utah at the time that the Aaronic Order was formally established and were married to Mormons, it was not until several years later that they followed the example of their parents by converting to it. It was largely through the efforts of the father of the first set of sisters that the parents of the second set learned about the Levitical Writings in the 1930s. In the case of two other converts, one male and one female, their interest in the order was largely stimulated by their fathers, who investigated the Order but did not actually join it. Both fathers became disillusioned because the Order did not officially condone the practice of polygyny.

### Influence of Spouses

Individuals to whom prospective converts were already married or later married appear to have been a strong factor in the conversion process—one which was present in fifteen of the thirty-five cases (43 percent of the sample). In a few cases it appears that both marriage partners would have influenced each other in the conversion process. For example, although a particular man had heard about the Aaronic Order first and had told his wife about it, for awhile she took the lead in investigating it. Four individuals in the sample were courting members of the Aaronic Order when they decided to convert to it or at least seriously to investigate it. Two women, who initially were not interested in joining the Aaronic Order, did so largely because their husbands had decided to do so. One man did not join the Aaronic Order until more than ten years after his wife had done so. During this interim period, however, they frequently discussed the teachings of the Order. That the conversion of one's spouse is an urgent concern of some Levites is evidenced by the great number of prayers certain members request the group to say regarding this matter.

### Influence of Other Relatives and Friends

Relatives other than parents and spouses and friends were influential in the conversion of twenty-seven individuals (77 percent of the sample). Siblings, uncles, and even children of converts played an especially important role in this regard. In some families two or more siblings joined the Order. In one case a woman learned about the Aaronic Order from an uncle and later was influential in the conversion of her mother.

A woman who accepted the Levitical Writings in the 1930s said that her husband's closest friends and her own intimates had also accepted them. A non-Mormon couple learned about the Aaronic Order while residing in Oregon from a neighbor who had been a Mormon but had later joined the Aaronic Order. When one man was told by a friend that there was a firstborn son of Aaron residing in Provo, he immediately investigated the matter. Although most Levites have refrained from evangelism, this man actively told others, particularly his friends, about the Levitical Writings and the Aaronic Order, and claimed that fifteen individuals joined the Order directly through his efforts.

Many social scientists have commented on the importance of a preexisting relationship between recruiter and potential convert in the spread of a social movement. In his study of the Divine Precepts cult, Lofland (1977, 51) found that "In order for persons who meet all four of the previously activated steps to be further drawn down the road to full conversion, an affective bond must develop or already exist between the potential recruit and one or more of the DP members." Luther P. Gerlach and Virginia H. Hine (1968, 30) found that relatives accounted for the recruitment of 52 percent and close friends for another 29 percent of the members of several Pentecostalist groups in their sample. Other important recruiters included neighbors, business associates, fellow students, and teachers. In a study on the growth of Soka Gakkai, a Japanese religious movement, Robert Lee (1967) shows that the most important initial recruiters attracting Tokyo converts were neighbors (35 percent), relatives (16.4 percent) and work colleagues (16.2 percent). Based upon his study of 152 Catholics who converted to the charismatic or Pentecostal movement within the church, Heirich (1977, 673) notes that "It seems clear that the process of conversion occurs through the use of available social networks."

The data collected on the Levite conversion experience also point out the importance of preexisting relationships in the recruitment process. In almost all cases a relative or friend introduced the potential convert to the Levitical Writings or the Aaronic Order. In the few cases where this did not occur, the individuals involved developed close relationships with members of the Aaronic Order before they formally joined. It appears that significant others played an even more important role in the recruitment to the Aaronic Order than in the groups studied by Lofland, Gerlach and Hine, and Lee. This is probably due largely to the small size of the Aaronic Order and its past philosophy on proselytism. Since proselytizing techniques such as those used by the Mormons were discouraged, members tended to recruit new members among relatives, friends, and acquaintances. It is possible that small religious groups, which place a great deal of emphasis on primary relationships, tend to rely heavily upon preexisting relationships as a method of recruitment. Some relatively large religious organizations, such as the Mormon Church, utilize full-time missionaries who seek converts by visiting strangers in a somewhat random and arbitrary manner. Seggar and Kunz (1972) found that prior to joining, converts to the Mormon Church in an urban Kentucky area did not experience much informal contact with Mormons.

Yet the Mormon Church is quite appreciative of the role of interpersonal bonds in recruiting new members, and actively encourages rank and file members to nurture intimate ties with non-Mormons with the goal of facilitating their conversion. In their examination of the statistics for all Mormon missionaries in the state of Washington during the year 1976–77, Rodney Stark and William Sims Bainbridge (1980, 1386) found that when the missionaries "merely go from door to door without the aid of social bonds, the success rate is only 0.1 percent. At the other extreme, if a Mormon friend or relative provides his home as the place where missionary contact occurs, the odds of success reach 50 percent."

## Elimination or Neutralization of Extra-Group Attachments

The existence of Lofland and Stark's third situational condition, namely, the elimination or neutralization of "extra-cult attachments" was somewhat difficult to establish definitely in my sample. Despite the fact that most active Levites interact primarily with others in the Aaronic Order, extra-group attachments are not totally eliminated or neutralized for many of them. Some active Levites are married to Mormons, a relationship which has a tendency to create certain tensions. Furthermore, some very ardent members of the Aaronic Order still retain an emotional and ideological attachment to the Mormon Church. During the early years of the Aaronic Order, some members attended both Levite and Mormon activities—a practice which now appears to have almost completely died out. In their study of the Nichiren Shoshu Buddhist movement in America, Snow and Phillips (1980, 441–442) note that its converts did not generally have to break off relations with nonmembers. They suggest that one reason for this may be related to the noncommunal nature of Nichiren Shoshu, in contrast to the communal structure of the group studied by Lofland and Stark. In the case of the Aaronic Order, one finds both communal and noncommunal forms of membership. In fact, generally Levite converts first become noncommunal members, and later may move to Eskdale (or to one of the other Levite cooperative endeavors during earlier years).

While the data on my Levite sample downplay the significance of the elimination or neutralization of extra-group attachments, this condition played a more crucial role in facilitating conversion to the sect during the 1930s and 1940s. This resulted not so much from a desire by the early Levites to break off relations with Mormons as proceedings by the Mormon Church during the 1940s to excommunicate church members who joined the Aaronic Order. For many Levites, excommunication translated into social ostracism not only by former ward members but also friends, relatives, and even spouses. An elderly Levite woman, whom I will call Joan, told me that friction developed with her husband when she began to investigate the Levitical Writings around 1939 or

1940. During this exploratory phase, she continued to attend Mormon services on Sunday mornings and afternoons but attended Levite meetings on Sunday evenings. After several weeks of this emerging pattern, Joan's husband reported her involvement with Glendenning's followers to their bishop. Due to her refusal to abide by the bishop's demand that she sever her connection with the Levites, her husband eventually divorced her. A Levite priest, now deceased, said that his excommunication, which he referred to as his "graduation" to a higher level of spiritual knowledge, prompted many people in Springville to cross the street when he and/or his wife came near. Furthermore, their sons were excluded from many social activities with their peers. In contrast, individuals, who joined the Aaronic Order after 1950 and constituted the bulk of my sample, generally were not excommunicated from the Mormon Church and encountered far less social ostracism. A Levite woman in her early thirties reported that she and her husband were not shunned by their suburban neighbors. She believed that this tolerant reaction was largely due to the strong prevalence of Jack Mormons and mixed (Mormon/Gentile) couples in their neighborhood.

### Intensive Interaction with Group Members

Lofland and Stark's fourth situational condition applies for almost all the conversions listed in the sample. But it does not apply in the case of one woman, who was exposed to the Aaronic Order and learned many things about it from her uncle. She experienced relatively little interaction with the other members of the Aaronic Order, except for her aunt, because she and her husband resided outside of Utah for about ten years following her conversion. During her investigation of the Aaronic Order, she interacted a great deal with her uncle and aunt but little with other members of the Order. It was only after she moved with her husband and children to Eskdale that she experienced intensive interaction with other Levites.

## *A Field View of the Levite Conversion Experience*

The Levite conversion experience, to a large degree but not completely, follows the steplike process delineated by Lofland and Stark in their "world-saver model." Levite conversions, however, do not simply involve a mechanical accumulation of predisposing and situational conditions, but result from a complex interaction of several variables at various levels of analysis. As David A. Snow and Richard Machalek (1984, 184) contend, "conversion is probably comprised of causal processes amenable to generalization. but merely to label a sequence of stages does not specify the causal relationships responsible for conversion." J. Milton Yinger (1965) argues that human behavior must be examined at four levels—biological, psychological, cultural, and social. His field perspective recognizes the existence of factors at various levels and attempts to explain behavior, such as religious conversion, as the result of the interaction of these factors. For example, relative deprivation, which is one factor predisposing individuals to convert, exists at several levels—the ethical (cultural), the social and economic (social structural), the psychic (psychological), and the organismic (biological). In the case of some Levite converts, four or even five forms of deprivation were present, whereas for others as few as one or two were present. In addition to the necessary condition of relative deprivation, factors which predisposed certain individuals to join the Aaronic Order include:

1. Being reared in a working class family
2. Being a member of the working class during adulthood
3. Receiving a strong or at least a moderate degree of exposure to a conservative Christian ideology (such as Mormonism or evangelical Protestantism) during childhood
4. Having a religious problem-solving perspective

As we have seen, all or most of these conditions were present in the bulk of Levites in my sample.

Thus far, these conditions characterize many other working class Mormons as well. While some of them may investigate other Mormon sects or even join non-Mormon religious groups, the great majority either will remain active Mormons, who cope with feelings of marginality or deprivation in a presumably wide variety of ways, or become inactive ("Jack") Mormons. Indeed, Lofland and Stark (1965, 867), in noting that "because people have a number of conventional and readily available definitions for, and means of coping with their problems, there were, in the end, very few converts to D.P.," recognize a similar pattern in their conversion sample. They also note that potential converts often "persist in stressful situations with little or no relief," "take specifically problem-directed action to change troublesome portions of their lives, without adopting a different world view to interpret them," or resort to "a number of maneuvers to 'put the problem out of mind' " (Lofland and Stark 1965, 868). Given the increasingly middle-class orientation of the Mormon Church, particularly since World War II, there is a pressing need to delineate the strategies that many working class Mormons adopt in dealing with their marginality, short of apostasy.

In their recent elaboration of the concept of relative deprivation, Stark and Bainbridge (1985, 6) introduce the notion of compensator, defined as "the belief that a reward will be obtained in the distant future or in some other context which cannot be immediately verified." In their view, religions offer compensators for scarce rewards or resources. In keeping with the common assertion that sects tend to exhibit an other-worldly orientation, Stark and Bainbridge (1985, 12) assert that the promise of eternal life as a compensator "can assuage worldly suffering by emphasizing the better to come. . . ." While indeed many sects function in this manner, the Aaronic Order cannot be characterized as a particularly other-worldly religion. As Stark and Bainbridge themselves observe,

> Any organization that provides a stage for human action and interaction will provide numerous direct rewards. . . . religious movements deal not only in compensators, but also in very tangible, direct rewards. Thus, people can gain a variety of rewards from religious commitment. They can earn a living from religion. Religions offer human companionship, status as an upright person of good character . . . leisure and recreational activity, opportunities for marriage, courtship, and business contacts—a whole host of things people value (Stark and Bainbridge 1985, 11).

The prospects of entering the celestial kingdom, achieving eternal salvation, recreating United Order, and witnessing the gathering of the tribes of Israel and the Second Coming of Christ all have served as compensators for Levites at one time or another. On a day-to-day basis, membership in a group that provides one with a sense of belonging, purpose, and psychsocial support has provided most Levites more immediate rewards—ones that they found blocked as Mormons or members of other religious bodies.

The presence of relative deprivation, a working-class background, and strong or moderate socialization into a conservative religious tradition, serve to predispose certain individuals to join the Aaronic Order, or perhaps one of various other Mormon sects. Ultimately, however, conversion will be completed only if one or more situational conditions are present. An inductive examination of the Levite conversion experience suggests the following situational conditions:

1. Experiencing some type of life crisis a relatively short time before or during the pre-convert's investigation of the new group
2. Having contact with significant others, such as parents, spouse, relatives and friends who are affiliated with the religious group
3. Interacting intensively with other members of the religious group
4. Elimination or neutralization of extra-group attachments

Recognizing the difficulty of differentiating between the "life crisis experience" or "turning point" and the lesser difficulties of everyday living, which in retrospect may be greatly exaggerated, it may be argued that the former constitutes a predisposing condition rather than a situational condition. At any rate, an increasing number of studies suggest that the crucial factor in facilitating commitment to a new religious group is the presence of preexisting interpersonal bonds between members and prospective converts. In an article that attempts to generalize the finding of some of these studies, including the one that Stark originally did with Lofland on the Divine Precepts group, Stark and Bainbridge argue the following:

> There is nothing contradictory between the deprivation and ideological appeal line of analysis and that which stresses the importance of social networks. Both seem obvious requirements of any adequate theory. If deprivation alone explained recruitment to cults and sects, millions more people would become members than actually do. Recruits must not only suffer relevant deprivations and be open to a radical group's ideological appeal; they must be placed in a situation where they develop social bonds with existing members of the cult or sect (Stark and Bainbridge 1980, 13).

As we have already seen, my data on the Levite conversion experience indicate that significant others played a vital role not only in introducing potential converts to the Aaronic Order, but also in promoting recruitment to it. This condition, perhaps coupled with intensive interaction with other Levites, appears to create a "network of faith" which bridges the gap between being a disaffected Mormon, who copes in one way or other with feelings of alienation and marginality within the church, and joining the Order. While the elimination or neutralization of extra-group attachments does not appear to be an absolutely necessary condition to facilitate conversion, during the 1940s it undoubtedly served to speed it up as a result of excommunication from the Mormon Church, and to some extent may have facilitated conversion after 1950 or so.

In order to illustrate the role of networking in ensuring conversion, I will refer to the conversion of Hilda. Hilda, who was born in Sweden and reared in the Midwest; and who after the age of seven, moved to Utah after her marriage broke up. In 1931, after being prayed over by Mormon elders during an acute illness, she joined the Mormon Church. Because she had only attended grade school for three years and worked in a nursery, she felt like a "crumb" in her predominantly middle-class ward. In 1940 Hilda moved across the street from Catherine, whose older sister was a follower of Glendenning. After Hilda moved again, she still maintained contact with Catherine, who in 1945 became a probationary member of the Aaronic Order, despite her husband's objections. In 1949 Catherine coaxed Hilda to attend the baptism of her two sons into the Order. Hilda signed an application for membership in the sect the following Sunday. Over a year later, on the very same day, both Hilda and Catherine were baptized into the Order. Hilda said that when she came into the group, the Levites were considerably closer than they have been in recent times. Glendenning appointed her to serve as the secretary of the Salt Lake branch. Hilda referred to the fruit canning sessions at the branch at this time as "so delightful" because the Levites were "just one." While she felt marginal in the Mormon Church and that the Mormons were no longer following the spirit of their scriptures, her friendship with Catherine and subsequent intensive interaction with the other Levites ensured her conversion.

The framework proposed above is based on data collected in interviews with converts to a specific type of religious organization. Both Richardson et. al. (1979) and Snow and Phillips (1980) have applied the Lofland and Stark's world-saver model to the respective religious groups that they studied. In both instances, their data did not confirm the world-saver model in its entirety. In the application of my own data to the model, I have found various points of congruence and divergence with the process of conversion that individuals who joined the Aaronic Order underwent. Overall, while the predisposing and situational conditions that Lofland and Stark delineate often contributed to the conversion of certain individuals to the Levite sect, all of these conditions were not always present in each case of conversion.

Given the proliferation of processual interpretations of religious conversion, Richardson (1985, 164) maintains that a new conversion paradigm which views "humans as volitional entities who assign meaning to their action and to the actions of others within a social context" has emerged in the past fifteen or twenty years. I believe that the field approach to conversion potentially allows for human subjectivism as a component of a convert's decision to join a religious group, or even to adopt a secular alternative to religion. Unfortunately, while it is true that some processual models of conversion have tended to be overly deterministic, the new paradigm that Richardson and others propose runs the serious risk of being reductionist. In this regard, let us be reminded of Marx's well-known assertion from *The Eighteenth Brumaire of Louis Boneparte* noting that "Men make their own history, but they do not make it as they please; they do not make it under circumstances chosen by themselves, but under circumstances directly encountered, given, and transmitted from the past."

A process of religious conversion similar to that experienced by recruits to the Divine Precepts cult or the Levite sect appears to be particularly useful in understanding conversion to other small religious bodies in western society. It seems likely that conversion to other types of religious groups, such as large churches, denominations, and certain middle class cults, would involve a somewhat different process. Indeed, Lofland and Stark never intended to apply their model of conversion to all religious groups. As Arthur L. Greil and David R. Rudy (1984, 318–319) observe. "There is no such thing as *the* conversion process; rather, there are as many conversion processes as there are organizational contexts in which conversion takes place." Consequently, there is a need to study conversion to a wide range of religious organizations. Only when this has been done both vertically (within a particular culture) and horizontally (cross-culturally) will social scientists be in a position to generalize about religious conversion.

In order to illuminate my framework of the Levite conversion experience more completely, I will apply it to Henry, an elderly man who was introduced to the Levitical Writings in 1930 and, except for Glendenning's widow, had been associated with the sect longer than any other living member.

**Henry the Pioneer**

Henry was born during the 1890s in a rural area of Switzerland. His parents were poor working and extremely religious people who converted from Lutheranism to Mormonism. When he was ten years old, Henry was also baptized a member of the Mormon Church. Henry described himself as a "self-educated man" with nine years of common grade school. As a Mormon, Henry encountered much ridicule and consequently studied his religion earnestly in order to defend his beliefs.

When he was nineteen years old, Henry became the first member of his family to migrate to Utah. He worked for two or three blacksmiths while residing in Cache Valley (Logan area), but became disillusioned with the behavioral patterns of many Mormons. He found them to be too worldly and was appalled that many Mormon leaders were more concerned about economic matters than religious matters. Henry also was disturbed that the Mormon Church failed to follow certain practices, such as the Law of Consecration and United Order. He felt that the Mormon Church should be working for social equality among its members and questioned how some Mormons could be millionaires while others were poor. He suspected that some Mormon leaders even used their church positions to become wealthier. Consequently, Henry felt that there was a need for the One Mighty and Strong to come and set the

House of God in order again. At one point, his despair caused him to doubt Mormonism. After two hours of intensive prayer on the matter, a voice directed him to be faithful to the Mormon doctrines and to disregard the behavior of many Mormons.

After working for two-and-a-half years in the Cache Valley, Henry attended a fall conference of the Mormon Church in Salt Lake City, at which time he obtained a job with the Rio Grande Railroad. A few months later he joined the aviation-mechanical branch of the army during World War I and served at several state-side locations. After his military duty he returned to his job at the railroad. In 1920 he married a woman seven years older than himself in the Salt Lake Temple. He and his wife settled down, and had five children.

In 1921 Henry was laid off from his job but later was called back to work again. After four days, however, another man with more seniority than Henry returned and displaced him. Henry was deeply disturbed by this incident and heard a voice say, "Why worry? Perhaps the Lord has something else." As he rode his bicycle home from work, the voice repeatedly said the word "south." That night Henry had a dream that made him realize that the voice had been directing him to work at the Koyle Relief Mine about fifty-five miles south of Salt Lake City. Until now Henry had ridiculed his brother-in-law for working at the Dream Mine. Henry was still somewhat unsure about the significance of his dream and teased his brother-in-law about the Dream Mine in order to learn more about it. In his dream, he had seen a translucent rock containing thousands of petrified animals. When he broke the rock, the petrified animals came to life and grew to their full size. His brother-in-law told him that the petrified animals in the dream were symbolic of the mining activities of the Nephites at the Dream Mine mountain during ancient times. When Henry accompanied his brother-in-law to the Dream Mine mountain, he immediately bore testimony that the story about the Dream Mine was true. Henry purchased some stock at the mine and worked there for the next fourteen months. He returned to his railroad job because he was unable to earn enough money to support his family from his job at the Dream Mine. Nevertheless, Henry worked intermittently at the Dream Mine thereafter for periods as long as eighteen months until his health began to fail.

In 1930, due to the Depression, Henry was again unemployed. During one of his many visits to the Salt Lake Temple, a friend, whom he had met at the Dream Mine, told him about a firstborn son of Aaron who was now residing in Provo. Henry gathered together about twenty people to hear the Writings while his friend brought to Henry's home Glendenning and a man who read the Writings to the meeting. After Henry heard three Writings, he knew that they were valid and immediately began to tell others about them. Many meetings at which the Writings were discussed were held at Henry's home during the 1930s. Although Henry's trades were carpentry and cabinetmaking, he worked at whatever jobs he could obtain during the Great Depression. He regularly visited the temple, and while there, told others about the Levitical Writings. Henry was active in his ward, having been a member of the elders' quorum for twelve years and high priests' quorum for ten years. He also taught various types of religious classes and was the president of his ward's genealogical society.

Shortly after the first consecrations were made in California, Henry consecrated his property and possessions to the Aaronic Order. The main office of the Aaronic Order was located in his home from late 1942 to 1951. He was a member of the Interceding Council for many years and was designated an Aaronite by Glendenning. Henry worked at the Alpha Colony for fifteen months and was instrumental in the establishment of Partoun. Although Henry was excommunicated from the Mormon Church in 1942 because of his belief in and promotion of the Levitical Writings, he still regarded himself to be a Mormon as well as an Aaronite.

Of the five forms of deprivation predisposing individuals to join the Order, it appears that all of them, with the exception of organismic deprivation, played a role in Henry's conversions. Henry also had a working class background, exhibited a strong religious problem-solving perspective, and experienced considerable stress before meeting Glendenning. Friends told him about Glendenning. While Henry accepted the Levitical Writings as valid almost immediately, intensive interaction with Glendenning's followers strengthened his commitment to the emerging sect. Henry continued to maintain some ties with some Mormons for most of his life, but found it difficult to do so during the 1940s after he was excommunicated from the Mormon Church.

## *Conversion as a Form of Problem-Solving Behavior*

Psychiatrists and psychologists often view religious conversion in a context of psychopathology. Other social scientists argue that conversion often performs various socially integrative and therapeutic functions for the individual. William James (1902) maintained that unification of the divided self is an optimum result of conversion. Conversion may involve a rebirth of submerged religious complexes with an acceptance of them (Maves 1963, 45–46). In other words, the individual turns to or intensifies the religious problem-solving perspective which he acquired during an earlier period of his life. In his discussion of conversion, Leon Salzmann (1953) focuses on the "regressive" form of conversion. Yet, he notes that the "progressive" form results in the positive fulfillment of one's powers with self-awareness, concern for others, and oneness with the world." In an analysis of one type of religious conversion, Wallace (1956b, 635) notes, "the process of mazeway resynthesis . . . seems to have the function of restoring an internal biopsychic equilibrium. It is, in a word, an autotherapeutic process that reduces stress."

Although this book deals primarily with a specific expression of conversion, namely, the decision to join a small religious group, conversion-like phenomena are recurring processes in the human condition. Conversion, which may be defined as a drastic change in attitudes and/or behavioral patterns, may also occur in other spheres of life. Conversion-like behavior is a common response to the frustrations, anxieties, and conflicts of life and should not be regarded necessarily as a psychopathological phenomenon. Indeed, conversion-like behavior is a process which can prevent pathology and have therapeutic effects on the individual.

This observation held true not only for rank and file Levite converts but also for Glendenning himself. In a sense, Glendenning was his own first convert. While many of the specifics of Glendenning's conversion will never be determined, the Levite prophet appeared to have experienced intense ethical, economic, social, psychic, and organismic deprivation prior to his public revelations. Like his followers, Glendenning belonged to the working class, received a conservative religious upbringing, and viewed the world from a religious perspective. In a sense, Glendenning and his early followers converted each other. Even after he moved to Utah and joined the Mormon Church, Glendenning continued to experience life crises. His daughter's conversion to the Mormon Church facilitated Glendenning's conversion to that group and his eventual encounter with disaffected working class Mormons. His ongoing interaction with the early Levites eventually convinced of the need to establish the Aaronic Order. As we saw in the previous chapter, the Order served as the partial solution to many of Glendenning's problems.

Although emotional factors are present in any case of religious conversion, it is a process which often involves a great deal of introspection, study and cognitive reorientation. This latter type of conversion has been greatly emphasized in the Aaronic Order. The belief systems of radical sects are often regarded to be irrational and illogical. If one makes certain assumptions, however, the Levite belief system is internally consistent and logical. It is only when the individual begins to question the assumptions of the belief system or accepts certain parts of other perspectives that contradictions emerge in his or her mind. As long as this does not occur, the Levite can use his or her belief system to impose meaning and order on reality.

Formal conversion does not necessarily reduce or eliminate the feelings of deprivation which predispose certain individuals to join the Aaronic Order are exposed to a multitude of viewpoints, particularly if inevitably arise and must be dealt with in order to insure the continuation of the convert's faith in and commitment to the group and its ideology. The group must provide mechanisms by which the convert's cognitive, social, and psychological needs are met. Since members of the Aaronic Order are exposed to a multitude of viewpoints, particularly if they live in an urban area and come into contact with nonmembers at work or school, it becomes necessary for the group to devise a method that reinforces belief in its ideology and negates conflicting input. The many study classes that are conducted at the various branches serve such a function as does the weekly discussion about world events presented by the Chief High Priest at Eskdale.

The Levite politico-religious hierarchy is a mechanism which provides status for at least certain members. A member of this hierarchy, even if he or she holds a relatively minor position in it, becomes a member of the most important ecclesiastical governing body in that world. Conversely, the existence of ranking in a group that espouses egalitarianism creates certain tensions. In other words, some people are "more equal" than others. It appears that some individuals have lost interest in the Aaronic Order because they were not able to obtain positions that they desired.

The rituals of the Aaronic Order are an important device for creating social solidarity among its members. Although there exists a considerable amount of diversity in the beliefs that members subscribe to, the various ordinances, such as the sacrament meeting and the worship service, tend to eradicate temporarily ideological differences among members. These rituals remind the individual that he is part of a group. Individuals who feel animosity toward one another occasionally settle their differences at these sessions and resolve to live in harmony.

The testimony sessions that occur on the first Saturday of the month and spontaneously from time to time are occasions when members express their dependence on the Order. Perhaps even more pronounced is the use of these sessions as a cathartic mechanism which permits individuals to express feelings of frustration and anxiety. Testimonies often take the form of confession of transgressions against others and failure to conform to the group's norms. Forgiveness is also asked of God and others during prayer circles. During testimony and prayer sessions, individuals experiencing marital or economic problems, doubts, temptations, and so forth are prayed for or given some type of moral support. The love one feels for the individual with a problem is often expressed at these times.

The fact that the Aaronic Order has a large number of inactive and semi-active members indicates that conversion is not always a process that solves all of the individual's problems. Several converts, including some at Eskdale, told me that they do not feel accepted by most Levites. This appears to be particularly true of individuals who have few or no relatives in the Order. One middle-aged man complained that many Levites have a "you come to them" rather than a "they come to you" attitude. Another male convert feels that some of the priests would rather not hear what he has to say. A female convert noted that although she felt accepted while she resided at Eskdale, she was unable to develop "close" relationships with any of its residents. When many Levites spoke of someone who is presently inactive in the Aaronic Order, they often stated tht he or she was "offended" by some person or persons and consequently discontinued attending group activities. With the advent of the "charismatic" movement within the Order during the summer of 1974, many Levites expressed publicly their concern about their past inability to be more open and supportive of others and vowed to overcome this tendency. The emergence of the charismatic movement was largely stimulated by contacts with a Jesus group from California known as the Order of the Lamb. A young man, who had joined the Aaronic Order several years earlier, emerged as the informal leader of the charismatic movement. In his efforts to win other Levites over to the revival, he was supported by his wife, Robert Conrad's eldest daughter. For awhile, the charismatic movement directed the Levites on the way toward greater unity. It integrated into the Order many of the young Levites who had not experienced the pioneering efforts of the older Levites. It even managed, at least in part, to transcend generational cleavages. However, as we will see in chapter 6, the charismatic movement in the end sowed the seeds of the most serious internal rift in the history of the Aaronic Order.

# 4

# *The Levite Community: The Search for* Gemeinschaft

The communitarian tradition has appealed throughout history to the alienated and disenfranchised living on the margins of civilization. Their search for a return to *Gemeinschaft* is a universal and ancient impulse—one that has accompanied the development of state or class societies. According to John Bennett (1975, 63), the communitarian tradition is the "oldest 'new' and the most traditional 'experimental' social movement in the West." It reaches back at least to the time of the Essenes, who practiced a rigid communism of property in Palestine. Many revitalization movements that emerged both before and after the Protestant Reformation, including the Lollards, the Labadists, the Waldenses, and the Anabaptists, practiced communalism of one sort or other. Communitarianism was practiced by groups such as the Shakers, Oneidans, the Harmonists, the Rappites, and the Amana colonies of nineteenth century America. Indeed, early Mormonism was very much influenced by the communitarian spirit of the 1830s and 1840s as was evident by its emphasis on the Law of Consecration and United Order. In the late 1960s, a new communal movement emerged in the United States as an outgrowth of the "hippie" counterculture and the anti-Vietnam War movement. This movement came to include those who sought salvation in Eastern mysticism or in Christian fundamentalism.

The search for *Gemeinschaft* on the part of communalists has resulted in a variety of ideological rationales. Rosabeth Moss Kanter identifies three rhetorical styles, namely, religious, political, and psychological, underlying communal groups:

> The religious view holds that the established society is out of touch with meaningful values, preventing people from being close to God and to the true purpose of life. The sharing and love of a commune thus promises a more *spiritual* existence. The political view is based on an analysis of the distribution of power and resources in the established society, arguing that the have's dominate and exploit the have-not's, preventing most people from sharing fully in the proceeds of their labor or making the decisions that affect their lives. To people with socialist leanings the commune provides a more *egalitarian* existence. The psychological view holds that the existing society is inherently alienating, keeping people from meaningful contact with each other, with their own bodies, and with their innermost selves, making love and trust impossible. In the commune people feel they will find increased possibilities for more *intimate* relationships (Kanter 1973, 6).

Of these rhetorics, the religious one obviously serves as the guiding principle for Levite communalism. Members of the Aaronic Order believe that they are continuing the long communitarian tradition characteristic of Israelites throughout the ages. The Law of Consecration, which embodies "giving all one's possession of this world's goods" and "all one's time, talents, and energy to the service of God," was given to the tribe of Levite in 1736 B.C. (Beeston 1966, 246). The ancient Levites and some other Israelite groups, both in the Old World and the New World, lived communally, as did Jesus Christ and his early followers. According to Robert Conrad, the Israelites—who include the Essenes of Qumran, the Incas, the Polynesians and the Micronesians, the Hutterites, the Waldenses, and Glendenning's ancestors in Scotland—have a very rich communitarian tradition. Non-Levites may live communally by becoming "Levites-by-adoption."

The desire of the early Levites to resurrect the communitarian tradition of nineteenth century Mormonism served as an important rationale for the establishment of the Aaronic Order. In fact, Glendenning's followers attempted to live communally near Alton in southwestern Utah during the early 1930s—a full decade before the incorporation of the Order as a religious body. After this initial effort failed, several other attempts to live either cooperatively or communally were made during the next two decades. This chapter will discuss these various ventures as well as the creation of the Eskdale commune and the social structure of the Aaronic Order.

## *Early Levite Cooperative and Communal Efforts*

Both religious and secular utopian ventures have found the task of community construction an ardous one. Most communal and cooperative groups tend to collapse within a few years of their establishment. The Levite search for *Gemeinschaft* has not been easier than that of many other groups. Unlike many other communitarian ventures, the Levites have been able to start over again when one of their social experiments either collapsed or foundered. In addition, when certain parties became weary of the search for community, others were willing to take their places.

### The Communal Experiment at Alton

The Great Depression placed a severe economic strain on Glendenning and his followers. At this time, many of the people who exhibited an interest in the Levitical Writings asked themselves why their church was not living the Law of Consecration and United Order. Glendenning may not have been the first one to suggest to the early Levites the possibility of living communally. Instead it appears to have been an idea that was in the air at the time. According to Henry, whose biographical sketch was presented in the previous chapter, some of Glendenning's followers persuaded him to join them in the creation of a communal venture on a farm about eleven miles from the small village of Alton, which is located a short distance south of Bryce Canyon National Park in southwestern Utah. Glendenning and another man in turn tried to persuade Henry to join them at Alton. Since Henry was unemployed at the time, this seemed to be a logical step for him to take. He decided, however, not to join the group planning to move to Alton after a voice told him, "Not this time; you will be up north." Shortly thereafter, Henry went to work at the Brigham Dream Mine, located about eighty miles north of Salt Lake City, and made three new converts to Glendenning's message there.

In June 1932, the Glendennings joined a couple with four young children in the establishment of the Alton Colony. Since the Glendennings were the smaller of the two families, they lived in a tent, whereas the other family stayed in the farm house on the premises. A third couple with three young children joined the small settlement later in the summer and also lived in a tent. This couple had owned a small dress shop but lost most of their customers after they started to investigate the Levitical Writings. The three families ate communally and took turns preparing meals. Initially the three families agreed not to discuss the revelations that Glendenning had received with the residents of Alton so their children would not be harassed at school. Glendenning found work on a road crew and other odd jobs. According to one Levite, Glendenning was ill much of the time during the first summer and unable to do his share of the work.

When one of the men became angry with Glendenning, he told the residents of Alton that the Levite prophet claimed to be the recipient of revelations from a supernatural source. Upon learning this, the townspeople allegedly became hostile toward Glendenning and his followers. In response to the hostility of the villagers, Glendenning received a Writing in February of 1934 which placed a curse upon them (Book of Elias 1944, Sec. 199). Another family, which had lost its construction business, joined the group for about a year, and yet another couple stayed with the group for a summer. Shortly thereafter the people at Alton became disillusioned with the communal venture and looked for other ways to deal with economic deprivation. None of the people who joined the Glendennings in Alton became permanently committed to the "work of Levi and Aaron." When the Glendennings decided to move to Hurricane in the summer of 1934 so that their daughter could attend high school in a nearby town, the fate of the Alton social experiment was sealed.

### Alpha Colony and the Levite Sawmill

Bliss Childs, the Second High Priest of the Order until his death in the spring of 1975, initiated the next Levite communal venture. He and his wife had consecrated their 107 acre farm on the outskirts of the small Mormon town of Springville in the Utah Valley after they joined the Order. In early 1949 Childs invited another family to join the Alpha Colony. The Childs family continued living at the old homestead. The second family initially resided in a tent as did several other newcomers over the years. Families at the colony lived in separate quarters, and ate their meals communally in a large tent. At one time or another, at least five families, as well as several individuals, lived and worked at the Alpha Colony. After the erection of a church building on the grounds, two families occupied apartments on each side of the new structure. Even after the colony dissolved as a commune per se sometime in the mid-1950s, families and individuals other than the Childs family lived on the premises. The site of the colony has continued to serve as the meeting place of the Springville branch of the Aaronic Order. Glendenning spent about a year or so at the colony during the early 1950s, again for awhile in the late 1950s, and reportedly spent much of the last seven years of his life there.

The members of the Alpha Colony were engaged in various economic projects. The community raised hay for its beef cattle and dairy cows, some grain crops, and vegetables for the members of the Springville branch. The men often worked outside the community. Two or three Levite men worked at a small coal mine near Price, Utah, and two others worked for awhile at the large Baker Ranch at the base of Wheeler Park in Nevada and near the present site of Eskdale.

The single most important economic project of the Alpha Colony was a sawmill which was established in 1950. The sawmill was located in the Huntington Canyon section of the Wasatch Plateau in central Utah, near the town of Fairview. Due to its location at an elevation of 9,500 feet, the sawmill could be operated only from late spring until early fall. Many young people spent their summers working at the sawmill; it provided them with the opportunity for courtship. For most of its ten years of operation, the sawmill was directed by its founder, a former agricultural teacher at Snow College, a two-year junior college in Ephraim, Utah. During this period, the administration of the sawmill was transferred from the Alpha Colony to the Christian Aid Society of America, a Levite organization involved in various work and charity projects. The lumber produced at the sawmill was used primarily for the construction of houses and other buildings at Partoun and later at Eskdale. Surplus lumber, which tended to be of marginal quality, was sold on the open market. The sawmill was forced to close in the early 1960s when the U.S. Forest Service ceased permitting the operation of private sawmills on national forest land.

The dissolution of the Alpha Colony appears to have been related to the diversion of energies into projects outside of the Springville area. The colony's cattle were sold so that trucks and equipment could be purchased for the sawmill operation. Work at the sawmill during the summer months shifted labor away from the colony during the most critical portion of the agricultural cycle. Perhaps even more significant in this diversionary process was the establishment of the desert community of Partoun only several months after the Alpha Colony was started. Eventually most of the residents of the colony moved to Partoun or Eskdale. In essence, the Alpha Colony not so much collapsed as withered away as its members moved to greener or, perhaps better stated, more arid pastures.

**Partoun, the First Levite Desert Community**

In the spring of 1949 the Levites established Partoun (named after an area in Scotland where Glendenning's ancestors once lived), their first community in the western Utah desert. A Writing entitled "Go ye into the lands of the earth" in part served as the community's creation (Book of New Revelations 1948, Chap. 23, 63–64). Thirty-seven homesteads (each

160 acres) were filed for, some by non-Levites, and of these thirty were actually settled for some time. Most homesteaders were required to install a deep well, which would provide water for farming, and to have forty acres under production within five years of their settlement as the conditions for receiving title to the land. Ex-servicemen could receive title to their homesteads by establishing and residing on them for one year. Eventually fourteen families or individuals obtained title to their homesteads, six of the titles having been obtained through the provision for ex-servicemen. Five "families," who were unable to improve their land according to the government regulations, took advantage of an option to purchase five acres of their original homestead claim for a nominal fee; one family purchased an additional thirty-five acres. One of these families consisted of two unmarried sisters who had converted to the Mormon Church in Sweden and later immigrated to Utah.

Partoun functioned as a cooperative rather than a communal venture, although most participants did consecrate their property and possessions to the Aaronic Order. According to one elderly man who had resided at Partoun since 1949, it was eventually to become a United Order or communal venture. His wife noted that Glendenning told the Levites that the homes at Partoun would be arranged in a semicircle, just as those at Eskdale are. Small groups of men and a female carpenter worked cooperatively in the establishment of various homesteads. Because of financial pressures, many of the male residents worked for wages during the week in the Wasatch Front area and improved their homesteads on the weekends. Some men were able to find work, often temporary, on nearby ranches or at Fish Springs National Wildlife Refuge. Occasionally young Levite men from the Wasatch Front area worked at Partoun. Some women did road work and farmed while their husbands were away from Partoun.

The West Desert School, which was part of the Tintic School District headquartered in Eureka, was established in the fall of 1949. Until the early 1950s the school offered some high school work, but since then it has been exclusively a grade school. Initially classes were conducted in the Levite chapel, but later a school house was constructed. The West Desert School had three teachers in the spring of 1975, one of whom was a member of the Order, and forty-three students from the communities of Partoun, Callao and Trout Creek.

Because of inadequate funds to sink deep wells and develop the land, the alkalinity of the soil, and the lack of agricultural expertise on the part of many of its residents, Partoun had many economic problems. Only a few homesteads became somewhat productive. Some of the older residents subsisted from Social Security payments, pensions, or various types of public welfare. One Levite male, who did not want to postpone the United Order any longer, attempted to establish a communal venture at Partoun with his family and several others sympathetic to his cause. Later he and his family returned to the main body of the Aaronic Order, but were required by Glendenning to be rebaptized to do so.

Like Alpha Colony, Partoun declined as a result of the diversion of energies and resources to other projects. In 1955 Partoun had some sixty residents; this number rapidly dwindled as people left for the new Eskdale commune fifty miles to the south. According to one elderly man who was involved in the development of Partoun, the first Levite desert community was left in a "desolate condition" as a result of the removal of equipment to the new commune. One longtime female resident of Partoun lamented that the cooperative community "had barely reached first base" when Glendenning decided to establish Eskdale. Despite the decline of Partoun, several individuals and families, most of them elderly, still reside there.

### Eskdale, the Second Levite Desert Community

The culmination of the Levite search for *Gemeinschaft* and United Order is the Eskdale commune located in a remote section of the western Utah desert.[1] Whereas the other Levite endeavors in cooperative and communal living either dissolved or, in the case of Partoun, became largely a retirement site for elderly Levites, Eskdale has managed to survive considerably longer than the majority of communitarian ventures. Since its establishment in 1955 Eskdale has served as the center of Levite economic, social, religious, and educational activities, as well as a source of hope for the future. It is the site of the Order's educational and musical facilities and of the annual June convocation, which brings together Levites from all over the country. Since its beginning, many urban Levites from the Salt Lake and Utah Valleys have made seemingly countless number of treks to this unpretentious desert settlement. Many of these Levites hope that some day, perhaps once they have paid off their debts, they too will be able to settle at Eskdale or one of the other desert communites planned for the future. For members of the Aaronic Order, Eskdale serves as a living, if not yet perfect, model of communalism.

The search for a general outline for a commune may have prompted Glendenning to visit the Hutterite colonies in Montana in 1948 (Beeston 1966, 204–210). Glendenning claimed that he earlier had received a revelation, which was transcribed in September of 1948, stating that the Hutterites are "Northern Levites." As a consequence, the Levites feel a strong spiritual bond with the Hutterites. In return, the Hutterites, who consist of three "peoples" or *Leuten* (the *Schmieden-leut*, the *Lehrer-leut*, and *Darius-leut*) refer to the Levites as *Glendenning-leut*. During the early 1950s, Glendenning and several other Levites made a number of trips to the Hutterite colonies in Montana. Since then the Levites have maintained regular contact with their spiritual brethren to the North.

Based upon information concerning the relatively easy accessibility to ground water in the central portion of the Snake Valley provided by a Levite man who had worked at the Baker Ranch in Nevada, Glendenning and several Levites visited the area in December 1954 to investigate the possibility of establishing a new community there. In mid-June of 1955 two cabins from Partoun and a house trailer were moved to the new community to house its first settlers. One cabin served as a cook house and dining hall and the other as a bunk house; the trailer was also used for sleeping accommodations (Beeston 1966, 219).

Eskdale was established under the guidelines of the Desert Entry Act, which enabled the community, unlike the case at Partoun, to concentrate the residences in one area rather than establish a homestead on each of the ten 320 acre entries. Eskdale gradually gained population, developed its land for agriculture, and added new buildings. Most early settlers of Eskdale lived in one-room houses which used coal, oil and gas lamps. Later the community acquired a 60,000 generator which provided electricity. In 1972 Eskdale hooked up its electrical system with the Mt. Wheeler Power Company of Nevada. In September 1956 Eskdale established a public grade school, with nine students, which became part of the Millard County School District (Beeston 1957, 223). A parochial high school was added to the community in 1960.

From a community with a handful of residents, Eskdale had grown to one with a population close to one hundred. In 1975 Eskdale consisted of thirteen houses arranged in two semicircular rows on the eastern portion of the community grounds, two small trailers housing two windows, and several public facilities. Except for the grade school, all the public buildings are located on the western portion of the community grounds. These include the dining hall-kitchen-laundry complex, a small high school building, the auditorium-school-music facilities complex, the Monterrori school, and the school dormitory. The dairy is located southeast of the community center and the shop buildings are directly north of it. Since the Eskdale commune constitutes the central focus of Levite activities, I will defer a more extensive discussion of its social organization and communal patterns for the following chapter.

## *The Social Structure of the Aaronic Order*

One of the major dissatisfactions that the early Levites had with modern Mormonism was its abandonment of certain egalitarian and communal ideals. The social structure of the Levite community represents an effort to recreate what the Mormon Church had forsaken. The Levites at first were more interested in reforming Mormonism from within than designing an alternative to it, but condemnation of their plan by the church hierarchy contributed to the notion that reform was not feasible. Their knowledge of the social organization of the Mormon Church, with its politico-religious hierarchy and system of mutual aid and cooperative networks, gave them a basis for the development of their own community. Furthermore, as we have seen, Glendenning may have used his familiarity with Hutterite communalism as a living model for the establishment of the Eskdale commune.

## Current Social Composition of the Aaronic Order

The present social composition of the Order differs somewhat from that of its early days. In addition to the surviving pioneers, it includes the children and grandchildren of the early Levites, as well as some individuals of a non-Mormon background who for various reasons migrated to Utah. Members of the Levite community can be divided into two principal categories—active and inactive. For purposes of my census, *active* members include individuals who attended Levite activities at least once every two months. Also included in this category are strongly commited Levites who cannot attend as regularly because of living outside of Utah or because of old age or poor health. Individuals (except for young children) who did not meet one of these criteria are classified as *inactive* members.

Because I was unable to contact most inactive adult members, their children were usually not included in the census.[2] The children of inactive members in almost all cases were inactive as well. Table 4-1 presents the results of the census of the Levite community I conducted during mid-1975. Since I usually had to rely on information given by active members in identifying inactive members, the census figures for the latter is probably somewhat conservative. Inactive members can be divided into two sub-categories—those who maintain some contact with the Levite community, often because they are related to active members, and those who apparently have broken all, or nearly all, ties with it.

Table 4.2 presents selected demographic characteristics of the Eskdale commune in May 1975. Because Eskdale has an appreciable number of school children whose parents are not residents of the community, its population is appreciably lower during the summer months. A few of the school children are not members of the Aaronic Order.

Table A-3 in the appendix shows the socioeconomic status of active Levites between twenty-five and fifty years of age during the summer of 1975. Most of the people in the sample are the offspring of the initial

Table 4-1
A Census of the Levite Community

| | Active Members | | Inactive Members |
|---|---|---|---|
| | Over Age 18 | Under Age 18 | Over Age 18 |
| Male | 56 | 50 | 51 |
| Female | 71 | 52 | 57 |
| Total | 127 | 102 | 108 |

Table 4-2
Selected Demographic Characteristics of the Eskdale Commune

| Category | Number |
|---|---|
| Nuclear families with children | 9 |
| Couples without children | 3 |
| Widows | 4 |
| Bachelors | 6 |
| School children whose parents do not reside at Eskdale | 17 |
| Eskdale population | 94 |

members of the Aaronic Order, although some are individuals who joined the Order at a later date. Table A-3 shows that ten out of twenty-one can be classified as laborers (most of whom are skilled); six were teachers, one a medical doctor, one an engineer, one a lawyer, one a salesman, and one a graduate school student. Five of the males had graduate school degrees and six had undergraduate college degrees. Except for one individual, who had a high school degree, all the males in the sample had some formal education beyond high school. Table A-3 lists the occupations of women before most of them became primarily homemakers. In four cases women worked primarily as homemakers almost immediately after completing high school or attending college. Fourteen women were skilled, semiskilled, or unskilled workers, four professional teachers, and one a law student. Five women had undergraduate college degrees, one a master's degree, and only one had not graduated from high school. Two males, who joined the Order within the past twenty years but are not included in Table A-3, held doctoral degrees. A comparison of Tables A-1, A-2, and A-3 shows that whereas the older Levites were or are primarily members of the working-class, younger Levites (fifty years and younger) have considerably more formal education and have gravitated to professional occupations. As H.

Richard Niebuhr (1929) and others have contended, the socioeconomic status and the social attitudes of the membership of a sect changes over time if it manages to survive. This generalization, as we will see in chapter 6, also applies to the Aaronic Order and has had important implications for its development as a religious organization.

### Levels and Symbols of Membership

Because of the difficulty and sacrifices in living communally, the Levites believe that most individuals or families must pass through a series of steps before successfully achieving this ideal. They have instituted three degrees of membership in their community: (1) tithing membership (2) consecrated membership and (3) United Order membership.

Like the Mormons, the Levites believe that tithing of a "dedicated tenth of one's possessions or increase" is expected of all. This is a "lesser law" than "full consecration"—the act of turning the title to all of one's possessions over to the church (Beeston 1966, 260). An individual who is accepted for membership will be first baptized and confirmed as a tithing member in the "Kingdom of God." After a probationary period of one year, application may be made for full membership in the True Church of God as a consecrated member. Before an individual becomes a fully consecrated member, he or she undergoes a probation of at least one year and tentatively deeds his or her property to the Aaronic Order. An applicant may extend his probationary period. A consecrated member receives a "stewardship" over, or responsibility to care for, property. Unless a member lives at Eskdale, he usually is given a stewardship over the property and possessions owned before consecration. The probationary consecrated member may reclaim his property and possessions, but not large sums of money if he decides to leave the Aaronic Order. Full consecration papers act as a legally permanent transfer of title which theoretically cannot be reclaimed. Robert Conrad, however, stated that some fully consecrated members had requested a return of title in the early days of the Order, and in every case that he was familiar with, an effort was made to return "as much as possible."

After an individual has become a fully consecrated member of the Aaronic Order, he or she may be called to be a "disciple." The branch priest generally recommends a particular individual for discipleship, and the Chief High Priest and the Supreme Council accept or reject the recommendation. Male disciples receive certificates acknowledging their status. While women may become disciples, they are not given a certificate.

According to one Levite, the term "United Order member" refers to a fully consecrated member who lives in a community. A Levite newsletter defines a United Order member as one "who has consecrated and is returning 100 percent of his time and talents to the Lord and is working with others in a collective effort for the benefit of the Church" (*Aaron's Star*, July 1965). It appears that this term is largely defunct; members of the Order have various opinions about its definition.

The Aaronic Order requires that an individual or family who resides at Eskdale be fully consecrated and free of debts; however, the Eskdale Community Council has made some exceptions to this regulation. The Order recognizes two forms of stewardship—individual and collective. Many Levites living outside of, and most living in, the desert communities have individual stewardships. In the case of those at Eskdale, families are permitted the primary use of certain items, such as a house, an automobile, and household furnishings. Individual stewardship is regarded as a probationary step leading to collective stewardship or total communalism, in which all the members of a community share its possessions, with the exception of certain items such as clothes. Bethel, a satellite community five miles southwest of Eskdale proper, was established in late August of 1975 as a collective stewardship by four young families. In order to qualify for collective stewardship, an individual or family must be completely free of debts.

One of the primary devices that people use in marking their sociocultural identity and differentiating themselves from other sociocultural groups or categories are "ethnic boundary mechanisms." As Frederik Barth (1969, 15) observes, "If a group maintains its identity when members interact with others, this entails criteria for determining membership and the way of signalling membership and exclusion." Since ethnic groups cannot simply be identified on the basis of territorial or linguistic criteria, they must use a variety of other symbols in order to distinguish themselves from others. These may include highly stylized forms of address and greeting, clothing, and dietary prohibitions, as well as participation in distinctive customs and rituals. For the active Mormon, the observance of the Word of Wisdom—a proscription on the consumption of alcoholic beverages, coffee, tea, and tobacco—and the wearing of certain styles of underclothes, known as "temple garments," provide powerful symbols indicating membership in a particular group (King and King 1984; Alexander 1986, 258–271).

The uniform constitutes the most distinctive Levite ethnic boundary mechanism. As I have noted elsewhere, uniforms also are a device by which males exert sexual dominance over females (Baer 1982). In essence, there exists a double standard in this area; greater social pressure is placed on females to wear a more distinctive uniform than that worn by males. In 1948 Glendenning formally proposed that the female members of the Aaronic Order wear a uniform. On one occasion, one man refused his sister-in-law permission to attend his wedding because she did not wear the cap that is considered to be an especially important part of the female uniform. Glendenning himself apparently exerted considerable pressure on women to wear the uniform as in the case when he photographed the women, placing those wearing the cap on one side, and those not on the other side.

Compared to the uniform worn by the females, the uniform for the males is not particularly distinctive. It essentially consists of a blue or white shirt with the word "Aaron" or "Levi" embroidered on the pocket. Only a male who has been designated as a lineal descendant of Aaron can have the word Aaron inscribed on his shirt; all other males can use the word Levi. A fair number of males, particularly those who do not demonstrate a strong commitment to the Order, do not follow this practice. Males are free to wear whatever style of pants and dress suits they choose. According to an elderly Levite woman, at one time it was proposed that the males of Eskdale wear white overalls and white shirts as a work uniform, but this met with general opposition on the part of the men. She maintained that Glendenning was willing to wear the proposed uniform at Eskdale but not in non-Levite settings.

The Aaronic Order has three basic uniform styles for females. One, which is regarded by some as the "official" Order uniform, consists of a light blue dress with buttons in the front and a ribbon with fringe above the breast. According to many Levites, this uniform is the only style that a woman should wear when she is involved in the performance of certain rituals. A uniform consisting of a blue jumper and a white blouse serves as a "work uniform" or "school uniform," although this is the only uniform many females generally wear. The most recent uniform to be designed—one with many practical advantages and which is probably the most stylish by secular standards—consists of blue slacks, a blue tunic, and a white blouse. Most widows wear a white uniform similar to the Order dress, but to do so must make a pledge that they will never marry again. Girls attending Eskdale grade and high schools are required to wear uniforms, even if they are not members of the Aaronic Order.

Part of the complete uniform is the white "cap of honor" which is modeled after the Mennonite cap. This cap includes a visor with the word "Levi" embroidered in gold stitching. Once a female decides to wear the cap of honor, she makes a pledge that she will never take it off (except in certain situations such as washing one's hair or bathing) and will never again cut her hair. The act of removing the cap after one has made a pledge is considered to be a fairly serious offense, but it appears that the only forms of social control to deal with it are disapproval and gossip. Rationales given for the women wearing a uniform are that it is more *modest* than secular dress styles, that it *unifies* the Levites, and is a method of *witnessing for Christ*.

Levite females have found various mechanisms for resisting the uniform policy. Some females who don't reside at Eskdale seldom wear the uniform, and others wear the uniform primarily to Levite meetings but not elsewhere. Some women feel particularly self-conscious about wearing the cap in non-Levite settings. Modifications of the uniform which attempt to make it more stylish by secular standards have been undertaken by some of the women.

### Affiliative Ties: Family and Marriage

Despite the fact that family life and marital patterns among Mormons exhibit many of the same stresses found in the larger society, most people acquainted with Mormonism recognize that familialism is one of its core values (Christensen 1972). As Thomas F. O'Dea (1957, 14) notes, "such loyalty to and identification with family and extended relations assumes a form which, to an outsider, often seems to approach ancestor worship in homage to the pioneers of settlement and the progenitors of family." In keeping with the tradition of their Mormon forefathers, the Levites also place a strong emphasis on familialism.

To a large extent the Aaronic Order consists of a number of interrelated families. Many offspring of the Levite pioneers intermarried and their children have in turn started to intermarry. Despite a preference for endogamy, it is not uncommon for young Levites to marry non-Levites, particularly Mormons. In many cases, marriage with outsiders results from a lack of commitment to the Aaronic Order. Given the limited number of potential mates to choose from within the Order, some Levites marry outsiders. In some cases, a young Levite with little initial commitment to the Order marries an outsider but later decides that he or she should return to the fold, a situation which may also cause certain marital tensions.

The Aaronic Order attempts to instill a sense of familialism among all its members. Like Mormons and many other small Christian groups, Levites address each other as *brother* or *sister*. Unlike Mormons, the Levites do not use forms of address which distinguish members on the basis of their status in the politico-religious hierarchy. Although Glendenning was addressed as Bishop, both young and old Levites address the current Chief High Priest as "Brother Bob." While there is an attempt to create a sense of familialism, some Levites admitted to me that they felt somewhat marginal because they had no or few relatives in the Order.

## Politico-Religious Organization

The Levites claim that their politico-religious organization is identical to that of the ancient Israelites and was revealed to Glendenning by the Angel Elias. Yet it bears some striking similarities to that of the Mormon Church. The Levites and the Mormons both have theocratic and hierarchical politico-religious organizations modeled after that of the ancient Hebrews. Divine authority is believed by Mormons to be delegated to the prophet-president of their church and by Levites to the Chief High Priest of the Aaronic Order. Advances in the religious hierarchy of the Aaronic Order are made by "calls" in a similar manner to that of the Mormon Church. Both religious groups claim to hold the Aaronic and Melchizedek priesthoods. Mormons believe that the Aaronic or "lesser" priesthood was conferred on Joseph Smith and Oliver Cowdery by John the Baptist. In the Mormon Church, the Aaronic priesthood is ranked into three grades—deacon, teacher, and priest—which are generally assigned to males between the ages of twelve and eighteen years. When a Mormon male reaches eighteen years of age, he can enter the Melchizedek priesthood, which is ranked into the grades of elder, and high priest.

Unlike the Mormon Church, the Aaronic Order places strong emphasis upon the Aaronic priesthood but gives minimal attention to the Melchizedek priesthood. According to Levite belief, in March of 1938 Glendenning climbed to the top of a small hill near Crystal Springs, Nevada. There the Angel Elias restored to him "all of the keys and authority vested in the Priesthood of Aaron" unto which he had been ordained in the spirit (Book of Elias 1944, Sec. 217, 94). Glendenning was further told that he would have the power to confer the keys and authority of the Priesthood on others who were lineal descendants of Aaron. Later the hill where Glendenning had received the keys was named "Mount Aaron," and a small monument was erected there. Mount Aaron has also been the site of several Levite pilgrimages and the marriage ceremony of a young Levite couple.

Members of the order believe that the Aaronites and Levites were officiants of religious rituals for the Israelites during Old Testament times. It is believed that God gave the Levitical priesthood to Levi and his male descendants (Deut. 10, 8–9). Later God gave the Aaronic priesthood to Aaron, the great-grandson of Levi and the elder brother of Moses, and to his male descendants (Exod. 40, 13–15). Consequently, all Aaronites are Levites, but not all Levites are Aaronites; the Aaronic priesthood "comprehends the Levitical priesthood" (Beeston 1957, 207). Levites not of Aaron are to assist the Aaronites in their priestly duties. Also, others, referred to as the "sons of Aaron by adoption," will be given the right to assist in the lesser offices of the Aaronic priesthood after the Second Coming of Christ (Beeston 1957, 207–208; Book of New Revelations 1948, Chap. 7, 24–25).

In addition, it is believed that only one lineage of the descendants of Aaron did not "pollute their inheritance"—the sons of Zadok. Consequently, according to Levite belief, only males who are patrilineal descendants of Aaron and Zadok can hold the lineal Aaronic priesthood today. Furthermore, all Aaronites are born with the priesthood, which is hereditary and was "ordained" to them in the "pre-existence," but can officiate in it only if authorized or "given the keys" which generally occurs after one has reached twenty years of age. A pamphlet written by an early member of the Aaronic Order states that the Aaronic priesthood was to be taken from the Mormon Church when the "sons of Levi" came (Weight, "The Aaronic Order," n.d.). The Melchizedek priesthood became corrupted after the time of Malachi and, according to one male informant, has not been yet "set in order."

Figure 4-1 illustrates the councils of the Aaronic Order and their relationship to other offices and associates. The Levites believe that Jesus Christ is the Great High Priest of all Christians. The Chief High Priest is in charge of the "spiritual affairs" of the Aaronic Order, and the First High Priest and Robert Conrad the First High Priest. The Office of Sec- "almost equal" (Beeston 1966, 64). Both offices have been held by Robert Conrad since the death of Glendenning in 1969. At one time Glendenning held the title of First High Priest, but later he was designated the Chief High Priest and Robert Conrad the First High Priest. The office of Second High Priest consists of a principal Second High Priest and his assistants, also technically referred to as Second High Priests. The Second High Priest and his assistants are responsible for the performance of certain ordinances. In 1975 the Aaronic Order had four Second High Priests—three of whom, including the principal Second Priest, were brothers. The former principal Second High Priest, now deceased, was the father of these three men.

The Priest of the branch is responsible for the "spiritual and temporal affairs" of a particular branch. The Salt Lake and Springville branches both have a permanent Priest. The branch priest of the Eskdale commune is called the "acting priest," a position which is rotated every three months among the priests residing at Eskdale. The branch priest is assisted by other priests and disciples in the performance of ordinances and other branch functions. Although Partoun has had resident branch priests in the past, it did not have one during the mid-1970s. A male resident of Partoun, referred to as the "lead" or "acting" disciple, carries out many of the spiritual and temporal functions ordinarily conducted by a branch priest. An attempt is made to have

Figure 4-1
The Councils of the Aaronic Order and Their Relationship to Other Offices and Organizations

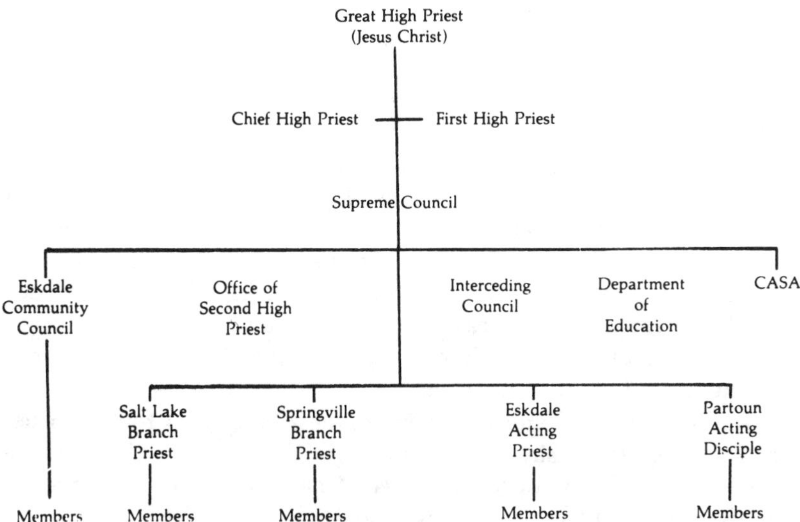


priests from the Eskdale commune visit the Partoun branch at least twice a month so that certain rituals may be performed.

Fully consecrated males generally are disciples, and male disciples are organized into a "brotherhood" which regularly meets in the various branches. Female disciples are not organized into a "sisterhood." All priests and male disciples in the Aaronic Order are married. Table 4-3 below shows the distribution of priests and disciples and married men not holding these positions in the Aaronic Order.

Table 4-3
Distribution of Theocratic Positions among Active Married Males

| Branch | Priests | Disciples | Males neither Priests nor Disciples |
|---|---|---|---|
| Eskdale | 9 | 5 | 3 |
| Partoun | 0 | 4 | 1 |
| Salt Lake | 5 | 1 | 2 |
| Springville | 2 | 1 | 1 |
| At Large | 4 | 0 | 0 |

The Aaronic Order has an elaborate system of councils which it is believed will some day administer the religious affairs of the tribes of Israel. The Supreme Council is the legislative body which passes rules and regulations and controls the funds of the Order. It consists of ten members, including a chairman, who must all be full consecrated Aaronite priests. Either the Chief High Priest or the Supreme Council may appoint the chairman of the council, but both must concur on the appointment. The principal Second High Priest is always a member of the Supreme Council.

According to Robert Conrad, the "real power" of the Aaronic Order lies in the Supreme Council. The Chief High Priest and First High Priest review and approve or veto the decisions of the Supreme Council which in turn can override a veto. Theoretically the Supreme Council will eventually consist of seven Divisional Supreme Councils, which will "preside over all the geographical areas of the Church and Kingdom" (Beeston 1966, 66). The Order has only one division—the Utah division, but at one time had a Colorado Division.

The Interceding Council coordinates the affairs of the four branches and "shall pass the desires and pleadings of the people to the Supreme Council" (Book of New Revelations 1948, Chap. 22, 62). It consists of ten members and is chaired by the Second High Priest. Only priests and disciples can belong to the Interceding Council. Table 4-4 shows the distribution of the membership of the various councils of the Aaronic Order during the summer of 1975. A relatively large proportion of the members of the Supreme and Interceding Councils are Eskdale residents—40 percent in both cases. It is interesting to note that three individuals hold dual membership on the Supreme and Interceding Councils, and one individual holds membership on all three councils.

The Supreme and Interceding Councils generally meet once a month, although additional meetings may be called. Supreme Council meetings are alternated between the Salt Lake and Eskdale branches while Interceding Council meetings alternate among the Salt Lake, Eskdale, and Springville branches. Most proposals are approved by majority vote. Council meetings are closed, except for secretaries who are obligated not to discuss proceedings with others. The Eskdale Community Council, which will be discussed in greater detail in the next chapter, exercises much latitude in making formal decisions for Eskdale and is seldom overruled by the Interceding Council or the Supreme Council. The Community Council generally convenes every other Sunday evening (comparable to Monday evenings in the larger society).

The two major official departments of the Order are the Christian Aid Service of America (C.A.S.A.) and the Department of Education. The C.A.S.A. functions in a manner similar to the Women's Relief Soci-

Table 4-4
Membership of the Aaronic Order Councils

| Individual | Supreme Council | Interceding Council | Eskdale Council |
|---|---|---|---|
| A Second High Priest & Salt Lake Branch Priest | X | X | |
| B Chairman of Supreme Council | X | | |
| C Asst. Second High Priest | X | X | X |
| D Asst. Second High Priest | X | | X |
| E Priest | X | | X |
| F Priest | X | | X |
| G Priest | X | | |
| H Priest | X | | |
| I Priest | X | | |
| J Springville Branch Priest | X | X | |
| K Priest | | X | X |
| L Priest | | X | |
| M Priest | | X | X |
| N Partoun "Presiding" Disciple | | X | |
| O Disciple | | X | |
| P Disciple | | X | |
| Q Disciple | | X | X |
| R Disciple | | | X |

ety in the Mormon Church. The C.A.S.A. sponsors sewing and quilting sessions for women in the various branches and also is responsible for the storage of used clothing. In the past the C.A.S.A. was involved in the picking and canning of fruits and vegetables and the operation of a sawmill at Huntington Canyon in the Wasatch Plateau of Utah. C.A.S.A. projects occasionally involve men; this was much more the case when it operated a sawmill during the 1950s and early 1960s. Occasionally members of the Aaronic Order state that there is a need to revitalize the C.A.S.A. The Department of Education is responsible for the religious and musical education of the Order and the operation of the Eskdale school system. The Levite educational system will also be discussed in detail in the following chapter.

The existence of an elaborate politico-religious organization in a small group such as the Aaronic Order very likely has struck the reader as both baffling and superfluous. After all, why would the members of a tiny religious sect, whose members are well-acquainted with one another and often related to one another, choose to construct such a bureaucratically top-heavy governing structure. Ironically, it appears that the Levite politico-religious organization is by no means an idiosyncratic phenomenon. Victor Turner (1969, 190–191) observes that: "Although the literature on religious and semireligious movements does not lend complete support to the view I have been taking, and many problems and difficulties remain, there is nevertheless strong evidence that religious forms, clearly attributable to the generative activities of structurally interior groups or categories, soon assume many of the external characteristics of hierarchies." Referring to an unpublished bachelor's thesis by Allan C. Spiers (1966), Victor Turner (1969, 192) mentions the Aaronic Order as one instance of "liminal movements" that "have a multitude of offices but a small number of members." Liminal movements exhibit many of the features, such as homogeneity, equality, absense of property, abolition of rank, and total obedience to one or more authority figures, characteristic of the liminal phase in what Arnold van Gennep termed "rites de passage." *Communitas* or an intense feeling of social solidarity is characteristic of both the liminal or intermediate phase in rites of passage and liminal or millenarian movements.

According to Turner, the hierarchical structure of liminal movements inverts the hierarchical nature of secular society. In other words, whereas the members of a liminal or millenarian movements in actuality exist on the margins of society, within the confines of their own social universe they create a pseudo-reality that permits them to see themselves as an elite or superior category. In essence, what liminal movements like the Aaronic Order do for their adherents is to instill in them a sense of community that they are unable to obtain in the larger society. To a large extent, the Levites have achieved a strong feeling of *Gemeinschaft* or *communitas* both in the various communal and cooperative ventures that they have established over the years as well as in the creation of an elaborate system of politico-religious offices, councils, and auxiliaries.

# 5

# *The Eskdale Commune: An Enactment of Levite Ideals*

The infrequent traveler crossing the Utah-Nevada border along US 6-50 generally is unaware that only a few miles to the north of this lonely stretch of highway lies a settlement of people who believe that they are literal descendants of the Levites and Aaronites of Biblical times. This wind-blown land, literally filled with sagebrush, greasewood, rattle snakes, and surrounded by stark mountains, constitutes the New Jerusalem of the modern Levites of Utah. The Snake Valley of the Great Basin is the site of Eskdale, a living enactment of Levite communal ideals. The Levites believe that Eskdale and the other desert communes that are to be established are places where they will be "purified as gold and silver" and prepare for the Second Coming of Jesus Christ. They maintain that many other similar refuge areas are being prepared not only for Israelites but also for worthy Gentiles. During the annual convention of the Order in June 1974, Robert Conrad stated that Christians throughout the world are gathering together in cooperative and communal settlements. Many Levites believe that during the period of premillennial disaster, strife, and corruption, thousands will leave the cities and come to the Snake Valley. The Levites living in the desert communities will have to be prepared to meet the physical and spiritual needs of these urban refugees. Just as the Salt Lake Valley was viewed as Zion by the

Mormon pioneers, the Levites view the Snake Valley, referred to as "Shiloah," as a refuge from the "wickedness of Babylon." Ironically, for many of them, Babylon refers to the Salt Lake and Utah Valleys that were settled by their Mormon forebears.

An examination of Eskdale is important not only in that it gives us a concrete example of how the Levites have attempted to revitalize the communitarian and egalitarian ideals of nineteenth century Mormonism, but also in that it contributes to a further understanding of communal groups and the factors that contribute to their survival or collapse. In addition to considering economic, educational, and social activities at Eskdale, this chapter will examine the commune's capacity for survival. As a commune, Eskdale is unique in several ways. First of all, it has already endured longer than the vast majority of utopian ventures. Furthermore, it did not emerge as a part of the recent communal movement that appealed to many white, middle class youth. Instead, Eskdale and its predecessor communities (the Alton Colony, the Alpha Colony, and Partoun) were established at a time when communalism was not a national phenomenon. Whereas most rural American communes are located in rather fertile areas, such as New England, northern California, and the Pacific Northwest, Eskdale is situated in the Great Basin, one of the most inhospitable areas for human occupation in the country. Finally, unlike most communal ventures, Eskdale is part of a larger religious organization with a noncommunal membership. As we will see, this fact alone has had important implications for its ability to survive.

## *Economic Organization*

While it is mandatory that communal groups satisfy basic subsistence requirements, it is not clear as to how economically efficient they must be in order to survive. According to Zablocki (1980, 45), "Few communes have ever succeeded in carving out comfortable and secure niches for themselves within the larger economy or apart from it. But even fewer, in the past as now, could trace their disintegrations to economic difficulties." Indeed, Rosebeth Moss Kanter (1972, 157) argues that: "For nineteenth century communities at least, financial prosperity may be associated with the decline of the community—partly because it indicated the growth of efficient *Gesellschaft* organization and partly because of the social consequences of prosperity, such as emphasis on individual consumption." At any rate, even though the Eskdale commune has developed a system of agricultural and dairy production as its primary economic endeavor, its capacity to remain economically viable apparently depends ultimately on subsidies received from noncommunal members of the Order.

## Geographic Setting

Unlike most of the newer communal ventures as well as many of the well-established ones, such as the Hutterite colonies and the Bruderhof of New York State, Eskdale is located in a semiarid environment—one which requires tremendous hardship and financial investment in the effort to acquire water, grow crops, and feed livestock. In his comparative study of contemporary American communes, Zablocki (1980, 68–77) lists the following clusters of rural communes: (1) the Taconic cluster of upstate New York and western New England, (2) the Appalachian cluster of the southern highlands, (3) the Hutterian cluster of the Dakotas and southwestern Minnesota, (4) the Rio Grande cluster of north central New Mexico, (5) the South Coast cluster between San Francisco and Los Angeles, (6) the North Coast cluster of northern California, and (7) the Cascade cluster of the Pacific Northwest. Each of these clusters, including that of the Rio Grande Valley of New Mexico, are located in areas of higher precipitation than that of the Eskdale commune. In the establishment of the Levite desert communities, Glendenning chose one of the most arid regions in an essentially arid state. Considering that the Levite pioneers were people of limited financial means, this choice was a logical one since the land was free, subject only to the ability to satisfy homesteading legislation.

Both Eskdale and Partoun are located in the Snake Valley of west central Utah and east central Nevada (See Figure 5-1). Eskdale is situated at an elevation of about 4,900 feet in the central portion of the Snake Valley, about six miles north of combined US Highway 6-50, and five miles from the Utah-Nevada border. Partoun is situated at the southwestern base of the Deep Creek Range, which rises to over 12,000 feet, and in the northern portion of the Snake Valley, about forty-five miles by gravel road from Eskdale.

Although somewhat drier, the physiography of the Snake Valley resembles that of the Salt Lake Valley. Both areas are surrounded by mountains on three sides with the valley open on the north. One cannot help to wonder whether Maurice Glendenning did not see himself as a twentieth century Brigham Young, thinking to himself that "this is the place" as he envisioned the establishment of the Levite kingdom. During the Pleistocene the Snake Valley was covered by Lake Bonneville, the remnant of which is the Great Salt Lake (Hunt 1967, 309). The Snake Valley is 3,480 square miles in area and runs 135 miles in a north-south direction (Hood and Rush 1965, 1–4). It has a maximum width of about forty miles near Garrison, Utah (several miles south of Eskdale). The southern portion of the Snake Valley ends about ten miles north of Modena, Utah, and its northern end opens into the Great Salt Lake desert. The valley is bordered by a series of high mountains on both its

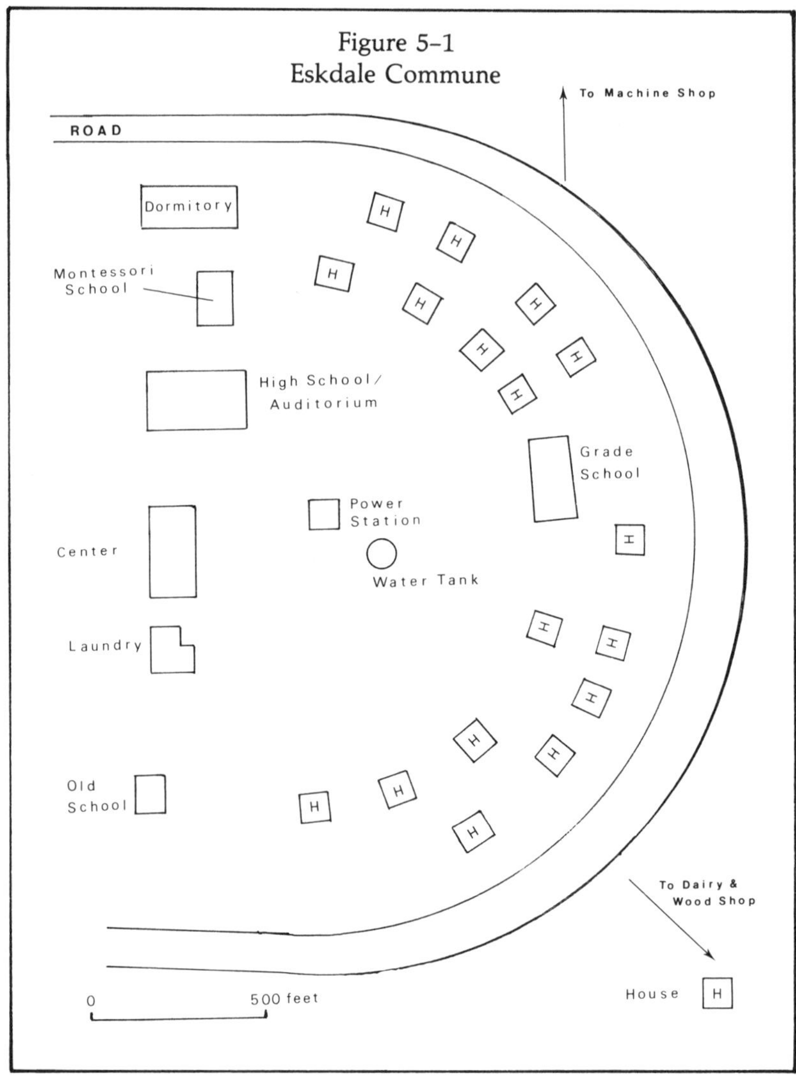


west and east sides. To the west of Eskdale lies the southern portion of the Snake Range, which includes Wheeler Peak (13,061 feet elevation)—the second highest peak in Nevada—and Mount Moriah (12,067 feet elevation). Directly east of Eskdale are the Confusion and Conger Ranges, the latter being a spur of the former. The foothills of the Conger Range begin about one mile East of Eskdale. The mountains on the eastern edge of the Snake Valley are generally much lower than those on its western edge; King Top Peak (approximately 8,300 feet elevation) is the highest mountain in the Confusion Range. About fifteen miles south of Eskdale are the Burbank Hills.

The Snake Valley has a semiarid climate with relatively hot dry summers (temperatures in excess of ninety degrees Fahrenheit are not infrequent) and relatively (but not extremely) cold winters. The Snake Valley may have several snowfalls during the winter months. Because the snow generally melts within a day or two, dirt roads in the Partoun area are often impassable, or at least difficult to drive on. The average annual precipitation for Garrison (near Eskdale) was 6.7 inches during the period 1952–1963; while it was 5.21 inches for Partoun during the period 1951–1963 (Hood and Rush 1965, 6–7). The annual precipitation in the Snake Valley varies appreciably from year to year. For example, the precipitation at Callao (about twenty miles north of Partoun) was 9.03 inches in 1945 but only 0.94 inches in 1953. In contrast, the mountains west of the Snake Valley may receive as much as twenty to thirty inches of precipitation. About 50 percent of the precipitation in the valley comes from summer thunderstorms. The Snake Valley has a growing season of about 150 days.

Most of the streams which flow into the Snake Valley originate in the mountains west of it. A number of small settlements were established near these streams, but both Eskdale and Partoun were not. Consequently, both communities draw most of their water supply from deep wells. The Deep Creek and Snake Ranges produce most of the runoff and ground water recharge in the Snake Valley. In several places, wet meadowlands are found for most of the year. Due to hot summer temperatures, these areas become relatively dry during the summer months.

The primary forms of vegetation in the lowlands include sagebrush, greasewood, bunch grass, and short grass. The only relatively lush lowland areas are found near streams. The lower elevations of the Snake and Deep Creek Ranges and some areas of the Confusion Range and other eastern mountains are covered with pinyons and junipers. In the higher elevations of the Snake and Deep Creek Ranges are found thick stands of aspens and various conifers, including Douglas fir, Ponderosa pine, spruce, and bristlecone pine.

### Production and Labor

Eskdale's primary productive activities are crop and dairy agriculture. The Eskdale commune filed for ten desert entries (320 acres each) and fulfilled the requirements on seven of them, dropping its claim on the other three. In 1956 the Eskdale commune acquired the South Ranch property, which is located several miles south of Eskdale proper and is now called "Bethel." Eskdale also purchased a small parcel of land, about one-half mile East of the central community, called "Black Mountain" where various religious rituals are conducted occasionally. The Eskdale commune, including its satellite community, Bethel, owns about 3,500 acres. The Order also owns about 1,500 acres in the Partoun area, a 107-acre farm outside of Springville, Utah, and the Pleasant Valley Ranch (about 200 acres) located on the Utah-Nevada border.

In order for Eskdale residents to acquire title to each of the desert entries, the Bureau of Land Management required them to have forty acres under production and a deep well installed on each entry. Eskdale acquired the final deed to its entries in 1972. In the spring of 1975 Eskdale proper had nineteen wells—three of which served the central community—and Bethel had two wells. During 1975 about 450 acres were under cultivation at Eskdale proper and about 300 acres at Bethel. Eskdale's principal crop is alfalfa which generally yields three or four crops a year. Most of the alfalfa is used to feed cattle but some is sold commercially. Other crops grown at Eskdale include corn, wheat, and barley. Eskdale also has two vegetable gardens which provide potatoes, corn, onions, carrots, beans, peas, pumpkin, squash, beets, and parsnips for Eskdale residents and other Levites.

In 1975 Eskdale owned about seventy milk cows and about 100 calves, springers, and dry cows. Several years earlier Eskdale owned about thirty head of beef cattle, but this number decreased to a handful. During 1974 the Order grazed another ninety to 100 head of beef cattle at its Pleasant Valley Ranch on the Utah-Nevada border during the summer months and at Bethel during the winter months. Eskdale cannot go into large-scale cattle raising because additional rangeland in the southern portion of the Snake Valley is unavailable. Eskdale's modern dairy was completed in December 1972; milk and cream are picked up at Eskdale and trucked to Delta, about eighty-five miles northeast of the commune. Prior to the completion of the dairy, most of Eskdale's alfalfa crop was sold commercially. In the spring of 1975 Eskdale owned about 300 chickens which provided eggs primarily for Eskdale residents and other Levites. Several years earlier Eskdale owned about 2,500 chickens, sold eggs to residents of the Snake Valley, and delivered eggs to stores between Eskdale and Ely, Nevada, once a week. Because the price of chicken feed went up, Eskdale found that the egg business was not profitable and reduced the size of its operation.

Table 5-1 lists Eskdale's full time work force in May 1975. The composition of the work force shifts from year to year, primarily because bachelors may move in and out of Eskdale at any time of the year. The work manager is voted into office for a period of one year and makes the work assignments for the men. Bachelors are generally members of the work pool, which means they may be assigned to agricultural work, construction, repair work, dairy work, or short-term assignments depending on the need. Male high school students are part-time members of the work pool and may be assigned specific tasks, such as milking and cleaning the dairy. Although married males are assigned specific tasks, they also are part of the general work pool and may be given temporary assignments. The males conduct a meeting each work day after breakfast to discuss work tasks for the day. All Eskdale teachers function under the Department of Education of the Aaronic Order.

Table 5-1
Eskdale's Full-Time Work Force

| Males | Positions | Females | Positions |
|---|---|---|---|
| A | Music teacher, beekeeper | A | Grade school teacher |
| B | High school principal & teacher | B | Grade school teacher |
| C | Work & shop manager | C | Kitchen supervisor, home economics teacher |
| D | Gardener | D | Montessori school directress |
| E | Agriculturist | E | Community secretary, center pool member |
| F | Agriculturist | F | Community accountant, center pool member |
| G | Work pool member | G | Student music teacher |
| H | Work pool member | H | Montessori school teacher |
| I | Maintenance work | I | High school teacher |
| J | Work pool member | J | Center pool member |
| K | Work pool member | K | Center pool member |
| L* | Dairy Manager | L | Center pool member |
| M* | High school teacher, work pool member | M | Center pool member |
| N* | Asst. shop manager, work pool member | N | Center pool member |
| O* | Work pool member | O | Center pool member |
| P* | Work pool member | | |
| Q* | Work pool member | | |

*Indicates that an individual is a bachelor. All other individuals in the full time work force are married.

Eskdale females, except those who are full-time school teachers, are members of the center work pool. The term "center" refers to a cluster of buildings which includes the communal kitchen and dining hall, the communal laundry, and storage areas. The kitchen supervisor, who is appointed by the Community Council, prepares the center work schedule, meal menus, and the grocery shopping list, shops once a month in the Salt Lake Valley, and coordinates the state-funded school lunch programs. Most center pool tasks are performed on a rotating basis. Each day two different women prepare meals. Women wash their family's laundry at assigned times; the dormitory laundry is washed several days a week on a rotating basis, with two women assigned to each day. Two women perform secretarial and bookkeeping tasks two days a week, and are assigned to the center work pool schedule only three days a week. Eskdale couples rotate as dormitory dean and matron about every month. Because the dormitory matron is expected to be in the dormitory most of the time, she usually does not participate in the center schedule.

Both grade school and high school girls work in the communal kitchen and dining hall, usually starting to wash dishes in the first grade and graduating to more complicated tasks as they mature. Some elderly women have no specified work tasks but can work whenever they choose. Sometimes women are assigned to work in the community nursery. During the summer months women and high school girls can vegetables which are raised at Eskdale and fruits which have been picked and purchased elsewhere, perhaps the Salt Lake and Utah Valleys. According to the kitchen supervisor, Eskdale budgets about $1,000 per month for groceries, which provide for about half of the community's food consumption. Eskdale produces its own meat, milk, butter, eggs, and vegetables, but must purchase some canned vegetables because it does not have facilities for pressure cooking vegetables.

Despite its goal to become, as the work manager noted, "self-sufficient," since its establishment the commune has not operated at a profit, and is heavily subsidized by the tithes and contributions of non-communal members of the Order. According to one prominent Eskdale resident, the community is operating at about "50 percent self-sufficiency," indicating that close to half of its operative budget is derived from outside subsidies. For example, a member who works as a metallurgist in Idaho contributed a substantial amount of money for the construction of Eskdale's dairy in the early 1970s. The Supreme Council controls and allocates funds which subsidize Eskdale. In contrast to the low wages earned by most early Levites, in the past few decades an appreciable number of Levites have become well-paid craftsmen, contractors, and professionals. This improvement in the general socioeconomic status of the members undoubtedly increased the financial resources of the Order. In theory the Order opposes going into debt; in reality it will borrow money if it has assets that can be used as collateral.

There are a large number of reasons for Eskdale's failure to operate at a profit during any fiscal year since its establishment. One is the constant expansion of the community's physical facilities—the construction of family dwelling units, school buildings, a school dormitory, a dairy, a community center, a shop building; the drilling of wells; the purchase of farm equipment; the installation of plumbing, heating, and electrical systems; the development of desert land for agricultural production; and so forth. Some noncommunal Levites work at Eskdale periodically. In reality it would have been advantageous for Eskdale to have developed one desert entry at a time. Instead, in order to comply with requirements of the Desert Entry Act, the community had to develop forty acres at a time and install a deep well on each desert entry. A significant factor preventing greater development of land is limited farm equipment. According to the work manager, it takes three to five years of planting for the alkaline soil of the Snake Valley to become productive.

Table 5.1 demonstrates that a large proportion of Eskdale's labor force works in its educational system. The low tuition, room, and board fees paid by nonresidents of Eskdale who send their children to school there makes income from this source insignificant. Eskdale's music program, which includes a fully equipped, forty-five piece orchestra, imposes a substantial financial burden on the budget of the Order. Trips made by the orchestra and chorus, often to places over 200 miles away from Eskdale, require even more expenses.

One of Eskdale's principal economic problems, as one Levite openly admitted, is that many of its residents are inexperienced agriculturalists. When I was involved in various work assignments, I often sensed that work proceeded rather slowly and was not well-coordinated. The work manager complained that men do not work as efficiently as they would on a job outside the community. In order to overcome problems of coordination, an engineering planner, who works in Idaho and whose wife is a member of the Order, advises the community in the formulation of its "Five Year Plan" of economic development.

Due to a variety of internal conflicts, there has been a considerable amount of turnover in work management positions at Eskdale. Since some farm managers were inexperienced in agriculture and were not respected by those under their supervision, there often was a serious discontinuity in the productive process. During much of its existence, Eskdale has experienced a tension between the "college men," who gravitate to positions of community leadership, and the "farmers." According to one Levite man, this tension is at present less pronounced than it has been in the past. Several men left Eskdale because of disputes over how to operate the community in the most efficient and economical manner. Two men, who possess a fair degree of farming experience and expertise, refuse to participate in the commune's primary agricultural endeavor because of tensions with the college men. One of these men was the farm manager for awhile, but withdrew from this position when he found it difficult to work with the college men. He does maintenance work and grows a small garden adjacent to his house. He bitterly complained that while the college men essentially run the agricultural activities, he could triple the output of any one of them. He feels further estrangement because his family is not related to any of the members and because he sacrificed a well-paying job in a steel mill to live at Eskdale. The other individual who has withdrawn from the main agricultural effort has found a more comfortable niche working alone in the community garden. Here he feels tht he can carry out farming properly, unhampered by the incompetence of the college men.

## Distribution of Goods

The Eskdale Community Council devised various guidelines for the distribution of community goods. When Levites move to Eskdale, they theoretically are required to consecrate their finances and possessions to the community. In reality, a few "unconsecrated" families and individuals reside at Eskdale. If housing is unavailable, the finances which the community received may be used for its construction. If there is any money left over, it can be used for other community expenditures. Retired people or widows at Eskdale turn their Social Security or pension checks over to the community. Eskdale requires that gifts, either monetary or material, be turned over to the community; exceptions to the rule are made by the Community Council.

Some people live in better housing than others, even though it is intended that all families will live in similar housing eventually. As Eskdale grew, no attempt was made to build each house according to a basic design. Some people who have built houses at Eskdale do not presently live in them. The community grants permission to others to live in them temporarily. Housing is made available on the basis of need and availability; no family has exclusive claim on a particular dwelling unit. Each family furnishes its house in whatever manner it desires.

At one time Eskdale distributed needs money on the basis of a family's claim to it. According to an Eskdale resident, the "squeaky wheels" received the largest shares. Consequently, each adult and each child in the community now receives a specific amount. In 1974 the monthly allowances, if funds were available, were $10.00 per adult and $5.00 per child for living expenses, plus $3.50 per adult and $.75 per child for gasoline.

One area that has caused considerable ill feeling at Eskdale is the use of automobiles. Eskdale nominally owns all automobiles in the community. When families move to Eskdale, They generally retain use of the automobile that they brought with them. Some residents have been reluctant to release their vehicles for community use because they feel that others will not properly care for them. In 1974 the Community Council ruled that expenses for family-held automobiles would no longer be paid by the community.

## *The Levite Educational System*

In attempting to socialize their offspring, communalists have developed a variety of educational philosophies. On the one hand, we find secular approaches, such as those of the Israeli *kibbutzim*, which encourage their youth not only to become intimately familiar with the outside world but also to attend its institutions of higher learning (Spiro 1955). On the other hand, highly introversionist sects, such as the Hutterites in North America, attempt to limit formal education to the proverbial three R's, feeling that much more than this will inevitably have a corrupting impact (Baer 1976). The Levite approach to education lies somewhere between these poles, having been greatly influenced by both Mormonism and the thinking of Maurice Glendenning. From the Mormon perspective, "Knowledge is necessary to mastery, and the way to deification is through mastery, for not only does education aid man in fulfilling tasks, it advances him in his eternal progress" (O'Dea 1957, 147). Brigham Young University, the largest church-related institution of higher learning in the world, manifests Mormon commitment to formal education. Ironically, while the Great Tradition of Mormonism emphasizes educational achievement, the early Levites were simple and pragmatic people who viewed intellectual endeavors with a certain disdain and suspicion. Consequently, it was Glendenning, whose own educational background was highly unconventional, more than his early followers, who urged their children to seek as much education as possible, often at secular universities.

The Levites, whose motto is Education Unlimited, maintain that learning is derived from God and that education provides for a rational approach to religion. Many Levites intensively study the Bible, the Levitical Writings, and, in the case of some of the older members, the Mormon scriptures. The Levites do not discourage an awareness of the secular world, and theoretically a Levite may read the writings of such modern thinkers as Marx and Freud. They consider an awareness of world events as important in understanding the prophecies concerning the Second Coming of Christ.

A central focus of the Eskdale commune has been its school system, which consists of a Montessori school for children between the ages of two and six years, a grade school, and a high school. The Montessori school is directed by a woman who was trained at a Netherlands-based Montessori institution in Phoenix, and is the first person in Utah to have been certified as a Montessori teacher. She is assisted by a young woman who graduated from Utah State University with a bachelor's degree in education with an emphasis in child development.

Since its establishment in 1956 and until the end of the 1974–1975 academic year, the Eskdale grade school was part of the Millard County

School District and was supported by public funds. In the fall of 1975, the Eskdale grade school became a parochial school because the state of Utah wanted it to consolidate with the Garrison grade school. During the 1974–1975 academic year the subsidy for school personnel was $20,000; this change in status eliminated an important source of supplemental income from the deficit economy of the community. In February 1975, the grade school had twenty-two students, about half of whom were children of people not residing at Eskdale. The grade school enrollment fluctuates appreciably from year to year, as is made apparent by its enrollment of thirty students during the 1973–1974 academic year. There was an annual $60.00 tuition fee and a monthly $40.00 room and board fee for students of parents who did not reside at Eskdale.

The curriculum of the grade school adheres fairly closely to that of most public schools. Unlike many evangelical religious sects, the Levites do not explicitly oppose sex education. The head teacher of the grade school stated that sex in its "proper place," namely, marriage, is not a vulgar thing, and noted that sexual matters should be discussed openly with school children.

Eskdale's high school always has been a parochial operation and the only high school between Delta, Utah, and Ely, Nevada—a distance of 147 miles. The size of the student body and the faculty of the high school fluctuates from year to year. During the 1974–1975 academic year approximately twenty-five students attended the high school with two graduating in May, whereas during the 1973–1974 academic year thirty-two students attended with seven graduating. The high school enrollment approached forty in some previous years. During the 1974–1975 academic year, the high school had three full-time instructors (all with teaching degrees) and two part-time instructors (both without college degrees). During the 1972–1973 academic year the high school had eight full-time and part-time teachers, six of whom had college degrees, but not necessarily in education.

As Table 5-2 illustrates, the high school has emphasized college preparatory courses. Eskdale encourages students to take four years of communications (literature, composition, etc.), even though the state of Utah requires only three years of study in this area for graduation. Courses in mathematics, science and social studies generally are offered annually, and language courses are offered occasionally.

The modern Levites believe that they have inherited their predilection for music from the Levites of Old Testament times and view music as an important means for conveying "the word of the Lord." They frequently sing hymns at religious services, meals, and for recreation. In addition to an evangelical hymnal, they use a hymnal called *Songs of Levi and Aaron.* In 1973 the school orchestra became the community or-

Table 5-2
High School Schedule (Sunday-Thursday)

| Time | Class |
|---|---|
| 8:00 A.M. | Orchestra practice—both grade and high school |
| 8:55 A.M. | Bible Study<br>1. Upper class<br>2. Lower class |
| 9:40 A.M. | World Geography—Lower class<br>Algebra II—Upper class |
| 10:35 A.M. | Communications<br>1. Upper class<br>2. Lower class |
| 11:25 A.M. | Chorus—both grade and high school |
| 1:30 P.M. | Typing—Lower class<br>American History—Upper class |
| 2:30 P.M. | Driver Education |

chestra after some adults expressed a desire to learn to play a musical instrument. Consequently, the community orchestra consists of grade and high school students, young people who recently graduated from high school, and adults (most of whom are women). The forty-five piece orchestra plays primarily religious and classical music, and has performed at numerous places in Utah and eastern Nevada, including the University of Utah and Brigham Young University.

The Eskdale schools are housed in four facilities—separate buildings for the three schools and the community hall. The community hall includes: a small library, an auditorium that is used for the orchestra, religious services, study classes, and other community meetings, music rooms, and several classrooms. Eskdale also owns a bus which transports the community orchestra and students. The Eskdale schools lack many of the facilities of outside schools, but the low student-faculty ratio compensates for this. Eskdale graduates generally have been accepted readily by colleges and universities, despite the fact that the high school lacks accreditation. A disproportionately high number of Eskdale graduates receive college scholarships, and many students pass tests granting them the equivalent of one year's college course work.

Based upon two days of observation of the Levite schools during 1972, Frederick S. Buchanan and Larry W. Stott (1974, 230) posed the question: "Can a sect-type religion embrace the methods and values of higher education and still maintain its identity as a separate community of believers?" In responding to their article, Robert Conrad, who holds a doctorate in education, admitted that indeed a potential conflict may exist between Levite religious beliefs and a strong emphasis on secular higher education. Until at least the mid-1970s, possibly over 50 percent of Eskdale high school graduates went on to college. Even prior to the establishment of the high school, young Levites, largely due to encouragement from Glendenning, were attending colleges and universities. Consequently, many middle-aged Levites are college graduates or have attended college. Eskdale high school graduates generally have attended either the University of Utah in Salt Lake City or the Utah State University in Logan. The few young Levites who have enrolled briefly at Brigham Young University generally have found that being a member of an "apostate" sect in a Mormon university causes considerable personal hardship. Of the two state universities that young Levites generally attend, the University of Utah is the larger and more cosmopolitan, and the one where they are more likely to experience cognitive dissonance.

There are a number of factors which tend to minimize the possibility of ideological conflict for these students. Levite students have not tended to be attracted to the social sciences and humanities—disciplines in which views at variance with Levite beliefs are most likely to be presented. With a few exceptions, they, like most Mormon college students, have majored in various vocational disciplines, such as education, engineering, agricultural science, medicine, and law. Since these disciplines rarely involve a direct challenge to the Levite world view, the young student finds the major portion of his college experience to be cognitively consonant. The Levite student is exposed to conflicting ideas in required courses in the humanities and social sciences and from the larger student culture. The Aaronic Order has created a number of formal and informal mechanisms by which this conflict could be reduced.

For several years, until the fall of 1975, many students who attended the University of Utah lived in a "mission home" adjacent to the Order's chapel in the Salt Lake Valley. The mission home, which was operated on a cooperative basis, housed single students and a few nonstudent couples. In addition to the religious ethos of the home, students attended religious study classes on Tuesday evenings and Saturday services at the Salt Lake branch. Since Robert Conrad spends much of his time in the Salt Lake Valley and has a small apartment and office in the basement of the Salt Lake branch chapel, students were readily able to consult with him about religious questions. Levite students attending the Utah State University also resided in a mission home.

As we have already seen, another tension that has resulted from the Order's emphasis on secular education is related to the occupational structure of the Eskdale commune. During the spring of 1975, three out of the seventeen male members and six of the sixteen female members of the commune's full-time work force were teachers. In addition, the educational background of many workers has not provided them with agricultural and technical skills. In the fall of 1974, a middle-aged man became the supervisor of the Levite school system and the principal of the high school. He held a master's degree in counseling and had extensive teaching and counseling experience in a number of schools. Following ideas gained in his academic training in community education, the new supervisor concluded that the existing Levite educational system did not adequately meet Eskdale's needs. Robert Conrad, the previous supervisor of the Levite educational system, concurred with this assessment. Consequently, they decided that the strong emphasis of the Order on higher secular education was maladaptive in the following areas: (1) the exposure of young Levites to values, beliefs, attitudes, and lifestyles incompatible with those of the Order; (2) the training of an excessive number of teachers; (3) the training of individuals for occupations that the Eskdale commune has little or no need for; and (4) the failure to train sufficient numbers of individuals for various occupations that are crucial for the operation of a modern rural commune.

In response to this new educational philosophy, plans were made to expand existing vocational training. Shortly after the Levites decided that there was a need to alter drastically certain aspects of their educational system, a schism of many young and some middle-aged members, including the new school supervisor, occurred. Ironically, as we will see in greater detail in the next chapter, it was not the impact of secular education per se that resulted in the break of many young people from the Order. Instead, it was the failure of the Levites to indoctrinate their young members sufficiently, as well as the contact of the young Levites with outside religious groups, which were the major factors contributing to the schism.

## *Community Decision-Making, Social Sanctions, and Community Interaction*

Communal ventures inevitably must create some type of policy for the purpose of decision-making, social control, and arbitration of internal conflict. Kanter identifies four general strategies that communes have used for carrying out these functions: anarchism, organized democracy, charisma, and variants of traditional systems:

> Anarchism involves a resistance to imposing any system of authority, setting any limits on behavior, or allowing any person or segment of the group to make decisions for any other. Organized democracy in-

> volves contracts or agreements whereby the group makes some decisions as an entity based on a stated principle (majority rule, two-thirds vote, unanimity) and delegates others to agents, individuals, or committees chosen by and responsible to the group. Organized democracies generally involve a definable structure of positions of responsibility and some rotation of people holding the positions. Charisma as a basis for decision-making involves guidance of the group by one person who inspires devotion in followers. Other people attain authority by their connection with the charismatic leader. Traditional systems include the rights of persons to "rule" by virtue of ownership of the land or position in family or tribal councils. They resemble medieval baronies or familial patriarchies (Kanter 1973, 143–144).

Aspects of each of these four strategies exists within the governing system of the Eskdale commune. Although Glendenning was the epitome of the typical charismatic leader, he exerted little direct influence on the Community Council. He occasionally placed favorites on the Council, or at least persuaded the Council to do so. Robert Conrad's leadership style involves considerable delegation of authority, making him in essence a respected first among equals.

The Community Council exhibits a traditional dimension in that its members are exclusively married males who are "called" rather than elected to office. In the spring of 1975, the Council consisted of eight of the eleven married men who were permanent residents of Eskdale. Two of the three married men not on the Council were in their early twenties. Although the third of these men had been a longtime resident of Eskdale, he was excluded from the Council in large measure due to some of his unorthodox religious views, and his tendency on occasion to react emotionally when feeling strongly about a particular matter. Adult males who are newcomers to Eskdale must undergo a probationary period before they can be admitted to the Community Council. According to an Eskdale priest, this is a precaution taken to prevent a newcomer who does not yet understand the complexities of communal living from disrupting a smoothly-operating decision-making process. A man should be, theoretically, a resident of Eskdale for one year before he can become a member of the Community Council, but this requirement can be waived.

The Council exhibits a democratic dimension by virtue of the fact that its composition includes a large proportion of the adult population of Eskdale. The Community Council receives input from the residents of Eskdale at the monthly community meetings. During these meetings the Council may announce new policies or recent decisions and present community financial reports. The residents of Eskdale may discuss community needs and take a vote of all adult members on proposed recommendations to the Council. Considering that females can perform only secretarial duties on the Council, and that there exists no system of popular election to the Council, it at best can be described as a "limited democracy."

Finally, the Eskdale commune exhibits an anarchistic strain in its general lack of formal social sanctions. While Council decisions act as precedents for future decisions, they are not codified, making them subject to considerable reinterpretation as new situations arise. Individuals at Eskdale often follow their own inclinations.

The principal forms of social control at Eskdale appear to be gossip, disapproval, and appeals to follow the dictates of one's conscience. Public statements may be made during study or testimony meetings that a particular individual or certain people, without mentioning their names, are not acting properly. If a young person or group of young people, such as the high school boys, are not conforming to the accepted norms of the community, group prayers may be said to correct the situation. Expulsion from the community is, theoretically, the most severe social sanction that can be imposed—one which is determined by the Community Council. It appears that expulsion seldom, if ever, occurs. When one priest was asked what types of behavior would warrant expulsion, he said one would be a "sin of the flesh." An Eskdale bachelor, who was discovered smoking several times, was in jeopardy of being expelled, but decided to leave before he was formally expelled. The Aaronic Order does not have a formal preocedure of excommunication such as the one utilized by the Mormon Church.

Most social interaction among adult members of the Eskdale commune occurs in work settings, the communal dining hall, religious meetings, and other public gatherings. Table 5-3 shows the daily schedule at Eskdale during the latter part of 1974 and the first half of 1975.

Table 5-3
Daily Schedule at Eskdale

| Time | Activity |
|---|---|
| 6:30 A.M. | Breakfast |
| 7:00 A.M. | Men's work meeting; men generally start working sometime after it becomes light outside |
| 7:30 A.M. | "Breakthrough" (a religious meeting for school children also attended by some adults) |
| 12:00 P.M. | Dinner (main meal of the day) |
| 7:30 P.M. | Community sing |

On Tuesday evenings Eskdale has a study class which is attended by most members of the community; school children are required to attend. Prayer meetings may be held spontaneously in the evenings during the week and have lasted late into the night and the early morning hours. Occasionally during the week a musical performance may be presented or a movie shown.

Just as active Mormons spend several hours attending various religious activities on Sundays, the Levites do the same on Saturdays. Since 1958 when Glendenning received a revelation on the matter, the Levites have observed Saturday as their Sabbath, imitating the ancient Hebrews in this regard. Eskdale's working and school week is from Sunday to Thursday, and Friday is similar to Saturday in the outside society. Friday is regarded to be "clean-up day" and "time to prepare for the Sabbath." On Fridays the females prepare as much food as possible for the Sabbath meals. Table 5-4 shows the Sabbath schedule during the latter part of 1974 and the first half of 1975.

Table 5-4
Sabbath Schedule at Eskdale

| Time | Activity |
|---|---|
| 7:00 A.M. | Breakfast |
| 9:30–10:30 A.M. | Study Class |
| 10:45–12:30 P.M. | Worship Service |
| 1:00 P.M. | Dinner |
| 4:00 P.M. | Prayer Meeting |
| 6:00 P.M. | Supper |
| 7:30–8:20 P.M. | Sacrament Meeting |
| 8:30–9:30 P.M. | Sabbath Study Class |

In contrast to interaction in work settings and community public areas, visitation patterns are much more irregular. Although children visit each other in their homes rather frequently, adults generally do not. Partoun residents appear to be more receptive to visiting than Eskdale residents. This may be related to the distance between homesteads at Partoun, the greater amount of leisure time that many of its residents have because they are retired, and fewer opportunities for social contact. According to an Eskdale widow, after the chores and community activities are over, there is little time for visiting. Some Eskdale residents expressed a desire for more visiting in homes among the adults. Also some Partoun residents stated that they sometimes feel like intruders or that the Eskdale residents are indifferent to their visits. A male resident of Partoun told me that he feels that there is more "fellowship" in his community than at Eskdale and that some Eskdale residents give him the impression that they prefer not to be visited at home.

I found much more visiting in homes among adults when I did fieldwork in a Hutterite colony in South Dakota (Baer 1976). It should be pointed out that many Levites were not reared communally, and concepts which they previously held about privacy are probably deeply ingrained. Eskdale's high school principal noted that it is relatively easy to construct some buildings, but it takes more time to develop a sense of "brotherhood and community"—a quality which he felt had been strengthened gradually at Eskdale. Even though tensions may exist between individuals or families, the intention to overcome them is often expressed in religious meetings, particularly during testimony meetings or at times when people spontaneously decide to give testimonies.

## *Relationship between Eskdale and the Outside World*

In their attitude toward the larger society, communal groups have tended to adopt either an introversionist posture or an activist posture. Those adopting the first posture, termed "retreat communes" by Rosebeth Moss Kanter (1972, 175), "seek geographical isolation, they discard technology, they develop pastoral visions embodying a return to nostalgically viewed past." The second type, the "service commune," sees itself as having a mission to the larger society, or at least to a constituency within it. According to Kanter (1972, 191), "the service adaptation makes possible for a community to interact with the environment not out of weakness but out of strength, for the commune has something valuable to offer society."

In its relationship with the larger society, Eskdale exhibits dimensions of both of these postures in theory, although in reality the first is more pronounced than the second. The Levites maintain that ideally it is desirable to avoid as much of the outside world as possible in order to "purify" themselves for the Second Coming of Christ. Some Levites maintain that they are attempting to pay off their debts so they can move to one of the Levite desert communities. Some Eskdale residents at one point opposed having the Mount Wheeler Power Company supply electricity to their community because it is a form of dependence on the outside world. At the same time Eskdale purchased fuel from the outside to run an electrical generator—a practice that proved to be more expensive than the former.

Levites consider many *worldly* recreational activities to be "of Satan." Glendenning labelled various recreational activities as "wreck-reation" and warned the Levites that when Christ returned to the earth, he would not look for people in movie theaters, dance halls, and public swimming pools. An Eskdale grade school teacher stated that one of the "evils" of public schools is dancing, an activity which Mormons generally highly condone. Eskdale students are forbidden to listen to rock music, but are encouraged to listen to songs with religious themes. On the other hand, some recreational outlets, such as hiking, biking, hayrides, sightseeing, and singing are considered to be necessary and desirable. Eskdale residents occasionally view educational films and *wholesome* entertainment films.

Most Levites reject or are indifferent to the idea of changing society through structural reform or revolution. Like most Mormons and evangelical Protestants, the Levites reject the concept of the 'Social Gospel' advocated by liberal Christians. Instead, they emphasize repentance and personal change. For them, Jesus Christ will revolutionize society by creating a perfect society on earth upon his Second Coming. Although many Levites maintain that they value secular education and being informed about current events, most appear to be relatively unconcerned about social issues. During the Saturday evening study class at Eskdale, Robert Conrad often discusses the relationship of current events to prophecies about the imminence of the Second Coming. Most people in the audience merely listen without comment to his discussion. Many Levites tend to be politically conservative and occasionally some express annoyance with big government intervention. One Levite admitted to me his ultra-conservative orientation and said that he would probably belong to the John Birch Society if he were not a member of the Aaronic Order. Although it appears many Levites vote, they generally consider one's political views a personal matter which need not be discussed with others in the Aaronic Order. One of the revelations received by Glendenning advises the Levites to "obey the law" but "leave the court to the world" (Book of Elias 1944, Sec. 171, 44).

Despite the political conservatism of most elderly and middle-aged Levites, they do not exhibit the strong commitment to militant nationalism characteristic of many conservatives in American society. The members of the Order believe in pacificism and nonviolence and maintain that the Levites of Old Testament times were exempt from military service. An Eskdale priest was the first person to be granted conscientious objector status in the state of Utah. Because this individual's local draft board resisted his request for a CO classification, Glendenning and the then Chairman of the Supreme Council personally visited the director of the Selective Service Board in Washington, D.C., about the matter. Since this time many other young Levite men have received a CO classification. Others have joined the armed forces, evidently because of a lack of commitment to the beliefs of the Aaronic Order at the time of their decision. According to Robert Conrad, Levites must be free to decide whether or not to serve in the military.

Despite a strong retreatist tendency within the Aaronic Order, the Levites recognize that they cannot escape the larger society. The Levites as the priesthood tribe of Israel believe that they have an obligation to the outside world and eventually will have to deal with its evil, as migrants to the desert from the cities will attempt to exploit and persecute them. Eskdale interacts with a considerable number of outside individuals, groups, businesses, and government agencies.

Over the years Eskdale has developed relationships with its non-Levite neighbors, many of whom are Mormons, in the sparsely populated Snake Valley. Some Snake Valley children have attended school at Eskdale or have taken lessons from Eskdale's music teacher. Some Snake Valley residents also attend some of the musical performances that are conducted at Eskdale. Eskdale's most unique neighbors reside at the Home Farm—a community located several miles west of Baker, Nevada, and on the lower slopes of Wheeler Peak. The Home Farm is the headquarters of the School of the Natural Order—an esoteric organization which attempts to integrate "much of the Egyptian, Greek, Christian, Oriental, . . . Wisdoms and Teaching with modern scientific theories and findings" ("School of the Natural Order," n.d.).

Ralph M. DeBit, known as Vitvan to his followers, became interested in New Age philosophy in the 1920s and established the School of the Natural Order in the late 1940s. Several decades ago the headquarters of the School was transferred from southern California to its present location. In 1975 the director of the school was a woman in her eighties who had worked closely with Vitvan. When I visited the Home Farm in late March 1975, there were about fifteen individuals, most in their twenties and thirties, present for dinner in the community's dining room. The primary reason that people stay at the Home Farm is to study the esoteric knowledge which the School of the Natural Order offers. While people stay at the Home Farm, they farm in order to communicate with Mother Earth. The School conducts correspondence courses, manufactures tapes of lecture series and publishes books and booklets relating to its philosophy. Despite the quasi-communal nature of the School of the Natural Order, its members have little interaction with the Levites. Some children from the Home Farm have attended school at Eskdale. Some young Levite men occasionally visit the Home Farm, and a middle-aged Levite man presented a slide show about Eskdale there. Many Eskdale residents tend to be suspicious of the School of the Natural

Order because it maintains that Jesus Christ is only one of many great teachers, and because it syncretizes Western and Eastern religious traditions.

A wide variety of groups and individuals have visited Eskdale, including social scientists, newspaper and magazine reporters, college students, and religious groups. In 1965 a reporter visited the Eskdale commune, and wrote an article on it which appeared in the religious new section of the *Los Angeles Times.* A *National Geographic* reporter visited Eskdale several times to compile information for a book called *Rural America,* but only two pages of it dealt with the community. Occasionally Levite university students invite other students to visit Eskdale. One such visitor was a young man who was interested in communal living, started dating a young Levite woman whom he later married, and became an extremely dedicated member of the Aaronic Order. The residents of Eskdale are cordial toward and tolerant of visitors, and the presence of visitors is a common occurrence which causes little excitement.

## *The Survival Capacity of the Eskdale Commune*

Despite economic difficulties, internal conflicts, and even schisms of disaffected members, Levites accept the survival of Eskdale as a matter of faith. Like Job of Old Testament times, they will be tested again and again in order to prove their steadfastness to God's word. The Levites maintain that a large number of communities similar to Eskdale will be established in the Snake Valley. One Levite stated that Glendenning claimed that there would eventually be over 250,000 people living in the desert of western Utah. In anticipation of a mass migration, the Levites feel that divine intervention will play a role in the development of the desert communities as the time of the millennium draws nearer. When I asked an Eskdale priest, given the present dependence of Eskdale on the national economy and the environmental conditions of the Snake Valley, how the growth that the Levites envision will be possible, he replied that some "minor miracles" would have to occur such as the discovery of an artesian well which would supply an unlimited amount of water without the use of a fossil fuel-powered pump.

For the immediate future, the Levites have made some more modest plans for expansion. Since a large population is believed to result in a breakdown of primary relationships and a loss of economic efficiency, the leaders of the Order maintain that Eskdale should not exceed a population of approximately one hundred. As an outgrowth of this idea, four young Levite families, only two of which had children (three children in each family), became in August 1975 the residents of the new Bethel commune. Although Bethel functions as a satellite community of Eskdale, it is anticipated that eventually it will have its own Community Council and be economically self-supporting. The Levites also plan to establish another community named Petra several miles north of Eskdale. In 1975 an unoccupied dome-shaped, cement building, which was originally designed to be a shop building, sat on the future site of Petra. An Eskdale resident noted that the building could be converted into a communal residence housing several families. Also, according to Robert Conrad, Partoun will be "resurrected" and become a collective rather than a cooperative community.

While one may be tempted to view the expectations that the Levites have for the development of their communities in a remote valley of the semiarid Great Basin as grandiose and utopian, Eskdale has already endured longer than the majority of communal ventures. Of 130 communal ventures that existed in the United States prior to the "communal explosion" of the 1960s, ninety-one lasted less than a decade, fifty-nine less than five years, fifty only two years, and thirty-two only one year (Deets 1939, 22–23). The Amana Society, the Ephrata Cloister, the Shakers, and Old Economy functioned for over a century as communal groups. Of all the communal groups that existed during the nineteenth century in the United States, only the Hutterites continue to function on a communal basis. In fact, the Hutterites, with the exception of a few short disruptions, have been practicing communalism since 1528, making them the oldest communal group in Western society. The longevity pattern of the new communal movement is roughly similar to those exhibited by earlier phases in the history of communitarianism. Zablocki (1980) and his coworkers examined the life expectancy of a sample of 120 American communes (sixty rural communes and sixty urban comunes). With the exception of eight groups, all of these were founded between 1965 and 1975. Discounting two communes that could not be contacted after two years, "All in all, fifty-nine percent of the 118 communes that were followed had disintegrated by 1978" (Zablocki 1980, 149). Of the twenty-nine communes in a "zero-year cohort," which consists of those groups that were in existence less than half a year period to the investigators' initial contact with them, "Half the communes in the cohort had disintegrated in little over two years, and almost half those remaining were gone by the end of the following two-year period" (Zablocki 1980, 148).

If we compare the Eskdale commune, which was established in 1955, with most other communal ventures, we must conclude that it has been a relatively successful social experiment (at least if we define "success" in terms of longevity). Based on a sample of thirty nineteenth century communes, Kanter (1972) concluded that the "successful" groups (those existing for over twenty-five years or more) exhibited a greater prevalence of "commitment mechanisms," defined as organizational-structural characteristics which function to promote group commitment, than did "unsuccessful" groups (those lasting less than twenty-five years). As might be expected, the Eskdale commune exhibits many of the practices, such as sacrifices and investments made by members for the community, the building of a strong family sense within the community, the sharing of property and work, the observation of rituals of communion, and the construction of an elaborate ideology and authority structure, also deemed necessary by Kanter for the promotion of commitment. While Eskdale also contains serious contradictions and conflicts, such as factionalism, doctrinal differences, and a tendency toward privatism, it compares favorably with other long-enduring communes in its development of group continuance, cohesion, and control.

A major flaw of Kanter's analysis, however, is its tendency to gloss over the importance of economic arrangements in the maintenance of communal experiments. While it is perhaps true that most utopian societies have failed for many other reasons and even sometimes due to economic prosperity, the inability of any communal venture to meet minimal subsistence needs in one way or another inevitably will result in its demise. In light of this fact, it is surprising that virtually no attention has been given to the role played by financial contributions in their survival. Nevertheless, it appears that some if not many communes have been dependent at some stage of their development on assistance from sympathetic patrons. For example, New Harmony, a secular commune which existed for a few years in Indiana during the 1820s, was in large measure sustained by the philanthropy of Robert Dale Owen, a wealthy Scottish industrialist and patron of several utopian schemes. The Kaweah Cooperative Commonwealth, a California commune combining Marxist and anarchist principles during the 1880s, was given financial support in the form of fees, donations, and gifts by the members of its supporting clubs in cities such as San Francisco, Los Angeles, Denver, and New York (Hine 1966, 83–84). Alturia, another nineteenth century California utopian colony, received a considerable portion of its financial support from "subordinate councils," a network of clubs in various California cities (Hine: 110).

Based on a study of thirteen rural communes in four western states (Colorado, New Mexico, California, and Oregon), Hugh Gardner suggests that subsidies in the form of free land, donations from sympathetic benefactors, new members, and parents, and public welfare, have played a significant role in the modern commune movement:

> . . . In understanding why some communes have succeeded and others failed, there is at least one more important factor to be considered: the role of gifts and subsidies played in the destiny of the modern commune movement. I credit my own suspicions about their importance to a conversation with a man named John Allen, leader of a New Mexico commune . . . Allen told me in 1973, when it was becoming clear that the New Mexico commune scene had all but completely collapsed, that the single most dangerous threat to the commune movement—or "former commune movements" as he put it—was not authoritarian repression, immaturity, or bad social design but subsidies taken from outsiders. Subsidized groups, he argued, are always subject to controls or expropriation at the whims of the subsiders (Gardner 1978, 235–236).

Gardner (1978, 236) goes on to argue that: "The specific historical cause behind five of the seven communal failures in this study was the withdrawal by benefactors of this support." In the light of Gardner's findings, it is important to stress the role of subsidies in the survival of the Eskdale commune. Unlike most communal ventures, Eskdale is part of a larger group with three non-communal branches. The Eskdale commune is to a large extent maintained by the financial tithes and contributions of members of the two urban branches located in the Wasatch Front area.

In addition to the issue of outside subsidization, another factor contributing to Eskdale's capacity for survival is its partial solution to the problem of high turnover that has plagued many communal ventures. Over the years, Eskdale has experienced a relatively high turnover rate in that some families will reside there for several years and then will return to an urban area. Unlike most communal ventures, the Aaronic Order has a pool of non-communal members who are committed to a communal ideology and fill vacancies which may arise at Eskdale. This practice does not completely eliminate the problems that are associated with high turnover rates, but it does ease them.

The success of the Eskdale commune is also partly ensured by the functions that it serves for non-communal Levites. In addition to actualizing utopian visions, many Levites view Eskdale as a place where they will eventually reside and find a serenity which they cannot find in an urban environment. For elderly people, the community theoretically provides freedom from economic deprivation and loneliness. The Eskdale school system provides a social environment which many non-communal members perceive as being desirable for the rearing of their children. For many members, the community is a place where they can retreat from their daily routines for a weekend or several days and regenerate a feeling of religious commitment. This function is perhaps especially true in the case of young Levites attending Utah's two state universities who may experience a certain degree of cognitive dissonance due to their secular surroundings.

# 6

# *The Development of the Aaronic Order as a Mormon Sect*

Religious movements are dynamic phenomena which are subject to events both in their external and internal environments. Just as Mormonism underwent a transformation between its beginnings in the 1830s and the twentieth century, the Levite religious system is not the same today as it was in the 1930s and 1940s. In this chapter, I will discuss the development of the Aaronic Order as a religious sect subsequent to its initial efforts to revitalize modern Mormonism. I will consider various influences upon its evolution, particularly those that moved it away from Mormonism and toward evangelical Protestantism as well as patterns of sectarian maintenance, stagnation, revitalization, and fission within the Order.

## *Influences on the Development of the Order*

New religions are always syncretistic in that they combine elements from older religious traditions with the idiosyncratic teaching of their prophet-founders and early members. Previously we saw that early Mormonism incorporated dimensions of Puritanism, frontier evangelicalism, primitivism, utopian socialism, and American folklore. The Levite religion also constitutes a syncretic ensemble—one which includes not only many elements of Mormonism but also of evangelical Protestantism, British Israelism, and Anabaptist communalism. Maurice Glendenning admitted his own religious eclecticism when he wrote the following remarks to an inquirer interested in the Aaronic Order:

> However, as for the Book of Mormon, we recognize this book—also the LDS D&C (Doctrine and Covenants) and the Koran. We study and teach the Book of Noah, the Book of Enoch, the Book of Jasher, and the Old and New Testament, and the Dead Sea Scrolls, and many of the other religions of the world (dated October 7, 1965; reprinted in the *Aaron's Star*, September 1966).

By introducing the Levites to various Protestant groups and individuals, Glendenning contributed to the Order's movement away from Mormonism toward evangelical Protestantism. Certain individuals of a non-Mormon background who converted to the sect also played a significant role in this transition. The rank and file members of the Order, however, were not passive actors in the development of their religion. Instead, they reacted favorably to some of the ideological forces acting upon them and strongly resisted others. The susceptibility to new religious beliefs and practices also varied along generational lines and according to the structural position of members in the group.

## The Eclectic Religious Background of Glendenning

Other than the claims that Glendenning made about his religious experiences prior to 1930, relatively little is known about his religious background during his youth and early adulthood. While Glendenning's father was an itinerant Methodist preacher, it is not known if Glendenning was a Methodist himself at one time. During his late teens or early twenties Glendenning wanted to become a minister and attended a Bible college in Osceola, Iowa, but did not achieve his initial goal. Because of the Glendennings' many moves, they never attached themselves to any religious congregation for long, and apparently they sampled a variety of religious groups.

Glendenning's early contacts with the Hutterites probably provided him with some ideas for the establishment of a communal venture. For awhile, prior to moving to Utah, Glendenning had a chiropractic practice in Yankton, South Dakota, which is about eighteen miles from the Bon Homme Colony (the oldest Hutterite colony in North America) and near other Hutterite colonies. Some of Glendenning's patients were Hutterites. During the late 1940s and early 1950s, Glendenning visited some of the Hutterite colonies in Montana. Other Levites have over the years visited the Hutterites, and one Levite woman taught school and resided at three Hutterite colonies over a period of about thirteen years.

Some concepts held by both the Levites and Mormons bear resemblance to British Israelism. At one time, probably no later than the late 1940s, Glendenning received literature from the British Israelites. It appears that he had no direct contact with the movement. While it is difficult to prove to what degree Glendenning was influenced by this literature, there are some interesting parallels in the beliefs of the British Israelites and the Levites. British Israelism teaches that Anglo-Saxons are the descendants of the ancient Israelites and heirs to all the promises made to Abraham and the Old Testament prophets (Braden 1949, 385). In 1694 John Sadler wrote a book linking Britain with Israel, but the primary impetus to the British Israelite movement came from John Wilson, who published *Our Israelitish Origin* in 1840 (Braden, 1949, 388–391). According to the British Israelites, the ancient Israelites failed to abide by God's laws, became divided and disappeared from history, but made their way in several migrations to the British Isles. Like the Levites, the British Israelites believe that the Jews represent only one of the tribes of Israel—that of Judah (Braden, 399–400). One lineage from the tribe of Judah migrated to the British Isles, and came to provide the sovereigns of the British empire.

A different John Wilson states the following about the emphasis that British Israelism places on the notion that Anglo-Saxons are lineal descendants of Israel:

> There have, however, been some who have stressed the importance of physical descent, and have emphasized that God's promises to the seed of Abraham are not altogether cancelled despite the waywardness of the Jews, and despite their rejection of Christ. . . . The British-Israelite emphasis on heredity descent from those to whom God's promises were made is more specific, and puts its main weight on the continuance of the promises of those Jews not involved in the final disobedience of the rejection of Christ—namely, the house of Israel, which had gone into captivity before the New Testament era. It further seeks to establish an identity between those Hebrews who did not forfeit God's good will, and those who are held to have been traditionally receptive to the claims of Christ—in particular the British people and perhaps also the Protestant peoples of Europe and North America, and their offshoots . . . (John Wilson 1967, 347–348).

The Levites also maintain that Israelites migrated to the "northern lands" (Book of Elias 1944, Sec. 174, 48–49). They believe that Jesus Christ established a church with two branches—one for the Gentiles and the other for the Israelites (Beeston 1966, 140–148). Shortly after its establishment, the Gentile branch of the Christian church fell into apostasy. The Israelite branch was led by James the Just, purportedly the brother of Jesus, through whom the Levitical and Aaronic priesthoods continued (Book of Elias 1944, Sec. 206, 83–84). Somewhat similarly to the British Israelite belief that the Israelites were to receive their inheritance for all generations, the Aaronic Order teaches that the priestly duties of the Levites and Aaronites were to continue after the establishment of the Christian church. The Levites believe that James the Just and his son, Dan, migrated north from Jerusalem and that some of the Christian Israelites settled in the British Isles (Beeston 1966, 156–162; Book of Elias 1944, Sec. 139, 4–5). The tribe of Glen Dan passed on knowledge of its lineal descent from Levi, Aaron, and Zadok and the gospel of Jesus Christ (Beeston 1966, 171). As the following passage indicates, the Levite view of the British sovereigns is similar to that of the British Israelites:

> The kings of Great Britain have long been recognized to be the blood of Judah through the traditions, ecclesiastical history, and early records of her people. The lion, symbol of British royalty as found in the supporters of the Royal Arms of Britain, was the tribal emblem of Judah (Beeston 1966, 109).

### The Levites and the Evangelicals

Glendenning made explicit efforts to move the Levites away from Mormonism toward evangelical Protestantism. He was disturbed that many members of the Order remained attached to many Mormon beliefs and behaviorial patterns. In a letter dated November 6, 1953, addressed to a couple identified as his "cousins," he contemptuously referred to the "reformed Brighamite Mormon Church" as "an abominable church with such abominable teachings" (*Aaron's Star*, June 1969). In a letter dated June 3, 1959, Glendenning wrote "that the time a member of the True Church of God uses in the study of the Book of Mormon is lost time. . . . If we establish the Kingdom of God as we are supposed to do, it will take every moment of our time in the study of the Bible and its allied subjects" (*Aaron's Star*, September 1962).

The evolution of the Aaronic Order was significantly affected by contacts that its younger members had during the 1950s and the early 1960s with evangelical Christians in Colorado Springs, a place where Glendenning had once lived. During this period the young Levites were exposed to a variety of Protestant attitudes and behavioral patterns that were drastically different from their own. In 1954 Glendenning persuaded two young Levite males, who had recently graduated from high school, to enroll in a Bible college in Colorado Springs. The Bible college was operated by the Pilgrim Holiness Church, which also had a Bible college in Bartlesville, Oklahoma—another place where the Glendennings had lived for a short time. According to a male resident of Eskdale, Glendenning wanted to inject new ideas among the Levites because they were "so Mormonized." Also he wanted some of the young Levites to obtain a Bible college education so they could become "ministers and teachers" in the Order.

Because other young Levites, including some couples, desired to attend the Bible college, they rented a house which was named the "Colorado Springs Mission Home." The site of the home was relocated in December 1956 and again in August 1958, when it was moved to a seventeen room house on a three acre tract (*Aaron's Star*, July 1960). Tensions between the Bible college and the young Levites apparently developed when it was discovered that there were major doctrinal differences between the Pilgrim Holiness Church and the Aaronic Order. The school administration objected to the separate living arrangements of the Levite students, but also was concerned about the potential influence that the Levites might have on other students, especially in light of the fact that a member of the Pilgrim Holiness Church had married a young Levite man and shortly thereafter had joined the Order. The college expelled all of the Levite students, except for a man whose education was being funded by the GI Bill. He was the only Levite to graduate from the Bible college. Shortly after the expulsions, the Pilgrim Holiness Church closed the school due to financial pressures. Some Levites view this event, as well as the death of a particularly antagonistic professor due to a heart attack, as forms of divine retribution.

The expulsion of the Levites from the Bible college did not lead to the immediate demise of the Colorado Division of the Aaronic Order. The Colorado Springs Mission Home underwent constant turnover of individuals and families. Young Levites worked in the community and became involved in other activities. Some fell in love with one another, resulting in a string of marriages. Two men enrolled at Friends University in Wichita, Kansas, and took their families with them—an experience which introduced them to Quakerism. The mission home housed seven families at one time and often was visited by Glendenning, who was very fond of the young Levites there. According to an Eskdale priest, a former resident of the home, Glendenning "liked the young people and kept his hand on us pretty strong, guiding us through different things." The Colorado Division dissolved with the closure of the mission home in January 1966 and the departure of the last Levite family from Colorado Springs the following summer.

Despite the conflict with the administration of the Bible college, the Colorado experience had the effect which Glendenning intended it to, that of "de-Mormonizing" the Levites, at least partially. A Levite confessed that she, as when she first went to Colorado Springs, was basically still a Mormon in her views. She discovered that the Pilgrim Holiness Church placed a greater emphasis on a personal relationship with Jesus Christ than on respect for men, such as Joseph Smith and the Mormon authorities. The Holiness people worked for their "brothers and sisters" rather than for "things." Despite her initial shock at the emotionalism of the Holiness services, she gradually learned that evangelical Christians are "beautiful people."

Another important chapter in the development of the Order was its contact with an evangelist named Jerry Owens who, according to many Levites, was once referred to in a Ripley's "Believe It or Not" cartoon as "the walking Bible." Owens brought the Levites in contact with various evangelical groups. In 1963 a Levite woman attended a meeting in the Phoenix area at which Owens was preaching. Owens became weak from preaching and focused upon this woman since she "stood out from the others because a light was shining around her head" (*Aaron's Star*, January 1964). He asked her to pray for the congregation; as she prayed, Owens felt her strength flowing into him. Somewhat later the Levite woman took Owens to meet Glendenning, who often spent the winters in Arizona for therapeutic reasons. Glendenning invited Owens to speak to the Levites in Utah and announced that he had received a revelation fourteen years earlier prophesying this meeting with Owens, who, according to the Writing, would have the "word of the Lord . . . written in his forehead" (Disciple Book 1955, 35). Owens was baptized into the True Church of God and enrolled his daughter in the Eskdale school in September 1963 (*Aaron's Star*, July 1964).

During 1964 Owens conducted revival meetings, which were attended by some Levites, at the Full Gospel Assembly Church in Salt Lake City and at the Assembly of God Church in Provo, as well as revival meetings at the four branches of the Aaronic Order. Members of the Order and the Full Gospel Assembly Church purchased a small bus which was used to transport the Eskdale school children to sing at meetings conducted by Owens, who was now being referred to as the "Shepherd of the Hills." Some of the meetings were broadcast by a Utah Valley radio station (*Aaron's Star*, August 1964).

At first many Levites objected to Owens' exuberant preaching style, but gradually most adjusted to it. One Levite argued that the Lord directed Owens to break down the Levites' "over-dependence on intellectualism" and to urge them to express their faith more openly. Some Levites, particularly older ones, did not accept Owens, but many others were charmed by him.

In 1965 Glendenning established contact with a Pentecostalist congregation in Indiana and another Pentecostalist congregation a short distance away in Illinois. The ministers of these two congregations visited the Levites in Utah in late spring of 1965 and were baptized members of the "Kingdom of God" (*Aaron's Star*, September 1965). Several Levites visited these congregations and were invited back by their pastors so the congregations could be established as branches of the Aaronic Order. Glendenning preached at the two churches again in September 1965 (*Aaron's Star*, October 1965). After this visit, however, relations between Glendenning and the two ministers became strained. According to several Levites, the two ministers attempted to test Glendenning by requesting him to perform a miracle. Glendenning claimed that in 1931 he had received a relevation entitled "Lest They Tempt Thee With a Sign" warning about requests of this nature (Disciple Book 1955, 77).

In addition to introducing the Levites to the minister of the Full Gospel Assembly Church in Salt Lake City, Owens introduced them to the Order of the Lamb, a quasi-communal group from California. This group was formed by the Protestant minister who was working with young people, particularly drug addicts. He established a halfway house for these young people in Sonora, California, out of which the Order of the Lamb developed. Some members of the Order of the Lamb moved into a house in Provo and attempted to evangelize local residents and Brigham Young University students, apparently with little success.

## *The Charismatic Movement: The Seeds of a Schism*

Despite his recognition that many revitalization movements do not become fully institutionalized, Wallace (1972, 429) does not elaborate upon their possible outcomes. In their critique of the Weber-Michels model of movement organizations which predicts their bureaucratization, routinization, and accommodation to the larger society, Mayer N. Zald and Robert Ash (1966, 328) cite several other possible transformations, including "coalitions with other organizations, organizational splits, increased rather than decreased radicalism." They observe that schismogenesis and factionalization in particular have "received little attention from sociologists" (Zald and Ash 1966, 328). In a somewhat similar vein, Armand L. Mauss (1975, 64–65) proposes a model of the natural history of social movements that posits that fragmentation often follows institutionalization. While the Aaronic Order had managed to remain a sect as it entered its fifth decade, the group also had undergone a process of partial institutionalization. For the younger Levites, the pioneer phase of the Order had passed and the Levite prophet was a remote figure who did not hold the same attraction as he did for their grandparents and parents. Given this situation, contact with a neo-Pentecostal group from California enabled the young Levites, as well as some middle-aged Levites, to recognize their own sense of dissatisfaction with the Aaronic Order.

The Order, like the Mormon Church, has undergone a process of internal fission. The most significant of a series of schisms occurred during a late phase of my fieldwork. In this section, I will review the events that led to the emergence of a Pentecostal or charismatic movement within the Order, its impact on various generational units in the sect, the eventual expulsion of its leaders, and the subsequent desertion by a substantial portion of Eskdale residents. In attempting to account for this schism, I will draw upon several hypotheses that Zald and Ash (1966) propose in their seminal article on change in social movement organizations.

Members of the Order of the Lamb, an outgrowth of the Jesus People movement, visited the Levites in Utah several times during the early 1970s. Some Levites, particularly young ones, also visited the headquarters of the group in Sonora, California. The Order of the Lamb first visited Eskdale in the fall of 1973, and introduced some Levites to glossolalia. Because of this visit, a middle-aged couple and an adolescent male began speaking in tongues. According to a female Levite, the Levites did not raise their arms while praying until this practice was introduced to them by the Order of the Lamb. A young man stated that Jerry Owens and the Order of the Lamb transformed the Levites from a "deadpan group to one with life."

While a small number of Levites had spoken in tongues prior to the summer of 1974, they did so privately or in small groups. During the spring of 1974 a group of young Levites, primarily high school students, but some in their twenties visited the Order of the Lamb in Sonora. A young Levite, whom I will call Sam, was "turned on to Christ" after having doubts about his religion. Subsequently, he discontinued smoking and drinking alcoholic beverages.

Richard, who was destined to lead the charismatic movement within the Order, had been reared a Protestant and attended college for awhile in the Midwest. He first came to Utah in 1967 on a hitchhiking trip following his conversion to the Lord. During his travels in Utah he encountered several Levites who put him up for the night. The following year, after having broken up with his fiancée, Richard again encountered the Levites on a second trip west. This time he decided to join the Order and to marry Robert Conrad's eldest daughter. Despite his conversion, Richard went through periods of doubt. At other times, he attempted to combine Christianity and Zen Buddhism. Due to his feeling of marginality at Eskdale, he left and returned to the community several times.

Late in the summer of 1974 a small group of young Levites began to speak in tongues in secluded sessions. The young Levites, some of whom had not previously felt committed to religious ideals, made exuberent testimonies about their faith in Jesus. Robert Conrad approved of this new religious fervor, but noted that it must be tempered. He observed that the inability of most Levites to express joy and their innermost convictions hindered the proslytism of others. In the late summer or early fall of 1975 a middle-aged Levite man, who had learned glossolalia when the Order of the Lamb had visited Eskdale for the first time the previous year, publicly spoke in tongues. It seems that this incident encouraged the young charismatics to make public their commitment to the Holy Spirit. During the fall, Eskdale experienced a Pentecostal revival, despite the absence (other than occasional visits) of the leader of the charismatic movement. At first many Levites were skeptical of this new phenomenon which they felt was unbecoming for a Levite. Some Levites stood off in the distance during the revival meetings and ridiculed the participants' behavior. Gradually suspicions and reservations about the charismatic movement dwindled. A fair number of young people and some middle-aged and even elderly people began to receive the "gifts of the Holy Spirit" or at least were affected by the enthusiasm and emotionalism of the charismatic movement.

During the fall of 1974 and the fall of 1975, revival meetings frequently occurred at Eskdale, often lasting until the early hours of the morning. Particularly young people, including high school girls, preschool and grade school children, were captivated by the religious enthusiasm. For many of them religious meetings had been events which were tiresome and incomprehensible, but which one was required to attend. The body was unwilling and so was the spirit. Long discussions about the Aaronic and Levitical priesthoods, the signs portending that the world is in its latter days, and various fine points in the Bible and the Book of Elias were tedious, if not meaningless. But Jesus and the Holy Spirit—they were real and manifested in the behavior of people. Jesus was a personal friend who listened, understood and forgave the most hardened sinner. Jesus was not the vengeful God of the Old Testament, but rather a companion who teaches us to forgive and love our enemies. And he was coming soon, not so much to destroy the wicked but rather to be with his friends. Although there were various reactions by the young people to the revival, the only group of them that resisted it were the high school boys. For them the revivals were "uncool"; they still knew who controlled the community, made them attend religious activities, and cut their hair. However, even some adults who were skeptical about the revival admitted that it had changed the young people in a desirable way.

During the Christmas break of 1974–1975, Eskdale's high school students, accompanied by some middle-aged and young adults, attended the Deeper Life Convention in San Diego, California—an event which was discussed at great length by the Levites for some time. The convention was sponsored by Morris Cerrillo, a charismatic evangelist, and included talks by Dale Evans and country Western singer Skeeter Davis. Richard and his wife pledged several hundred dollars to promote Cerrillo's work, despite the fact that they were penniless. For a couple of months after the convention some Eskdale residents wore buttons with the words "I care" on them. The convention further extended the ecumenism that had been developing for twenty years within the Order—a phenomenon very atypical of Mormonism itself.

The first climax of the charismatic movement occurred during the fall of 1974 and the winter of 1975. By spring the intensity of the movement had subsided. Meetings were held less frequently in the community auditorium and more frequently in various homes, which permitted only a small number to attend them. By the late summer of 1975 the charismatic movement intensified its public activities again. Several Levites who had been inactive for some time became involved in the enthusiasm of a meeting in late September. Certain tensions arose at Eskdale and in the Order because of the charismatic movement. While a fair number of adults, even elderly ones, accepted it, some expressed a "wait and see" attitude and others were openly hostile to it. The now deceased Second High Priest warned the members of the Springville branch about the excesses at the Eskdale commune. An Eskdale widow told me that she was unable to speak in tongues, dance, and shout "Allelulia!" She added that Joseph Smith had said that the Gentiles have an "exuberant spirit" but the Israelites have a "quiet spirit," and that he had claimed that glossolalia was the least important of the "gifts of the Holy Spirit." Some Levites complained that those individuals who had received the "gifts of the Holy Spirit" often were cliquish and regarded themselves as better than others. When I asked the leader of the Pentecostalists about this allegation, he stated that a special bond existed among those who had received the Holy Spirit. Late in the summer of 1975 Richard confessed to an Eskdale congregation that at first he thought he was superior to others but now "everyone" was speaking in tongues, and he realized how lowly he really was. In response to the allegation that they felt superior to others, the Pentecostalists began to deny that one has to speak in tongues or interpret tongues to receive the Holy Spirit. Despite initial reservations, most Levites regarded the charismatic movement as a desirable phenomenon. Many middle-aged and elderly Levites commented favorably on the increased religious fervor among the young people. Many Levites also maintained that they had never before been so "drawn in love."

It seemed for awhile that in the long run that the charismatic movement would serve a cohesive function. It integrated into the Order many of the young Levites who had not experienced the pioneering efforts of the older Levites, and transcended the cleavages that existed among the three generations of the group. These points of unification, however, proved to be temporary and were negated by events that occurred during the fall of 1975 and the early months of 1976, which culminated in a schism of many young Levites and some middle-aged Levites from the Order.

Richard's wife and one of her sisters began to compare the Bible and the Levitical Writings sometime in the late summer of 1975. In the early fall about a dozen Levites attended a week-long Pentecostal conference in Anaheim, California. A prominent Pentecostal preacher, who was well-known in fundamentalist circles for his campaign against various cults, argued that Mormonism does not qualify as a Christian religion. Upon hearing this, two middle-aged Levites, who had been reared in the Mormon Church, rushed to the front of the assembly and renounced their Mormon roots. One of the young women doing comparative scriptural research concluded that this may mean that the Levite religion is not theologically valid either. The conference emphasized the idea of comparing the teachings of one's religious group with those in the Bible. Indeed, shortly thereafter the Levite researchers announced that the Levite scriptures are in error and argued that the Aaronic Order is a Mormon offshoot.

In contrast to his earlier marginality, Richard now found himself in the center of events at Eskdale as a result of his informal leadership over the charismatic movement. Nevertheless, he was astute enough to recognize, at least partially, the direction that the religious revival might take the Order. Richard predicted to me that the charismatic movement would cause a rift within the Order, with one faction perhaps being led by Bliss Childs, the Second High Priest, and the other faction being made up of the younger Levites. In August, 1975, Richard told me that his hope of becoming a priest had been dashed when the priesthood was granted to two other Eskdale residents, one a middle-aged man who had recently moved to the community with his family, and the other a man several years younger than himself. By November Richard had ceased attending many of the religious activities in the community and had begun to anticipate his eventual departure from Eskdale.

At any rate, the heated debates, which revolved around the claim by the scripture researchers that the Levite sect was in error, prompted the Community Council to expel the leaders of the charismatic movement. After milking the cows on December 7, 1975, a priest told Richard and Sam that the Council had voted to expel them from the commune, and that a car was ready to take them to Salt Lake City. Richard's wife followed him as did many others, including the other woman who had conducted the controversial scriptural research. Despite his reluctance, this woman's husband, who was the supervisor of the Levite educational system, also left Eskdale at the end of the 1975–1976 academic year.

At first the schismatics attached themselves to a Pentecostal congregation in Salt Lake City. The Aaronic Order had had ongoing contact with this group since the time that it was discovered by a Levite priest during his search for a place for Jerry Owens to conduct his revival meetings. Several young schismatics were baptized at this church and became active in its religious meetings for a brief time. Later in the early part of 1976, the schismatics transferred their allegiance to another Pentecostal congregation which held services in the Bread of Life Fellowship, a storefront church in a Salt Lake suburb. They found themselves attracted to the colorful style of the female pastor at the storefront church. She had been directed by the Lord during the summer of 1975 to leave Reno, Nevada, and establish a new church in the Salt Lake City area. By the summer of 1976 several of the schismatics had become elders and deacons in the storefront congregation. In the meantime, the remaining Levites declared that the schismatic movement was "of Satan" and referred to its leader as "the deceiver."

In their attempt to account for schimogenesis in social movement organizations referenced as MOs, Zald and Ash propose the following three hypotheses:

1. To the extent that a becalmed or failing MO is heterogeneous and must rely heavily on solidary incentives, the more likely it is to be beset by factionalism.
2. The more the ideology of the MO leads to a questioning of the bases of authority, the greater the likelihood of factions and splitting.
3. Exclusive organizations are more likely than inclusive organizations to be beset by schisms (Zald and Ash 1966, 337).

In considering the first of these propositions, our discussion thus far suggests that the charismatic movement, despite initial opposition from many members, came to be regarded by both young and old as a mechanism for regaining social solidarity. The ability of the charismatic movement to accomplish this objective was short-lived. Prior to the charismatic schism, the Aaronic Order consisted of three generational units. In 1975 the first generation or the "pioneers" included all members sixty years of age and older; the second generation, those between thirty and fifty-nine and the third generation, those under thirty years of age. Unification of beliefs tended to occur on a generational level rather than on a group-wide level. The differences between the first and third generations were considerable—the first generation having been a product of

Mormon culture, and the third having had little systematic exposure to Mormon ideology. The second generation stood with a foot in each camp—many of its members having been reared in Mormonism, but also exposed to fundamentalist Protestantism in late adolescence or early adulthood. Each generation also exhibited a diversity of viewpoints, a pattern particularly characteristic of the pioneers.

### The First Generation

In chapter 2 we considered some of the perspectives of the first generation of Levites. Some of the pioneers, including those still sympathetic to polygyny and the Koyle Relief Mine, were still alive in 1975. Almost all members of the first generation had been Mormons, either as result of birth or conversion. Most pioneers had been relatively active and had held minor positions in the Mormon Church, such as teachers, members of priesthood quorums, and members of the Women's Relief Society. Some pioneers still believed that the Mormon Church and the Aaronic Order would reunite before the millennium, and that the Levitical priesthood would be recognized by the Mormon Church. At least one elderly Levite regarded himself to be also a member of the Mormon Church, despite the fact that he had been excommunicated from it. Many pioneers viewed the functions of the Aaronic Order and the Mormon Church as complementary—the work of the former being directed toward the Israelites and that of the latter toward the Gentiles. The pioneers frequently cited the Mormon scriptures, and believed that Joseph Smith had been a prophet. Some of them refused to be rebaptized in the Aaronic Order because they considered their baptism into the Mormon Church to have been sufficient. Prior to 1951, even though the Order conducted baptisms, Levites who had been baptized in the Mormon Church generally were not rebaptized, but after 1951 this policy changed. The primary ideological unity of the pioneers rested in their strong Mormon roots. Various individuals of the first generation, however, held religious beliefs bearing no direct relationship to Mormonism or the Levite cosmology.

Some pioneers believed in reincarnation and maintained that Glendenning also believed it, but did not advocate teaching about it. Five pioneers admitted their belief in reincarnation directly to me, while some spoke of other pioneers who accepted this idea. Those who subscribed to the concept of reincarnation pointed to two Levitical Writings to support their position. Some of the pioneers believed in flying saucers. A Levite widow believed that Christ had been taken into heaven in a flying saucer and that he will return in one. An elderly Levite man collected "space people messages" from magazines and other sources. He maintained that there are many sources of 'Truth' besides the Bible, the Mormon scriptures, and the Levitical Writings, and that many earthlings are receiving Truth from these sources. Glendenning's reaction to these beliefs apparently was one of bemusement. He once threw a saucer across the kitchen in Eskdale's dining hall, exclaiming that he too believed in flying saucers. Some pioneers, such as a woman who reared her baby for awhile on spinach juice instead of milk, embraced various health food fads. In addition to the Levite proscription on the consumption of "swine's flesh," some pioneers advocated vegetarianism.

## The Second Generation

Many members of the second generation were reared as Mormons, but were exposed to the teachings of the Aaronic Order during their childhood or adolescence, usually because of their parents' interest in the Order. A fair number of them had shown little interest in the Order during their parents' investigations of it, but developed greater interest as they became older, especially as romances budded among them. The views of the second generation merged Mormonism and Christian evangelicalism. Many of them were exposed to evangelical Protestantism during early adulthood and developed a certain ecumenism. Although many adhered to various Mormon concepts and occasionally cited the Mormon scriptures, they generally regarded the Aaronic Order to be independent of the Mormon Church. Most of them believed that Joseph Smith was a prophet, but conceded that perhaps he had become a "fallen prophet" at some point. Many adhered to Mormon polytheism and the doctrine of the progression of gods, but others were ambivalent about these ideas. Members of the second generation often had a superficial understanding of Mormon theology. They generally expressed little concern with the idea of entering the celestial kingdom, the highest level of the Mormon afterlife, or achieving divinity. While a fair number of them believed in the existence of many gods, they stated that they were concerned primarily with Jesus Christ. They greatly emphasized a personal relationship with Jesus.

While many members of the second generation deemphasized or even disclaimed various Mormon beliefs, they generally subscribed to the official ideology of the Aaronic Order. An Aaronite priest told me, however, that despite his acceptance of most of Glendenning's revelations, he had "shelved" some. He said that he was more excited by the thought of being part of a community bound together in Christian love than by the idea of being a lineal descendant of Aaron or a member of a communal group. When a Levite pioneer stated that the "highest fulfillment" comes from being part of the House of Levi and Aaron, a middle-aged man objected, noting that there are "many ways to Christ." In addition to a tilt away from Mormonism, the second generation, particularly certain individuals, deemphasized the work of Levi and Aaron and placed greater stress on fundamentalist Protestant concepts and behavioral patterns. Members of the second generation tended to be much more conventional in their views than the pioneers. Few subscribed to reincarnation, flying saucers, or vegetarianism.

**The Third Generation**

Almost all members of the third generation were reared not as Mormons but rather as Levites. They generally knew little about Mormonism and often did not regard Joseph Smith as a prophet. Occasionally when Mormon doctrinal points were discussed by middle-aged and elderly Levites, the young people expressed surprise that some of these points were part of official Levite ideology. The formal religious training in the Eskdale schools tended to emphasize traditional Christian doctrines rather than those of the Aaronic Order. Eskdale's former high school principal stated that Bible study was stressed in the high school religion classes with the Levite scriptures being used only occasionally. He felt that the Book of Elias should only be studied in depth after the students have acquired a relatively solid understanding of the Old and New Testaments. Although the young people were often present at study meetings where various Levite beliefs were discussed, generally these discussions were not geared to include school children actively and consequently often became sessions to be patiently sat out by them. Some members of the third generation over twenty years of age had a greater comprehension of official Levite ideology than did the school children, but generally were not as interested in it as in a personal relationship with Jesus Christ and receiving the "gifts of the Holy Spirit." A Levite bachelor told me that he had neither read the Book of Elias nor was he sure where he could obtain one. For many of the young people, Glendenning was a rather remote figure, although they may remember having seen and having heard him at an earlier age.

There emerged a strong tendency among members of the third generation to deemphasize doctrines and stress a deep commitment to Jesus Christ. Specific doctrines often were viewed as being divisive of Christian unity. This new philosophy within the Aaronic Order probably formed partially as a reaction to the relatively weak exposure to official Levite ideology that many young people had received. A related issue was the "faith-works" debate. Some of the older members of the third generation argued that works without faith are like filthy rags, and for several months they strongly emphasized the importance of faith while almost ridiculing at times the value of works. Middle-aged and elderly Levites, whose Mormon background emphasized the value of works, argued that faith without works is of little value. This debate resulted in an angry exchange between the camps at a prayer meeting in early 1975, but was resolved with both sides agreeing that faith and works are equally important.

Although the Levite politico-religious organization includes a position called the "Aaronic Order Evangelist," which in theory is held by two middle-aged males, it is a nonfunctioning position. The general attitude of the Levites in the past has been that prospective converts will be directed to the Aaronic Order by the Lord.

With the advent of the charismatic movement, a change in this philosophy began to occur. A bachelor, who knew little about official Levite ideology, told me that the "work of the Levites is to go out into the world and teach about Jesus." The informal leader of the charismatic movement and his wife were involved in missionary work in Logan, Utah, during the fall of 1974 and the following winter. In late August 1975 he had contemplated the possibility of conducting missionary work in Nigeria. During the late spring of 1975 Robert Conrad told an Eskdale congregation that he had received a letter from a Hutterite who wrote that some Hutterites were receiving visions and speaking in tongues. He stated that these events were a "sign of the work of the Lord" and predicted that the Levites would soon be working together with the Hutterites.

Prior to the schism which began in December 1975, it was far easier to find heterogeneity than unity in the beliefs of members of the Aaronic Order, particularly along generational lines. Several informants wondered how I was going to determine what the Levite religious belief system really included. There were, nevertheless, a number of ideological points on which there existed a fair amount of unity in the Aaronic Order. Almost all Levites regarded the Second Coming of Jesus Christ and the millennium as imminent events. In this regard the first generation had intensified a Mormon belief, whereas the third generation had largely absorbed a common evangelical Protestant theme. There was also cross-generational agreement that the Mormon Church had "gone the way of the world." Members of all three generations tended to view communal living as an important vehicle for becoming "worthy of the Lord." The commitment to communal living in the first and second generations generally tended to be greater than in that of the third generation. Some members of the third generation, particularly those over twenty years of age, who had been assigned to relatively prestigious positions in the Aaronic Order, were more committed to communal living than were most members of the first two generations. To a large extent, communal living was a revitalization of the nineteenth century United Order for the pioneers, a revitalization of primitive Christianity for the third generation, and a combination of both for the second generation. Despite these perhaps superficial elements of unity, the generational differences proved to be too great to avert a schism. Many members of the third generation, who had received virtually no indoctrination in Mormonism and relatively little in the beliefs of the Aaronic Order itself, found evangelical Protestantism more meaningful and emotionally satisfying.

With respect to the second of Zald and Ash's propositions on fissioning in social movement organizations, it may not be immediately apparent that Levite ideology contributed to the questioning of Glendenning's revelations. The subversive dimension of Levite ideology lies in its motto, Education Unlimited. Education is a double-edged sword in that it may promote critical thought that challenges the existing social order. In the case of certain Levites of the third generation, the premise that a member of the Order is permitted to engage in free inquiry justified their comparison of the Levitical Writings and the Bible. When the former were perceived to be in contradiction with the latter, which was regarded as the ultimate standard of truth, the authority of the Aaronic Order was undermined.

As for the third of Zald and Ash's propositions, the relatively stringent membership requirements of the Aaronic Order, particularly in the case of becoming a consecrated member, indicates that the Aaronic Order is an "exclusive organization." According to Zald and Ash (1966, 33), "the inclusive organization with its looser criteria of affiliation and of doctrinal orthodoxy is more split-resistent than the exclusive organization. The inclusive organization retains its factions while the exclusive organization spews them forth." As we have seen, Richard, the leader of the charismatic movement, remained a marginal member of the Eskdale commune for many years, despite his marriage to Conrad's eldest daughter, in large part because of his unorthodox religious views. In time, some of his views coupled with those of the Order of the Lamb appealed to the young Levites whose own indoctrination in the official Levite belief system was rather superficial. Richard and his leading disciple were expelled from the Eskdale commune because the community's leadership believed that they were having a negative influence on the young people. The internalization of Pentecostalism by many young Levites and some middle age ones had progressed to such a degree that many of them preferred to forsake the faith of their grandparents and parents in order to continue their involvement in what they regarded to be a more meaningful religious experience.

## *The Maintenance of Sectarianism in the Aaronic Order*

Revitalization movements may undergo one of several developments: extinction, sectarian maintenance, or denominationalization. Once a new religion becomes somewhat institutionalized, forces different from those that contributed to its emergence affect its subsequent development. As we have seen in this chapter thus far, various factors moved the Aaronic Order away from Mormonism toward evangelical Protestantism between its formal establishment in the early 1940s and the mid-1970s. During this period, the Order neither disintegrated nor underwent a process of dynamic or even modest growth that might have propelled it toward becoming a denomination or church. Instead it remained a small sect that essentially maintained its numbers through the reproductive activities of its members and the occasional conversion of outsiders. The high birth rate of the Levites that should have contributed to the modest growth of the group was offset by the loss of many young members of the larger society.

In order to examine the development of the Levite sect, I will now turn to various concepts and hypotheses derived from research of the church-sect continuum. In chapter 1, I argued that the Mormon Church evolved into an "ecclesia" within the sociocultural context of the Intermountain West, particularly the areas of Utah and southern Idaho as well as certain sections of northern Arizona. In the larger context of the political economy of the United States, I proposed that the Mormon Church developed into a "corporate church." For our purposes, we can probably assume that it had reached this position by the onset of the Great Depression—the period during which we see not only the emergence of the Levite sect but also a number of Mormon Fundamentalist groups.

While the Aaronic Order has undergone an appreciable number of changes since its emergence, it has remained a sect in the classical sense. In making the argument that the Order constitutes a sect with respect to Mormonism, it may be useful to juxtapose various aspects of the two.

Max Weber's (1930, 144–154) concept of church-sect dichotomy views charisma in the church as being attached to the office, whereas in the sect it is attached to the religious leader. According to Weber, the sect develops into a church through the process that he calls "routinization of charisma." In Mormonism this process had been for all practical purposes completed by the early twentieth century. The average Mormon is not so much impressed with the personality of the President of the Church, who is formally referred to as the "Prophet," "Seer," and "Revelator," but rather by the power of the office he holds. In fact, at times Mormons express dislike for the personal attributes of a particular president, but still maintain that he has access to supernatural guidance. Maurice Glendenning, like Joseph Smith, possessed a tremendous amount of personal charisma. Like Brigham Young, Robert Conrad functions as a religious administrator and spokesperson. In contrasting Glendenning with the current Chief High Priest of the Order, it is evident that the process of routinization of charisma has begun.

According to Peter Berger (1954, 474), a sect "may be defined as a religious group based on the belief that the spirit is immediately present," whereas a church is a religious grouping based on the belief that the "spirit is remote." Berger's dichotomy applies well to a comparison of the Mormon Church and the Aaronic Order. Although the Mormon Church continues to claim modern revelations, the statements of its twentieth century presidents have not been accorded the same deference as those of Joseph Smith and Brigham Young. Twentieth century Mormon presidents do not claim that they receive revelations by hearing a voice or seeing a vision of a supernatural being. In contrast, Glendenning until his death in 1969 had revelations that involved a voice and visions. Furthermore, rituals, such as prayer circles and manifestations of glossolalia, are characterized by an attitude on the part of the Levites that the presence of the supernatural is near. This development resulted largely from contacts with various Protestant evangelical groups and individuals.

Despite my assertion that the Mormon Church does not constitute a denomination per se, David A. Martin's (1962, 8) distinction between the sect and the denomination with respect to eschatology is of use in contrasting it with the Aaronic Order, particularly if we bear in mind that the former does indeed exhibit certain denominational tendencies. According to this interpretation, sectarians are largely alienated and rejected people who expect some sort of millennium in the near future. Conversely, the denomination retains the traditional eschatological view of Christianity but does not regard it to be of imminent relevance. Members of the Aaronic Order regard the Second Coming of Christ as an event which will occur by A.D. 2000, if not earlier. Levites regard various world events, natural catastrophes, and an alleged decaying moral order as signs prophesying the imminence of the Second Coming. Conversely, the average Mormon does not live in a state of constant expectation of this event. As Gordon Shepherd and Gary Shepherd (1984, 195–196) observe, "eschatological rhetoric diminished drastically after 1920 as modern Mormonism became securely established in its course of accommodation to secular power. Even though an apocalyptic scenario of the last days is still a central Mormon doctrine, it is no longer enunciated by modern conference speakers with anything like the emphatic ferver of nineteenth century leaders."

The strong persistence of sectarian features in the Order supports the contention of both J. Milton Yinger and Bryan R. Wilson that a sect can become a relatively stable and enduring organization. Based on his study of the Elim movement in England, Bryan Wilson makes the following remarks with regard to this phenomenon:

> That there has been a cultural lag in the attitudes of sectarians generally seems likely: some, brought up to find satisfaction in the extreme emotional atmosphere of the sect will continue to do so in spite of much improved economic conditions: the sect may have important social functions for the individual long after the relation of religious expression and socioeconomic circumstances has ceased to hold in his case. The aetiology of origins is not, in such a case, the aetiology of continuance (B. Wilson 1961, 321).

These remarks may partially explain why some members of the second and third generations continue to find the Order satisfying as a sect and have no desire to transform it into a denomination by accommodating it to the larger society. The Aaronic Order does not serve the same functions for its middle class members as it did for its initial members. Instead, it provides a "repository of sentiments, ideals and associations, and an integrating and stabilizing factor in the individual's social life" (B. Wilson 1961, 321). The Aaronic Order remains largely a family religion—one to which the individual is often tied by actual and fictive kinship bonds. Levite meetings attended by relatively large numbers bear strong resemblances to family reunions in Western society. It appears that a similar phenomenon is part of Mormonism in which religious loyalty is often seen as synonymous with family loyalty.

Elsewhere Bryan Wilson (1964, 444–446) has noted that one of the principal sources of tension within sects is the coexistence of an ethic of separation from the world with a belief that the group should engage in proselyting. Conversionist sects generally admit members on the basis of belief in a loosely defined set of doctrines or mere acceptance of the savior. Adventist sects, which forewarn the world of the imminence of the millennium and attempt to gather the elect, require exacting standards of admission. Wilson argues that conversionist sects are more likely to develop into denominations than are adventist sects because the former encounter more contact with the world and consequently are more likely to accommodate to it.

The distinction that Wilson makes between conversionist sects and adventist sects in this regard may be useful in contrasting the development of the Mormon Church and the Aaronic Order. Despite Mormonism's strong features, its approach toward the world is largely conversionist. Thousands of Mormons, particularly young Mormon males in their late teens or early twenties, spend about two years as missionaries in many parts of the world. According to Rodney Stark (1984, 21), "By 1979 more than 260,000 Mormons had served a tour of mission duty since the founding of the church. In 1980 there were 30,000 Mormons on full-time missions." Baptism into the Mormon Church follows several weekly indoctrination sessions during which only the elementary teachings are presented. Conversely, the Aaronic Order, as was discussed in chapter 4, has several degrees of membership and much more stringent policies of admission. While some Levites, particularly those associated with the charismatic movement, expressed a desire to spread the gospel, the Aaronic Order has generally not been greatly concerned with evangelism or attracting large numbers.

In essence, the Aaronic Order has developed into what Yinger (1957, 150–152) calls an "established sect." Whereas most sects tend to be unstable and to disintegrate when the initial members die, others create a structure that allows them to persist beyond one generation. The Aaronic Order has developed a social structure, particularly in the creation of isolated communities, and an independent or semi-independent educational system, which guarantees the socialization, although not totally successful, of a certain portion of its young to its beliefs and ideals. It has also developed a politico-religious organization which guarantees routinization of charisma, transfer of leadership, and social control.

Yinger (1970, 267) argues that sects placing major emphasis on individual anxiety and sin are more likely to evolve into denominations, whereas those that originally stress the evils of society tend to resist this process. It is the latter type rather than the former that is perceived as being more dangerous by elites in the larger society. Consequently, they encounter greater opposition and persecution, which instills in them a stronger feeling of isolation and social cohesion. It appears that the primary reason for individuals joining the Order in its early years were various forms of dissatisfaction with Mormon culture or perhaps more accurately, with a discrepancy between actual and ideal Mormon culture. Mormonism rejects the Calvinist pessimism that characterizes much of American Protestantism. Rather than viewing human nature as depraved and sinful, Mormonism views it as basically good. The transgression of Adam and Eve is not a sin inherited by humanity, but rather a foreordained event necessary for humanity to progress toward the status of godhood (O'Dea 1957, 129–130). While in more recent years, largely because of their contact with evangelical Protestants, some Levites have come to view humanity as weak and sinful, this has not been the general attitude held by members of the Aaronic Order. Instead the Order challenges the authority of the Mormon Church and pointed out its weaknesses, much to the latter's consternation.

Another factor which has possibly contributed to the retention of sectarian features in the Order is the criterion of size. Georg Simmel (1950, 89–90) maintained that the social structure of religious sects made it impossible for them to support a large membership because they generally attempt to regulate strictly the behavior of their members. Examples of this in the Order are the establishment of isolated communities and the attempt to have members, particularly females, wear a distinctive dress style. Simmel (1950, 90) argued that "in such situations, extension to large groups would evidently break the tie of solidarity which consists of a large degree precisely in the position of being singled out of larger groups and being in contrast to them."

Liston Pope also considered the criterion of size when he challenged H. Richard Niebuhr's contention that the denominationalization of sects was largely a response to the changing class composition of these groups. "A sect, as it gains adherents and the promise of success, begins to reach out toward greater influence in society, whatever the roots of its ambition may be—evangelistic fervor, denominational rivalry, ministerial desire for greater income and influence, the cultural vindication of its peculiar faith, or what not" (Pope 1942, 119). In the process of doing this, the sect accommodates itself to the larger society and develops into a denomination. It appears that the membership of the Order has not increased appreciably since its emergence and still remains very small. The Order as a case study appears to support Pope's contention concerning the development of religious sects.

Whereas many proponents of church-sect theory contend that sects tend to evolve into churches or denominations, Stark and Bainbridge (1985, 137) argue that: "Most sects are, in fact, dead ends. They start small, remain small, and slowly wither away." In a survey of 417 American sects, they found that 51 percent of them are declining in size, 18 percent are stable, and 31 percent are growing. Furthermore, only 6 percent of the sects in their sample exhibit a pattern of rapid growth. Despite fluctuation in membership, including the loss of about two dozen members (largely residents of the Eskdale commune) as a result of the schism of 1975–1976, the Aaronic Order can probably be best described as a relatively stable sect. As we will see in the Epilogue, natural increase and a few conversions have for the most part counterbalanced the loss of membership due to the charismatic schism.

Sects are generally described by social scientists as religious groups with minimal organization and emphasis upon spontaneity in religious meetings. Bryan Wilson (1967, 10) points out that hierarchy rarely exists in religious sects, and where it does, it is usually not that of a professional clergy. He also maintains that adventist sects tend to deemphasize organization because they believe that the millennium is imminent and that more important tasks must be performed (B. Wilson, 16). Since its formal establishment, the Aaronic Order has had, at least in theory, a relatively elaborate organization (especially when one considers the group's small size) and, like Mormonism, has rejected a professional clergy. For the most part, the hierarchical nature of the Levite politico-religious organization does not preclude the existence of a strong sense of egalitarianism among members. The combination of an adventist or millenarian ideology and a relatively hierarchical organization, although apparently compatible at the present time, could result in certain internal tensions for the Aaronic Order if it were to gain an appreciable increase in members.

J. Milton Yinger (1970, 273–274) notes that some sects develop a complex, hierarchical organization from the beginning and suggests that this may be an important factor in determining whether or not the sect will become established. Both the Mormon Church and the Aaronic Order formulated an hierarchical organization shortly after their respective formal establishments. Contrary to what appears to be the case for most sects, the Aaronic Order also incorporated highly structured religious rituals, some of which were modifications of Mormon rituals and others of which were independently created. The existence of spontaneity at the religious meetings of the Aaronic Order during the early 1970's was a result of its contact with evangelical Protestant groups. This new trend did not lead to the elimination of traditional rituals.

## *Sectarian Stagnation and an Attempt to Revitalize the Aaronic Order*

Successful revitalization movements often become in time routinized or devitalized religions. Niebuhr recognized this pattern in his contention that the sect is a short-lived phenomenon:

> By its very nature the sectarian type of organization is valid for only one generation. The children born to the voluntary members of the first generation begin to make the sect a church long before they have arrived at the years of discretion. For with their coming the sect must take on the character of an educational and disciplinary institution, with the purpose of bringing the new generation into conformity with the ideals and customs which have become traditional. Rarely does a second

> generation hold the convictions it has inherited with a fervor equal to that of its teachers, who fashioned these convictions in the heat of conflict and at the risk of martyrdom (Niebuhr 1929, 19–20).

H. Richard Niebuhr (1929) also argued that the sect often adopts the discipline which in turn may lead to an improvement of its members' socioeconomic status. The occurrence of this phenomena in the Aaronic Order is demonstrated by a comparison of the socioeconomic status of its initial members and that of its adult members under fifty years of age. The emphasis that Glendenning placed on formal education appears to have contributed to the creation of a middle class or at least a relatively affluent working-class within the Aaronic Order. In contrast to Mormonism's strong emphasis on formal education, many of the early Levites didn't perceive a great need for it. However, due to Glendenning's influence, the Aaronic Order created an educational system that directed as many young people as possible to attend college and train for professional occupations. Despite this, the Order accommodated relatively little to the secular world. Some Levites who acquired college degrees and well-paying occupations severed most of their ties with the Order. But others in this category often moved into positions of leadership within the group. Many members of the second and third generations were as committed to millenarianism and communal living as were those of the first generation. This pattern even applied to many who became involved in the schism discussed earlier. For the most part, the schismatics did not call into question these ideals. While the Order has undergone some significant ideological changes, there is no evidence that it has moved in the direction of becoming a denomination. Nevertheless, Niebuhr's discussion of the generational issue offers some valuable insights for understanding the development of the Aaronic Order.

Despite the fact that the offspring of the first generation did not have the same reasons for belonging to the Order as their parents, they still shared in the excitement of establishing the House of Israel. Many of them, while they were adolescents and young adults, worked at the Alpha Colony, the sawmill in Huntington Canyon, and in the establishment of Partoun and Eskdale. The generational problem that Niebuhr discussed became a major problem primarily for the third generation.

Because the members of the third generation had nothing to do with the actual establishment of the Aaronic Order and the Levite desert communities, they generally lacked the religious fervor and idealism of their parents and grandparents. Although they had heard about the "work of Levi and Aaron," and the need to prepare for the Second Coming of Jesus Christ by living communally in the desert, it all seemed a little hard to believe for many of them. Some had lived at Eskdale for a large portion of their lives, and for most of them, it was basically a good life. There were many other young people there to interact with. There were the wide open spaces of the desert and mysterious hills a short walk east of the community. Work, while it had its tiring aspects such as waking in the early hours of morning to milk the cows, was often interesting and exciting. Some young people, who left Eskdale to attend college or to work, occasionally visited the community to relive the joys and the companionship of their school days.

Nevertheless, there were aspects of Eskdale and the Order that seemed downright oppressive and incomprehensible. All the talk about the Levitical Writings, the Bible, the things that Glendenning had said, and the priesthood often did not make much sense to them. Religious services and study classes were boring but mandatory. There were so many rules that seemed arbitrary and meaningless. In some cases children whose parents lived in the Salt Lake and Utah Valleys and *elsewhere* were sent to school at Eskdale. Sometimes these children preferred not to be at Eskdale. After they graduated from high school, many became inactive or semiactive members of the Order and often married outsiders—a decision which generally pulled them even further away from their religious roots.

The charismatic movement changed this situation for many young people. It first affected the young people in their twenties and late teens, but later its enthusiasm spread to the Eskdale school children, preschoolers, and other adults. The fervor of the movement within the Order can be viewed as a "revitalization movement within a revitalization movement."

Before it culminated in a schism, the charismatic movement lasted, despite fluctuations in its intensity, for well over a year. Despite initial opposition and reservations by many of the older members, it regenerated the sectarian vigor which the Order had been gradually losing, and temporarily integrated into the Order many of the young Levites who had not experienced the pioneering efforts of their grandparents and parents. For a brief moment, it transcended the cleavages which existed among the generations of the group. Nevertheless, even during this period of sectarian renewal, there appears to be a feeling among some that the generational differences were perhaps irreconcilable. As I noted earlier, Richard even predicted privately to me that it would cause a permanent rift in the Aaronic Order. It was not long after his forecast that indeed a schism occurred. That the schism did not occur earlier was largely due to the tact and diplomacy of the Chief High Priest who recognized the value of the charismatic movement in promoting the commitment of the young people to the Order. These points of unification, however, proved to be transitory and were negated by the schism of many young Levites and some middle-aged Levites after the ouster of the leader of the charismatic movement and of his chief disciple. As Stark and Bainbridge (1985, 101) observe, "Schisms in organizations or groups are most likely to occur along lines of cleavage. That is, when internal conflicts break out in a religious organization, they usually do so between sub-networks that existed prior to the outbreak of dispute." Anything that prevents the formation or maintenance of close ties within the social network of a group or organization can produce a cleavage. While various cleavages (e.g., the "college men" versus the "farmers," males versus females, familial loyalties, etc.) had existed for some time among the Levites, as we have seen, generational differences emerged by the mid-1970s as the most profound kind of cleavage within the Order.

The Aaronic Order has been no less subject to internal schisms than most other sects. Despite the relatively egalitarian ethos of the Order, one finds a fair amount of jockeying for position among its members. Many of those who joined or merely investigated the Order were seeking to substitute a prominent position within its hierarchy for the status that they lacked in the larger society. Several individuals claimed divine inspiration of some sort—a phenomenon that did not find favor with Glendenning. Nevertheless, only one of these claims resulted in the formation of a permanent religious organization, namely, the Sons of Levi led by Marl Kilgore (Shields 1982, 155–158). While the leader of the charismatic movement did not claim divine revelation per se, it is interesting to note that he felt frustrated by his exclusion from the Community Council at Eskdale. In lieu of the position that Richard was denied within the formal politico-religious organization of the Order, he found a calling in his role as the leader of the movement that caused a serious split within the Levite sect. It is ironic that while the early Levites viewed the Order as a revitalization of Mormon communitarian ideals, some of their grandchildren and children came to believe that the sect itself had become devitalized and needed to be rejuvenated in some way. Like their grandparents and parents, when it became apparent that they could not reform the Order in the manner they desired, they were forced to become schismatics. Thus, we see in the Aaronic order the same processes of revitalization, routinization, and schismogenesis that are seemingly axiomatic parts of sectarian development.

# 7

# *Epilogue*

This book presents an analysis of the emergence and development of the Aaronic Order as well as the process of conversion to the sect. In order to understand the sociocultural context within which the Order emerged, we have first considered the evolution of its parent church, namely, the Church of Jesus Christ of Latter-day Saints. Just as was true for the Levite sect in the twentieth century, I have argued that the Mormonism emerged during the early nineteenth century as a revitalization movement that responded to the strains and contradictions of the new American republic. In time, due to various external as well as internal pressures, the Mormon Church underwent a process of accommodation to the larger society that was encroaching upon its refuge in the isolated Intermountain West. Whereas Mormonism emerged as a utopian sect in the Midwest, it evolved into a religious state inthe Intermountain West, and eventually into an international corporate church that came to embody many of the beliefs and practices of capitalism which it once so vehemently had rejected. In other words, the Mormon Church became institutionalized and, in the minds of some of its twentieth century members, devitalized.

Also we have seen that throughout its relatively short history, the Mormon Church has spawned a large number of schismatic groups, many of which appeared during periods of crisis in its development. While a variety of factors contributed to the emergence of these sects, those that appeared after the Manifesto of 1890 emerged as protests to the accommodation of the church to the larger American society. Instead they attempted to revitalize the *Gemeinschaft* ethos which they perceived to have been characteristic of nineteenth century Mormonism. Some of these groups, which are referred to as Fundamentalists, view the preservation of plural marriage as being a significant avenue for revitalizing Mormonism. Their interest, as well as that of some early Levites, in polygyny rests not so much in the practice itself, but rather in what it represents, namely the Golden Age when Mormonism was characterized by ideals of egalitarianism, communalism, and millenarianism. While the Levite sect rejected the first principle, perhaps largely due to the background of its founder, it embraced the latter ones and consequently may be seen as part of the protest tradition of modern Mormonism. As Hansen (1981:213) observes, "perhaps no phenomenon establishes a former sect more firmly among mainline faiths than the fact that it spawns sects dedicated to its reform. Needless to say, Mormon leaders vigorously attempt to disassociate themselves from such movements."

The Levite sect appealed to a certain alienated segment of the Mormon Church because the latter no longer effectively satisfied the needs of many of its working class members. The Order emerged as a revitalization movement which attempted to rejuvenate certain ideals that its members believed to have been an integral part of early Mormonism. Like other revitalization movements, the Aaronic Order was started by a charismatic leader who experienced religious inspiration and formulated a new new for living. In his role as the Levite prophet, Glendenning was able to articulate in religious rhetoric the estrangement from mainstream Mormonism felt by the early Levites. The emphasis of the early Levites on cooperation and egalitarianism and their beliefs in the imminence of the millennium and revelation (and even in polygyny in some cases), indicates their strong desire to return Mormonism back to its nineteenth century ideals.

This book delineates various forms of relative deprivation, which predisposed certain individuals to join the Aaronic Order, and supports the contention, as proposed by several social scientists, including J. Milton Yinger (1970), David Aberle (1972), and Charles Y. Glock (1973), that deprivation is a significant variable in the origin of new religious groups. Many individuals who joined the Order experienced deprivation, particularly ethical, economic, and social forms, primarily within the context of Mormonism. Psychic deprivation was often not only a by-product of deprivation experienced within the context of Mormonism, but also was related directly to specific person problems and crises. Although deprivation was a necessary factor in drawing individuals into the Aaronic Order, it was not a sufficient one. An analysis of the Levite conversion experience revealed that it is the product of a complex interaction of several variables at several levels of analysis.

Between the mid-1950s and the mid-1970s, the ideological orientation of the Levite sect shifted away from Mormonism and toward evangelical Protestantism. This shift was related to the contact that the Levites had with various Protestant groups and individuals, and was promoted by Maurice Glendenning and later sustained by his successor. In attempting to explain the persistence of sectarian features in the Aaronic order, I have appealed to certain factors, such as what Bryan Wilson (1961, 321) terms a "cultural lag in attitudes" among middle class members, the rejection of a conversionist posture toward the world, and the criterion of size. In my discussion of the development of the Levite sect, I noted that Niebuhr's second generation dilemma really appeared more during the third generation of the group. Some members of this generation, who had been poorly socialized into Mormonism as well as Levite beliefs and values, embarked upon a revitalization effort of their own. Like the early Levites who attempted to reform Mormonism, these individuals attempted to reform the Aaronic Order from within, but were forced to break away from the parent body when it became apparent that their efforts were doomed. Thus, even in the case of a seemingly obscure sect, we see the processes of revitalization and institutionalization that appear to be characteristic of most religious movements, at least those that manage to survive for some time. The Levites, although to a lesser degree than their Mormon forebears, lost much of the organic ideal of the good religious life between the 1930s and the 1970s. This is in keeping with Barry Nigel Howe's (1981, 114) assertion that the prevailing pattern in American religion "has been one of the 'privatization' of religious life, the eclipse of a society dominated by collective religious values regulating interpersonal relations." Bearing these observations in mind, I would like at this point to examine recent developments within the Aaronic Order, including the continuing impact of the charismatic schism upon the group.

While most of the data that I collected on the Aaronic Order pertains to the period prior to mid-1976, it is fitting at this point to present a brief update on the group based upon information obtained during a recent visit to the Eskdale commune and the Salt Lake branch in December 1986. The schism of a substantial number of young adults and some middle-aged adults during the period of 1975–1976 acted as a shock wave upon the Order. Included among the schismatics, who questioned the legitimacy of Glendenning's revelations and therefore the Order itself, were four of Robert Conrad's eight children. Yet, as in the case of the Conrad family, kinship as well as affective bonds continued to connect the schismatics with those who chose to remain in the Order. The schismatics neither formed a new religious sect nor joined any one other religious group en masse. While a few actually returned to the Order, most joined various charismatic sects. Several of them joined the Bread of Life sect established by the dynamic woman referred to in the previous chapter. When she relocated her congregation in Seattle, Washington, most of them followed her and now serve as ministers in her church. Although Richard (the informal leader of the charismatic movement within the Order) and his wife (Robert Conrad's eldest daughter) also belonged to the Bread of Life sect for awhile, apparently irreconciliable differences developed between Richard and the sect's leader. These differences reportedly remain so severe that the Bread of Life pastor will not allow Richard to enter her church. Nonetheless, Richard, who pastored a congregation in Kansas for awhile, and now resides with his family in a Seattle suburb, continues to remain active in the charismatic movement. He and his wife have visited Eskdale several times over the past several years, and recently attended the Feast of Tabernacles at the commune in October 1986. Like Richard and his wife, many of the other schismatics have renewed their contacts with the Levites in Utah. One of the schismatics is a very active member of a charismatic congregation in a suburb of Salt Lake City, and several schismatics reside in various other parts of the western United States.

Despite an initial period of bitterness, most of the Levites have come to view the schism as a "growing thing." One Levite woman described the schism as a "blessing" in that ultimately it increased the Order's contacts with other religious groups. Robert Conrad stated that Levi and Aaron of Old Testament times were "service-oriented" and "we are learning to relate to a lot of groups." John Conrad, one of Robert Conrad's sons and the Eskdale Acting Priest, noted: "We came to see the body of Jesus Christ as bigger than our little spot." Although the Order still refers to itself as "The True Church of God," the young Conrad added, "we are in it rather than being it." In addition to their long-standing ties with the Hutterites, the Levites have extended their ties with evangelical groups, particularly of the charismatic variety. Levites regularly attend charismatic conferences around the country and host charismatic preachers at their various branches in Utah. Several Levites residing in the Phoenix area also "fellowship" with a charismatic congregation there. Jamie Buckingham, the pastor of the Tabernacle Church in Melbourne, Florida, and a well-known charismatic speaker and author, has taken a special interest in the Levites. During the summer of 1986, he introduced several Levites to an audience of some 3000 people attending a charismatic conference in North Carolina. The Levites are anxiously awaiting the publication of an article on the Aaronic Order that Buckingham has written for a magazine entitled *Charisma.*

In addition to growing interaction with charismatic groups, the Levites have established contact with several groups having a Hebraic-

Christian orientation. Some Levites also have engaged in study classes with members of the Reorganized Church of Latter-Day Saints in California, Illinois, and Missouri because, according to Robert Conrad, the latter two are interested in "the restoration of Israel and the work of Levi and Aaron." A Levite priest and his wife over the past year or so have been living and working with a Hebraic-Christian sect based in New Haven, Indiana. The sect, which is led by Shmuel ben Menachem, calls itself "Bet Hashem—The House of Yhweh, House of Ahron." Furthermore, the Utah Levites currently correspond with a group of people in New Zealand who also consider themselves Levites. Members of the Aaronic Order maintain that there are Levites in many parts of the world and their identification is an integral part of the restoraton of Israel.

Recognizing the weak indoctrination that young Levites had been receiving on concepts peculiar to the Order itself, the Levites now place greater emphasis than I found was the case in the mid-1970s on acquainting their children with the revelations that Glendenning received from the Angel Elias. In 1978 the Aaronic Order completed the compilation of the many Writings found in the Book of Elias, the Book of New Revelations, and the Disciple Book into a new sacred text entitled "The Levitical Writings." While older Levites traditionally have viewed the Writings as an important addition to the Mormon sciptures, and perhaps works that in some ways superceded them, many middle-aged Levites and young Levites today regard the Levitical Writings as "modern revelations" that serve as commentaries on the Bible and, more specifically, on the work of Levi and Aaron in the last days before the Second Coming of Christ. Since the schism of 1975–1976, some members of the Order have continued to question the meaning as well as the validity of the Writings, and some of these individuals have left the Order and even Eskdale in recent years because they could not accept them. According to one Levite woman, some Levites have placed the matter of the relationship between the Levitical Writings and the Bible on the "back-burner." Conversely, some elderly Levites continue to question the merits of the "Holy Spirit movement." While many Levites continue to believe that the Second Coming of Christ will occur before A.D. 2000, others, while admitting that the world is now in its last days, prefer not to speculate as to the exact date of Christ's return.

Whereas during the mid-1970s most Levites tended to view Eskdale as a refuge from the wickedness of Babylon and a place to purify themselves for the Second Coming of Christ, many Levites now regard Eskdale and the other desert communities as a training ground for outreach work. In contrast to the mid-1970s when Eskdale had a substantial number of middle-aged people, most Eskdale residents tend to fall in either the over sixty year-old range or the under forty year-old range. Whereas I found ninety-four residents at Eskdale in the spring of 1975, I counted eighty-six residents at Eskdale and its two satellite communities during my recent visit. Three young Levite families with a total of twenty-one individuals reside at Bethel. Two late middle-aged couples, each with one child still at home, and an elderly widow live at Petra, a second satellite community established in the late 1970s. Petra consists of four circular, stucco houses, one of which is unoccupied, situated about five miles north of Eskdale. Residents of the satellite communities work, worship, and attend school at Eskdale proper, making them in a sense commuters from the bedroom suburbs. Many of them feel somewhat isolated from Eskdale proper and find the constant commuting a burden. Eskdale proper, with a population of fifty-nine consists of sixteen household units eight families with children at home, five elderly couples, one widow, one bachelor, and one young single woman and three school children belonging to a California non-Levite family. In contrast to 1975 when Eskdale had nine nuclear families with children living at home, Eskdale and its satellites now have thirteen such households, with most of the children still in the preschool or grade school years. Although Partoun has not been revitalized as a cooperative community yet, a few young families have joined the few remaining elderly families there. The West Desert School, which some Levite children attend, is now housed in a new building. Despite the unavailability of exact figures, it appears that the membership of the Aaronic Order has neither significantly increased nor decreased during the past decade. While the Order has gained members through a few conversions and births, this growth has been offset by defections resulting from the schism of 1975–1976 as well as those in subsequent years.

In keeping with its new outreach thrust, the Aaronic Order began to review its economic activities a few years ago. Despite the loss of many workers as a result of the schism, Eskdale embarked upon a program of economic expansion during the late 1970s and early 1980s. The community's cattle herd grew to about 350 head, including some 175 dairy cows. In order to feed the cattle, the community increased its production of alfalfa, barley, and corn. According to Eskdale's work manager, the community came close to self-sufficiency during the early 1980s. However, a declining farm economy for small and medium-sized operators in recent years has forced Eskdale to reexamine its own agricultural endeavors. For a short time during the early 1980s, Eskdale developed a herd of some 300 sheep, but sold it off when the sheep market took a downward turn. Unfortunately, economic conditions came to affect adversely Eskdale's major source of income, namely, its dairy herd. As a result of dropping returns for dairy farmers, community leaders scrutinized the dairy operation. After long discussions and many prayers, the community members decided to accept the advise of John

Conrad, who now holds a doctorate in veterinary medicine, that high-technology cattle breeding might be a more profitable route to follow and also would be a capital-intensive as opposed to labor-intensive endeavor, thereby freeing up more community members for missionary and evangelical activities.

In August 1986 Eskdale sold most of its prize herd in the largest onetime sale of registered cattle in Utah history. Eskdale purchased five super cows, each valued at $10,000–20,000, with a portion of the $320,000 netted from the cattle sale in order to embark upon an agricultural experiment in embryo-transfer. The super cows will be artifically inseminated and then *flushed* for multiple fertilized eggs, which can be frozen for sale on the open market. The community has retained several bulls and heifers, the latter of which in time will function as surrogate cows that can carry embryos to term. While Eskdale could have earned about one million dollars by participating in the federal government's buy-out program, it decided not to do so since this would have required staying out of the dairy business for five years. Eskdale retains a small dairy herd of eighteen milking cows that provide milk for the community, and expects to increase its dairy herd to about fifty milking cows. Eskdale is considering developing a more diversified economic base than it has had in the past. In April 1984, the community opened a woodworking shop which is presently producing a small number of kitchen cabinets and glide chairs. A young Levite with a B.S. in Industrial Technology from the Utah State University supervises the shop and receives some assistance from two other men.

In keeping with the new policy of economic diversification, the Levites have returned to their earlier educational emphasis on college preparatory curriculum in the high school. Although the community experimented briefly with a vocational philosophy designed to prepare children for agricultural and technical pursuits, this phase barely was implemented before matters returned to the status quo. In large measure, the defection in the early summer of 1976 of the former Eskdale school system superintendent, who had brainstormed the vocational track for the community, contributed to its demise. With twenty-two or twenty-three students, the enrollment of Eskdale's grade school is almost identical to what it was during the early and mid-1970s. Conversely, the high school enrollment of six students is considerably less than what it was over a decade ago. The Order has not made an active effort in recent years to encourage nonresidents of the community to send their children to school there. As the grade school cohort increases in age, the enrollment of the high school will obviously increase.

Although mechanical repair services, veterinarian services, state vehicle inspections, and music lessons for non-Levite residents of the

Snake Valley provide supplemental income for Eskdale, the planned diversified economy remains a thing of the future. Due to the general economic downturn, Eskdale has generated only about 65–70 percent of its annual income in recent years, forcing it to draw upon monies from consecrations, tithes and contributions. Monies from consecrations also paid largely for the expenses of houses at Petra and a new dining hall-office-meeting room complex located near the former location of the old dining hall or center. While Eskdale prefers not to go into debt, it did take out a loan in order to purchase an automobile, a tractor, and a grain storage tank. Levite leaders readily admit that their new economic program entails serious risks. According to Robert Conrad, the new program involves a "leap of faith" and is not completely based on "economic knowledge." Many Levites now view Eskdale as a training site for evangelical activities in the larger society rather than as an economic alternative to earning a living in the latter. Robert Conrad told me that Glendenning "knew that living in the desert was going to be tough. We would have been better off economically in the Salt Lake Valley or Utah Valley."

In reviewing the evolution of the Levite sect from its emergence among working-class Mormons during the Depression of the 1930s to what some term the post-industrial, high technology age of the 1980s, we see a steady evolution away from Mormonism towards evangelical Christianity. Despite a divergence of beliefs between the Levites and the Mormons, both of their religions appear to be undergoing a certain convergence with evangelical Christianity as well. As Shepherd and Shepherd (1984, 198) observe, "The innovative vigor of early Mormon thought appears to have withered and become increasingly timid and conservative, less true to its original theological perspectives and more in tune with orthodox Christian fundamentalism." Nevertheless, considerable doctrinal tension persists between Mormonism and evangelical Protestantism.

At any rate, whereas from a social scientific perspective the Aaronic Order of the 1950s, 1960s, and even the early 1970s could be characterized as a Mormon sect, the Aaronic Order of the late 1980s has in large part shed its Mormon roots and become what we may term a "charismatic, Hebraic-Christian sect." Indeed, during the past decade the Order has begun to observe a number of quasi-Judaic festivals. For instance, in the late summer and early fall it conducts the Feast of Trumpets, the Day of Atonement, and the Feast of Tabernacles. While the few remaining pioneers and some middle-aged Levites still give credence of one sort or another to Mormon doctrines, most young Levites feel either indifference or even mild hostility toward Mormonism. Some of these young Levites eschew Mormonism in part because various evangelicals have told them that Mormonism is a "cult" and "of the Devil." Considering this, what will be the consequences of continuing interaction with various evangelical groups, particularly of the charismatic variety, for the Levites? In discarding their Mormon roots, will the Levites discontinue their adherance to communalism, despite the fact that few continue to refer to it as the United Order? Given their traditional pacifism and deemphasis of social issues, will their contacts with the largely right wing evangelical movement move them to become staunch reactionaries? Or will they become aligned with more liberal and progressive evangelicals, such as those found among the Mennonites, other Anabaptist groups, and various Christian communitarians?

Several Levite leaders admitted to me their somewhat qualified approval of the activities of Moral Majority stalwarts such as Jerry Falwell and Pat Robertson. One branch priest of the Order has become increasingly ultraconservative in his political views, and is an ardent admirer of W. Cleon Skousen, the Mormon founder of the Center for Constitutional Studies (formerly Freemen Institute)—a Salt Lake City-based think tank dedicated to the restoration of the American Constitution in the tradition of the Founding Fathers and of *laissez-faire* capitalism. According to Anson Shupe and John Heinerman (1985, 147), Skousen serves as the "lynchpin" in a series of channels between the New Christian Right and ultraconservative Mormons. Despite his close association with Ezra Taft Benson, Skousen's group remains on the margins of mainstream Mormonism, especially outside of Utah. The aforementioned Levite priest meets regularly in Provo with a group of ultraconservative Mormons who study the relationship between religion and the American Constitution. Conversely, at least some Levites are troubled by the hawkish orientation of many evangelicals as well as the latters' acceptance of a profit-oriented society. In stating his ambivalence about the American political economy, the Eskdale Acting Priest argued that: "Capitalism either creates a society built upon greed or incentives." He also noted, "I hate communism except when it is based upon love."

In conclusion, what do the Levite have to tell us about the Mormon success story and about revitalization movements that somehow become institutionalized and enter the mainstream of complex societies? In essence, successful revitalization movements, including early Christianity and nineteenth century Mormonism, come eventually to accept patterns of social stratification characteristic of complex societies and, as a consequence, produce alienation and estrangement among certain segments of their memberships. In the case of Mormonism, some of these alienated members initiated or joined a wide array of schismatic groups. While I find myself in agreement with Rodney Stark's (1984, 26) contention that "The 'miracle' of Mormon success makes them the single most important case on the agenda of the social scientific study of religion," not only in the United States but perhaps elsewhere in the world, I maintain that scholars need to make note of Mormonism's failures as well. Many, if not the majority of Mormons, do not share in the benefits of corporate or monopoly capitalism of which the Mormon Church has become an integral part. Despite the existence of a few historical and journalistic accounts about or at least touching upon certain Mormon sects, there exists a tremendous paucity of social scientific research on such groups. A perusal of Armand L. Mauss and Jeffrey R. Franks' (1984) extensive bibliography of social science literature contains only seven items on Mormon schismatic groups, four of which I authored. Just as Mormonism, as Stark implies, continues to constitute a relatively neglected topic in the sociology of religion (See Mauss 1984), one may argue with equal validity that Mormon sectarianism remains the forgotten theme of the social scientific study of Mormonism.

In closing, I hope that this book will prompt others to engage in the study of the origin and development of other Mormon schismatic groups and what their existence tells us about modern Mormonism and American society. As I indicated earlier, this in my opinion is the real value of studying a small sect that at most may occasionally attract a few of the "disherited" of its parent body.

# *Appendix*

**TABLE A-1**

Socioeconomic Background of Males Demonstrating Strong Interest in the Levitical Writings during the 1930s and 1940s

**TABLE A-2**

Socioeconomic Background of Females Demonstrating Strong Interest in the Levitical Writings during the 1930s and 1940s

**TABLE A-3**

Socioeconomic Background of Currently Active Levites (Ages 25–50)

### Table A-1
### Socioeconomic Background of Males Demonstrating Strong Interest in the Levitical Writings during the 1930s and 1940s

| Male | Occupation | Religious Background |
|---|---|---|
| 1 | Laborer, farm hand | LDS |
| 2 | Laborer | Convert to LDS Church |
| 3 | Laborer, rancher | LDS |
| 4 | Laborer | LDS |
| 5 | Truck driver | LDS |
| 6 | Custodian | LDS; many other religions |
| 7 | Laborer, farmer | LDS |
| 8 | Farmer | LDS |
| 9 | Laborer, rancher salesman | LDS |
| 10 | Laborer | LDS |
| 11 | Laborer | Lutheran; LDS convert at age 10 in Switzerland |
| 12 | Laborer | LDS |
| 13 | Salesman, office worker | LDS |
| 14 | Mechanic, trolley conductor | LDS |
| 15 | Swimming instructor, laborer | Protestant; LDS convert in South Africa |
| 16 | Farmer, laborer, post office employee | LDS |
| 17 | Laborer | LDS |
| 18 | Laborer | LDS |
| 19 | Laborer | LDS |
| 20 | Laborer | LDS |
| 21 | Laborer | LDS |
| 22 | Laborer | LDS |
| 23 | Laborer, rancher | LDS |
| 24 | Laborer | LDS |
| 25 | Laborer | LDS |
| 26 | Baker | LDS |
| 27 | Trolley conductor and motorman | LDS |
| 28 | Blacksmith, piano tuner | LDS |
| 29 | Laborer, farmer, factory guard | LDS |
| 30 | Teacher, barber, farmer, laborer | LDS |
| 31 | Teacher | LDS |
| 32 | Shop Owner | LDS |
| 33 | Deliveryman | LDS |
| 34 | Peddler | LDS |
| 35 | Laborer | LDS |

Table A-2
Socioeconomic Background of Females Demonstrating Strong Interest in the Levitical Writings during the 1930s and 1940s

| Female | Occupation | Religious Background |
|---|---|---|
| 1 | Domestic | LDS |
| 2 | Nurse, midwife | LDS convert in Germany |
| 3 | Homemaker | LDS |
| 4 | Domestic | Lutheran; LDS convert |
| 5 | Nurse | LDS |
| 6 | Domestic | LDS |
| 7 | Homemaker | LDS |
| 8 | Cashier | LDS |
| 9 | Seamstress | Lutheran; LDS convert in Germany |
| 10 | Book store employee | LDS |
| 11 | Homemaker | LDS |
| 12 | Domestic | LDS |
| 13 | Laborer | LDS convert in Sweden |
| 14 | Laborer | LDS convert in Sweden |
| 15 | Homemaker | LDS |
| 16 | Homemaker | LDS |
| 17 | Homemaker | LDS |
| 18 | Teacher | LDS |
| 19 | Bookkeeper | Protestant; LDS convert |
| 20 | Beauty shop operator | LDS |
| 21 | Homemaker | LDS |
| 22 | Secretary | LDS |
| 23 | Laborer | LDS |
| 24 | Teacher | LDS |
| 25 | Nurse's aide | Protestant |
| 26 | Telegraph & telephone operator | LDS |
| 27 | Domestic | LDS convert in Germany |
| 28 | Teacher | LDS |
| 29 | Telephone operator | LDS |
| 30 | Teacher | LDS |

Table A-3
Socioeconomic Background of Currently Active Levites (Ages 25–50)

| Male | Occupation | Education | Female | Occupation | Education |
|---|---|---|---|---|---|
| 1 | Eskdale laborer | Some college | 1 | Teacher | M.S., education |
| 2 | Carpenter printer | Some college | 2 | Eskdale teacher | B.S., education |
| 3 | Eskdale music teacher | B.S., education | 3 | Student | Law school |
| 4 | College music teacher | Ed.D., candidate in music | 4 | Clerical worker | Some college |
| 5 | Eskdale teacher | B.S., physics | 5 | Clerical worker | Business school graduate |
| 6 | Internist | M.D. | 6 | Clerical worker | High school graduate |
| 7 | Salesman | Some business & technical school | 7 | Salesclerk | Some high school |
| 8 | Corporation supervisor | B.S., Ch. Engr. | 8 | Eskdale worker; teacher | High school graduate |
| 9 | Lawyer | LL.B. | 9 | Clerical worker | Some college |
| 10 | Laborer | B.S., psychology | 10 | Eskdale bookkeeper | Some college |
| 11 | Teacher | M.A., geography | 11 | Laborer | High school graduate |
| 12 | Carpenter | High school graduate some Bible college | 12 | Pediatric nurse | B.S., nursing |
| 13 | Eskdale laborer | High school graduate | 13 | Partoun teacher | B.S., education |
| 14 | Laborer | Some college | 14 | Nurse's aide | High school graduate |
| 15 | Graduate school student | B.S., animal science | 15 | Nurse's aide | High school graduate |
| 16 | Laborer | High school graduate some Bible college | 16 | LPN | Technical school |
| 17 | Eskdale counselor and teacher | M.S., comm. education and counseling | 17 | Clerical worker | Some college |
| 18 | Eskdale teacher | B.S., education | 18 | Clerical worker | High school graduate |
| 19 | Laborer | Some college | 19 | Homemaker | Some college |
| 20 | Eskdale laborer | Some college | 20 | Teacher | B.S., education |
| 21 | Eskdale laborer | Some Bible college | 21 | Eskdale bookkeeper | High school graduate |
| | | | 22 | Salesclerk | High school graduate |
| | | | 23 | Homemaker | High school graduate |
| | | | 24 | Homemaker | High school graduate |

# Notes

## CHAPTER 1

1. The nature of James J. Strang's charismatic leadership and claims of religious inspiration strongly resembles those of both Joseph Smith and Maurice L. Glendenning. For example, all three men claimed that they received revelations from supernatural sources, and that they were able to dicipher cryptic or ancient scripts and recorded their revelations that were eventually incorporated into sacred books.

2. Members of the Reorganized Church of Jesus Christ of Latter Day Saints call themselves "Latter Day Saints" and reject the label "Mormon" as a term of self-reference.

3. For a more recent account of the Short Creek community, see Wiley S. Maloney (1974).

## CHAPTER 2

1. I collected all data in tables pertaining to the Aaronic Order; the data were not derived from the files of the Order.

2. The term "Israel" for the Levites of Utah refers to the patrilineal descendants of the twelve sons of Jacob. The Levites believe that Jews are patrilineal descendants of Judah, one of Jacob's sons.

3. Large portions of this section appear in a published article (Baer 1979).

4. The Levites do not regard Glendenning as a "prophet" but rather as a "mediator" or "recorder" who transcribed the words of the Angel Elias. In terms of Anthony F. C. Wallace's concept of revitalization movement, Glendenning qualifies as a prophet because he heard a supernatural voice, had visions, and formulated a new code for living.

## CHAPTER 3

1. This chapter includes revised and expanded portions of a published article (Baer 1978).

2. Although Mormons generally still claim that their prophet-presidents receive revelations, the mechanism for divine communication has changed since the nineteenth century. As Thomas F. O'Dea (1957, 160) observes, "organizational procedures under the direction of a strong authoritarian leader largely replaced visions and revelations, a process that had already started in the last days of Joseph's rule in Nauvoo."

3. The Aaronic Order uses wine in its sacrament services, which may constitute another attempt to revitalize nineteenth century Mormonism. Like Catholics, Eastern Orthodox Christians, Episcopalians, and Lutherans, the Levites believe that the wafer and wine used in the communion ritual are transformed into the physical body and blood of Jesus Christ. Although Catholics refer to this process as "transubstatiation," the Levites do not use this term.

4. The Council of Fifty was a secret organization formed by Joseph Smith to promote the establishment of a theocratic government which would, under the leadership of Jesus Christ, have supreme power during the millennium.

## CHAPTER 4

1. According to the Levites, the Eskdale refers to "part of the lands owned by the Glendonwyns, Maurice Glendenning's patrilineal ancestors in Scotland" (Beeston 1966, 213).

2. Although I was able to collect data on the approximate number of active and inactive members of the Order, I was unable to obtain reliable data on the rate of turnover in membership. In some cases members appear to be permanently inactive, and in other cases, members fluctuate between periods of activity and inactivity in the group.

# References

*Aaron's Star*

1972 Salt Lake City. July 1960, September 1962, September 1963, January 1964, July 1964, August 1964, July 1965, September 1965, October 1965, September 1966, June 1969, June-July 1971, January-February 1974.

Aberle, David

1972 A Note on Relative Deprivation Theory as Applied to Millenarian and Other Cult Movements. In *Reader in Comparative Religion*. 3d ed., edited by William A. Lessa and Evon J. Vogt. New York: Harper & Row.

Ahlstorm, Sidney E.

1972 *A Religious History of the American People*. New Haven: Yale University Press.

Alexander, Thomas G.

1986 *Mormonism in Transition: A History of the Latter-Day Saints. 1890–1930*. Urbana: University of Illinois Press.

Allen, James B. and Malcolm R. Thorp

1975 The Mission of the Twelve to England, 1840–41: Mormon Apostles and the Working Classes. *BYU Studies* 15:499–526

Anderson, C. Leroy

1981 *For Christ Will Come Tomorrow: The Saga of the Morrisites*. Logan: Utah State University Press.

Anderson, Nels

1942 *Desert Saints: The Mormon Frontier in Utah*. Chicago: University of Chicago Press; Phoenix Books, 1966.

Arbaugh, George B.

1932 *Revelation in Mormonism*. Chicago: University of Chicago Press.

Arlow, Jacob A.

1951 The Consecration of the Prophet. *Psychoanalytic Quarterly* 20:374–397.

Arrington, Leonard J.

1954 *Orderville, Utah: A Pioneer Mormon Experiment in Economic Organization*. Utah State Agricultural College Monograph Series, Vol. II, No. 2.

1958 *Great Basin Kingdom: An Economic History of the Latter-Day Saints 1830–1900.* Cambridge: Harvard University Press: Lincoln: University of Nebraska Press, 1967.

Arrington, Leonard J. and Davis Bitton

1979 *The Mormon Experience: A History of the Latter-Day Saints.* New York: Alfred A. Knopf.

Baer, Hans A.

1973 The Hutterites and the External World. *Platte Valley Review.* 1:33–43.

1976 The Effect of Technological Innovation on Hutterite Culture. *Plains Anthropologist* 21:187–197.

1978 A Field View of Religious Conversion: The Levites of Utah. *Review of Religious Research* 19:279–294.

1979 A Psychocultural View of a Modern Day Prophet Among the Mormons. *Journal of Psychological Anthropology* 2:177–195.

1982 Sex Roles in a Mormon Schismatic Group. In *Sex Roles in Contemporary American Communes.* Edited by Jon Wagner. Bloomington: Indiana University Press.

1984 *The Black Spiritual Movement: A Religious Response to Racism.* Knoxville: University of Tennessee Press.

Baer, Hans A. and Merrill Singer

1981 Toward a Typology of Black Sectarianism as a Response to Racial Stratification. *Anthropological Quarterly* 54:1–14.

Barth, Frederik

1969 *Ethnic Groups and Boundaries: The Social Organization of Cultural Difference.* Boston: Little, Brown, and Company.

Barzun, Jacques

1974 *Clio and the Doctors: Psycho-history, Quanto-history, and History.* Chicago: University of Chicago Press.

Becker, Howard

1932 *Systematic Sociology, on the Basis of the Baziehungslehre and Gebilderlehre of Leopold von Wiess.*

Beckford, James A.

1975 *The Trumpet of Prophecy: A Sociological Study of Jehovah's Witnesses.* New York: John Wiley.

Beecham, Bill and David Briscoe

1976 Mormon Money and How It's Made. *Utah Holiday,* March 22.

Bennett, John

1975 Communes and Communitarianism. *Theory and Society* 2:63–94.

Beeston, Blanche W.

1957 *Now My Servant.* Caldwell, Idaho: Caxton.

1966 *Purified as Gold and Silver.* Caldwell, Idaho: Caxton.

Berger, Peter L.

1954 The Sociological Study of Sectarianism. *Social Research* 21:437–485.

Berthoff, Rowland

1971 *An Unsettled People.* New York: Harper & Row.

Bible

1962 New York: Catholic Book Publishing Company (St. Joseph "New Catholic" Edition).

Boisen, Anton T.

1939 Religion and Hard Times: A Study of the Holy Rollers. *Social Action* 5:8–35.

Book of Elias

1944 Salt Lake City: Corporation of the President of the Aaronic Order.

Book of New Revelations

1948 Salt Lake City: Corporation of the President of the Aaronic Order.

Bradlee, Ben, Jr. and Dale Van Atta

1981 *Prophet of the Blood: The Untold Story of Ervil LeBaron.* New York: G.P. Putnam's.

Braden, Charles

1949 *These Also Believe.* New York: MacMillan.

Bringhurst, Newell B.

1981 *Saints, Slaves, and Blacks: The Changing Place of Black People Within Mormonism.* Westport, CT: Greenwood.

Brodie, Fawn

1971 *No Man Knows My History.* 2d ed. New York: Knopf.

Buchanan, Frederick S. and Larry W. Scott

1974 The Eskdale Commune: Desert Alternative to Secular Schools. *Intellect: Magazine of Educational and Social Affairs* 102:226–230.

Burridge, Kenelm

1969 *New Heaven New Earth.* New York: Schocken.

Bush, Lester E.

1973 Mormonism's Negro Doctrine: An Historical Overview. *Dialogue: A Journal of Mormon Insights* 8:11–60.

Bushman, Richard L.

1984 *Joseph Smith and the Beginnings of Mormonism.* Urbana: University of Illinois Press.

Campbell, Alexander

1832 Delusions: *An Analysis of the Book of Mormon . . . and a Refutation of Its Pretenses to Divine Authority.* Boston: B.H. Greene.

Campbell, Colin

1972 The Cult, the Cultic Milieu and Secularization. In *Sociological Yearbook of Religion in Britain*, Volume 5, edited by Michael Hill. London: SCM Press.

Cannon, M. Hamblin

1950 The "Gathering" of British Mormons to Western America: A Study in Religious Migration. Ph.D. diss., American University, Washington, D.C.

Carter, Kate B.

1969 *Denominations That Base Their Beliefs on the Teachings of Joseph Smith.* Salt Lake City: Daughters of Utah Pioneers.

Childs, Bliss

n.d. *The Church of Christ.* Unpublished pamphlet.

Christianson, James R.

1962 An Historical Study of the Koyle Relief Mine, 1894–1962. M.A. Thesis, Department of History, Brigham Young University.

Christensen, Carl W.

1963 Religious Conversion. *Archives of General Psychiatry* 9:207–216.

Christensen, Harold T.

1972 Stress Points in Mormon Family Culture. *Dialogue: A Journal of Mormon Thought,* 4:20–34.

Clark, E.T.

1929 *The Psychology of Religious Awakening.* New York: MacMillan.

Cohn, Norman

1970 *The Pursuit of the Millennium.* New York: Oxford University Press.

Coles, Robert

1975 *On Psychohistory: In the Mind's Fate.* Boston: Little, Brown, & Co.

Crane, Julia B. and Michael V. Angrosino

1974 *Field Projects in Anthropology: A Student Handbook.* Morristown, N.J.: General Learning Press.

Cross, Whitney R.

1950 *The Burned-Over District.* Ithaca, New York: Cornell University Press.

Darter, Francis M.

1954 *God Will Send a Man.* n.p. Pamphlet.

Davies, J. Kenneth

1963 The Mormon Church: Its Middle Class Propensities. *Review of Religious Research* 4:84–95.

1968 The Accommodation of Mormonism and Politico-Economic Reality. *Dialogue: A. Journal of Mormon Thought* 31:42–54.

Deets, Lee Emerson

1939 *The Hutterites: A Study in Social Cohesion.* Gettysburg, Pa.: Times and News Publishing Co.

DePilis, Mario S.

1968 The Social Sources of Mormonism. *Church History* 37:50–79.

*Desert News*

1905 Salt Lake City, November 13. Salt Lake City, March 19.
Devereux, George
1955 Charismatic Leadership and Crisis. In *Psychoanalysis and the Social Sciences* Vol. IV, edited by Warner Muensterburger. New York: International Universities Press.
Deutronomy
1962 *Bible.* New York: Catholic Book Publishing.
DeVoto, Bernard
1936 The Centennial of Mormonism: A Study in Utopia and Dictatorship. In *Forays and Rebuttals,* edited by Bernard DeVoto. Boston: Little, Brown, & Company.
Diamond, Stanley
1974 *In Search of the Primitive: A Critique of Civilization.* New Brunswick, N. J.: Transaction Books.
Disciple Book
1955 Salt Lake City: Corporation of the President of the Aaronic Order.
Doctrine and Covenants
1963 Salt Lake City: Church of Jesus Christ of Latter-Day Saints.
Dowd, Douglas F.
1977 *The Twisted Dream: Capitalist Development in the United States Since 1776.* Cambridge, MA: Winthrop.
Ellsworth, George S.
1951 History of Mormon Missions in the United States and Canada, 1830–1860. Ph.D. diss. University of California., Berkeley.
Ericksen, Ephraim Edward
1922 *The Psychological and Ethical Aspects of Mormon Group Life.* Chicago: University of Chicago Press.
Erickson, Ralph D.
1969 History and Doctrinal Development of the Order of Aaron. MA Thesis, Department of Religious Instruction, Brigham Young University.
Exodus
1962 *Bible.* New York. Catholic Book Publishing.
Faris, Ellsworth
1955 The Sect and the Sectarian. *American Journal of Sociology* 60 (supplement): 75–89.
Fife, A.E.
1940 The Legend of the Three Nephites Among the Mormons. *Journal of American Folklore* 53:1–49.
Flanders, Robert Bruce
1965 *Nauvoo: Kingdom on the Mississippi.* Urbana: University of Illinois Press.
Foster, Lawrence

1981 *Religion and Sexuality: Three American Communal Experiments.* New York: Oxford University Press.

Fuchs, Stephen

1965 *Rebellious Prophets: A Study of Messianic Movements in Indian Religions.* New York: Asia Publishing House.

Gardner, Hamilton

1922 Communism Among the Mormons. *Quarterly Journal of Economics* 37:134–174.

Gardner, Hugh

1978 *The Children of Prosperity: Thirteen Modern American Communes.* New York: St. Martin's Press.

Gerlach, Luther P. and Virginia H. Hine

1968 Five Factors Crucial to the Growth and Spread of a Modern Religious Movement. *Journal for the Scientific Study of Religion* 7:23–40.

Glendenning, M.L.

1955 *The True Church of God (With His Levites).* Salt Lake City: Corporation of the President of the Aaronic Order.

Glock, Charles Y.

1973 On the Origin and Evolution of Religious Groups. In *Religion in Sociological Perspective: Essays in the Empirical Study of Religion,* edited by Charles Y. Glock, Belmont, CA: Wadsworth.

Gottlieb, Robert and Peter Wiley

1984 *America's Saints: The Rise of Mormon Power.* New York: G.P. Putnam's Sons.

Greil Arthur L. and David R. Rudy

1984 What Have We Learned from Process Models? An Examination of Ten Case Studies. *Sociological Focus* 17:305–323.

Hansen, Klaus J.

1967 *Quest for Empire: The Political Kingdom of God and the Council of Fifty in Mormon History.* Lansing: Michigan State University; University of Nebraska Press, 1974.

Hansen, Klaus J.

1981 *Mormonism and the American Experience.* Chicago: University of Chicago Press.

Heinerman, John and Anson Shupe

1985 *The Mormon Corporate Empire.* Boston: Beacon Press.

Heirich, Max

1977 Change of Heart: A Test of Some Widely Held Theories about Religious Conversion. *American Journal of Sociology* 83:653–680.

Hill, Marvin S.

1969 The Shaping of the Mormon Mind in New England and New York. *BYU Studies* 9:351–372.

Hilton, Jerold A.
1965 Polygamy in Utah and Surrounding Areas Since the Manifesto of 1890. M.A. Thesis, Department of History, Brigham Young University, Provo, Utah.
Hine, Robert V.
1966 *California's Utopian Colonies.* New York: W. W. Norton and Company.
Hood, James W. and F. Eugene Rush
1965 *Water-Resources Appraisal of the Snake Valley, Utah and Nevada.* Technical Publication No. 14, Utah State Engineer.
Howe, Barry Nigel
1981 The Political Economy of American Religion: An Essay in Cultural History. In *Political Economy: A Critique of American Society,* edited by Scott G. McNall. Glenview, IL: Scott, Foresman.
Hunt, Charles B.
1967 *Physiography of the United States.* San Francisco: W. H. Freeman.
James, William
1902 *The Varieties of Religious Experience.* New York: The Modern Library.
Johnson, Benton
1967 On Church and Sect. In *The Sociology of Religion: An Anthology,* edited by Richard D. Knudten. New York: Appleton-Century-Crofts.
Journal of Discourses
1855 London: Richards. Lithographed by Grater Printing and Litho Company, Los Angeles, 1956.
Kanter, Rosabeth Moss
1972 *Commitment and Community: Communes and Utopias in Sociological Perspective.* Cambridge: Harvard University Press.
1973 *Communes: Creating and Managing the Collective Life.* New York: Harper & Row. Kanter, Rosabeth Moss, ed.
Kardiner, Abram
1945 *The Psychological Frontiers of Society.* New York: Columbia University Press.
King, Robert R. and Kay Atkinson King
1984 the Effect of Mormon Organizational Boundaries on Group Cohesion. *Dialogue: A Mormon Journal of Thought* 17(1):61–75.
LaBarre, Weston
1972 *The Ghost Dance Religion: The Origins of Religion.* New York: Dell.
Lee, Robert
1967 *Stranger in the Land.* London: Lutterworth.

Leone, Mark P.
1979 *Roots of Modern Mormonism.* Cambridge: Harvard University Press.
Linton, Ralph
1943 Nativistic Movements. *American Anthropologist* 45:230–240.
Lloyd, Wesley P.
1937 The Rise and Development of Lay Leadership in the LDS Movement. Ph.D. Diss., Faculty of Divinity, University of Chicago, Chicago, Illinois.
Lofland, John and Rodney Stark
1977 *Doomsday Cult.* Irvington Press, Inc., N.Y. (2nd edition).
Lofland, John and Rodney Stark
1965 Becoming a World-Saver: A Theory of Conversion to a Deviant Perspective. *American Sociological Review* 30:862–875.
Lynch, Frederick R.
1978 Toward a Theory of Conversion and Commitment to the Occult. In *Conversion Careers: In and Out of the New Religions,* edited by James T. Richardson. Beverly Hills, CA: Sage Publications, Pp. 91–122.
Maloney, Wiley S.
1974 Short Creek Story. *American West* 11:16–23.
Martin, David A.
1962 The Denomination. *British Journal of Sociology* 12:1–14.
Marx, Karl and Friedrich Engels
1964 *On Religion.* New York: Schocken.
Mauss, Armand L.
1975 *Social Problems as Social Movements.* Philadelphia: Lippincott.
1981a White on Black among the Mormons: A Critique of White and White. *Sociological Analysis* 42:277–282.
1981b The Fading of the Pharaoh's Curse: The Decline and Fall of the Priesthood Ban Against Blacks in the Mormon Church. *Dialogue: A Mormon Journal of Thought* 14(3):10–45.
1984 Sociological Perspectives on the Mormon Subculture. In *Annual Review of Sociology,* Volume 10, edited by Ralph H. Turner and James F. Short, Jr. Palo Alto, CA: Annual Reviews Inc.
Mauss, Armand L. and Jeffrey R. Franks
1984 Comprehensive Bibliography of Social Science Literature on the Mormons. *Review of Religious Research* 26(1):73–115.
Maves, Paul B.
1963 Conversion: A Behavioral Category. *Review of Religious Research* 5:41–48.
McBrien, Dean DePew
1929 The Influence of the Frontier on Joseph Smith. Ph.D. Diss., George Washington University, Washington, D.C.

McConkie, Bruce R.
1966 *Mormon Doctrine* Salt Lake City: Bookcraft.
Michaelsen, Robert S.
1977 Enigmas in Interpreting Mormonism. *Sociological Analysis* 38:145–153.
Morgan, Dale L.
1949 A Bibliography of the Church of Jesus Christ Organized at Green
/50 Oak, July, 1862. *Western Humanities Review* 4:45–70.
1953 A Bibliography of the Churches of the Dispersion. *Western Humanities Review* 7:255–266.
*Newsweek*
Polygamy in the Desert, May 19, 1975.
Niebuhr, H. Richard
1929 *The Social Sources of Denominationalism.* New York, Holt, R. & Winston.
Oberschall, Anthony
1973 *Social Conflict and Social Movements.* Englewood Cliffs, N.J.: Prentice-Hall.
O'Connor, James
1973 *The Fiscal Crisis of the State.* New York: St. Martin's Press.
O'Dea, Thomas F.
1954 Mormonism and the Avoidance of Sectarian Stagnation: A Study of Church, Sect, and Incipient Nationality. *American Journal of Sociology* 60:285–293.
1957 *The Mormons.* Chicago: University of Chicago Press.
Persons, Stow
1958 *American Minds: A History of Ideas.* New York: Holt.
Peterson, William J.
1973 *Those Curious New Cults.* New Canaan, CT.: Keats.
Pierce, Norman C.
1958 Dream Mine Story. Mimeo.
Pope, Liston
1942 *Millhands and Preachers.* New Haven, CT.: Yale University Press.
Prince, Walter Franklin
1917 Psychological Tests for the Authorship of the Book of Mormon. *American Journal of Psychology* 22:383–389.
Quinn, Dennis Michael
1976a The Mormon Hierarchy, 1832–1932: The American Elite. Ph.D. Diss., Yale University.
1976b The Mormon Succession Crisis of 1844. *BYU Studies* 16(2):187–233.
1985 LDS Church Authority and New Plural Marriages, 180–1904. *Dialogue: A Journal of Mormon Thought* 18(1):9–105.

Rich, Russell R.
1959 *Those Who Would be Leaders.* Provo, Utah: Brigham Young University Lecture Series, Extension Publication.
Richardson, James T.
1985 The Active vs. Passive Convert: Paradigm Conflict in Conversion/Recruitment Research. *Journal for the Scientific Study of Religion* 24:163–179.
Richardson, James T., Mary White Stewart, and Robert B. Simmonds
1979 *Organized Miracles: A Study of a Contemporary, Youth, Communal, Fundamentalist Organization.* New Brunswick, NJ: Transaction.
Robertson, Roland
1970 *The Sociological Interpretation of Religion.* New York: Schocken.
Roof, Wade Clark and William McKinney
1987 *American Mainline Religion: Its Changing Shape and Future.* New Brunswick, N.Y.: Rutgers University Press.
Runyan, William McKinley
1982 *Life Histories and Psychobiography: Explorations in Theory and Method.* New York: Oxford University Press.
*Salt Lake City Tribune*
July 4, 1976; December 3, 1983.
Salzmann, Leon
1953 The Psychology of Religious and Ideological Conversion. *Psychiatry* 16:177–187.
Scharf, Betty R.
1970 *The Sociological Study of Religion.* New York: Harper & Row.
Schneider, Herbert
1952 *Religion in 20th Century America.* Cambridge: Harvard University Press.
School of the Natural Order
n.d. *The School of the Natural Order: A Brief Description Concerning Intent. Objectives, Work, Etc., for the New Cycle.* Baker, Nevada: School.
Seggar, John and Phillip Kunz
1972 Conversion: Evaluation of a Step-Like Process for Problem-Solving. *Review of Religious Research* 13:178–184.
Shapiro, David
1965 *Neurotic Styles.* New York: Basic Books.
Shepherd, Gordon and Gary Shepherd
1984 *A Kingdom Transformed: Themes in the Development of Mormonism.* Salt Lake City: University of Utah Press.
Shields, Steven L.
1982 *Divergent Paths of the Restoration: A History of the Latter Saint Movement.* 3d ed. Bountiful, Utah: Restoration Research.

Shipps, Jan
1985 *Mormonism: The Story of a New Religious Tradition.* Urbana: University of Illinois Press.
Shupe, Anson and John Heinerman
1985 Mormonism and the New Christian Right: An Emerging Coalition? *Review of Religious Research* 27:146–157.
Sillito, John R. and John S. McCormick
1985 Socialist Saints: Mormons and the Socialist Party in Utah, 1900–20. *Dialogue: A Journal of Mormon Thought,* 18(1):121–131.
Simmel, Georg
1950 The Significance of Numbers for Social Life. In *The Sociology of Georg Simmel,* edited and translated by Kurt H. Wolff. New York: Free Press.
Singer, Merrill
1979 Nathaniel Baldwin, Utah Inventor and Patron of the Fundamentalist Movement. *Utah Historical Quarterly* 47:42–53.
1980 The Use of Folklore in Religious Conversion: The Chassidic Case. *Review of Religious Research* 22:170–185.
Smelser, Neil J.
1963 *Theory of Collective Behavior.* New York: Free Press.
Snow, David A. and Richard Machalek
1984 The Sociology of Conversion. In *Annual Review of Sociology,* Volume 10, edited by Ralph H. Turner and James F. Short. Palo Alto, CA: Annual Reviews Inc.
Snow, David A. and Cynthia L. Phillips
1980 The Lofland-Stark Conversion Model: A Critical Reassessment. *Social Problems* 27:430–447.
Spiers, Allan C., Jr.
1966 Village in the Desert: The Aaronite Community of Eskdale. B.A. Thesis, Department of Anthropology, University of Utah. Salt Lake City.
Spiro, Melford E.
1965 *Children of the Kibbutz.* New York: Schocken.
Stannard, D.E.
1984 *Shrinking History: On Freud and the Failure of Psychohistory.* New York: Oxford University Press.
Stark, Rodney
1984 The Rise of a New World Faith. *Review of Religious Research* 26:18–27.
Stark, Rodney and William Sims Bainbridge
1980 Networks of Faith: Interpersonal Bonds and Recruitment to Cults and Sects. *American Journal of Sociology* 85:1376–1395.
1985 *The Future of Religion: Secularization, Revival, and Cult Formation.* Berkeley: University of California Press.

Stark, Werner
1967 *The Sociology of Religion: A Study of Christendom,* 3 Vols. New York: Fordham University Press.
Stone, L.
1981 *The Past and the Present.* Boston: Routledge and Kegan Paul.
Sunstone
1986 Polygamists Enter Political Arena. *Sunstone* 10(11):43.
Talmon, Yonina
1965 Pursuit of the Millennium: Between Religious and Social Change. In *Reader in Comparative Religion* 2d ed., edited by William A. Lessa and Evon Z. Vogt. New York: Harper & Row.
Taylor, Samuel W.
1956 *I Have Six Wives: A True Story of Present-day Plural Marriage.* New York: Greenburg.
1978 *Rocky Mountain Empire: The Latter-Day Saints Today.* New York: MacMillan.
Troeltsch, Ernst
1931 *The Social Teaching of the Christian Churches,* 2 vols. London: George Allen and Unwin.
Turner, Victor
1969 *The Ritual Process.* Chicago: Aldine.
Turner, Wallace
1966 *The Mormon Establishment.* Boston: Houghton Mifflin.
Van Wagoner, Richard S.
1986 *Mormon Polygamy: A History.* Salt Lake City: Signature Books.
Wach, Joachim
1944 *Sociology of Religion.* Chicago: University of Chicago Press.
Waeldner, Robert
1951 The Stucture of Pranoid Ideas: A Critical Survey of Religious Inspiration. *International Journal of Psychoanalysis* 32 (Part III):167–177.
Wallace, Anthony F. C.
1956a Revitalization Movements. *American Anthropologist* 58:264–281.
1956b Mazeway Resynthesis: A Biocultural Theory of Religious Inspiration. *Transaction of the New York Academy of Sciences* 18:626–638.
1966 *Religion: An Anthropological View.* New York: Random House.
Wardwell, Walter I.
1952 A Marginal Professional Role: The Chiropractor. *Social Forces* 30:339–348.
Webber, Everett
1959 *Escape to Utopia.* New York: Hastings House.

Weber, Max

1930 *The Protestant Ethic and the Spirit of Capitalism.* London: Unwin.

1947 *The Theory of Social and Economic Organization.* New York: Free Press.

1963 *The Sociology of Religion.* Translated by Ephraim Fischoff. Boston: Beacon.

Weight, Claude

n.d. *The Aaronic Order: Restoration of the Sons of Levi.* Unpublished Pamphlet.

n.d. *The House of Israel—To Be Restored in the Last Days.* Unpublished Pamphlet

Whalen, William J.

1964 *The Latter-Day Saints in the Modern Day World.* New York: John Day: University of Notre Dame Press, 1967.

White, Jr., O. Kendall

1969 Mormonism—A Ninteenth Century Heresy. *Journal of Religious Thought* 26:44–55.

1978 Momonism in America and Canada: Accommodation to the Nation-State. *Canadian Journal of Sociology* 3:161–181.

1980 Mormon Resistance and Accommodation: From Communitarian Socialism to Corporate Capitalism. In *Self-Help in Urban America: Patterns of Minority Economic Development,* edited by Scott Commings. Port Washington, New York: Kennikat Press.

White, Jr., O. Kendall and Daryl White

1980 Abandoning an Unpopular Policy: An Analysis of the Decision Granting the Mormon Priesthood to Blacks. *Sociological Analysis* 41:231–245.

Wilson, Bryan R.

1961 *Sects and Society.* London: William Heinemann.

1964 An Analysis of Sect Development. In *Readings in General Sociology* 3d ed., edited by Robert W. O'Brien, Clarence C. Schrag, and Walter T. Martin. Boston: Houghton Mifflin.

1967 *Patterns of Sectarianism.* London: William Heinemann.

1970 *Religious Sects.* New York: McGraw Hill.

1973 *Magic and Millennium.* New York: Harper & Row.

Wilson, John

1967 British Israelism: The Ideological Restraints on Sect Organization. In *Patterns of Sectarianism,* edited by Bryan R. Wilson. London: William Heinemann.

Wesley, Roger

1968 *The Trumpet Shall Sound.* New York: Schocken.

Wright, Lyle O.

1963 Origins and Development of the Church of the First-Born of the

Fulness of Time. M.S. Thesis, Department of History and Philosophy of Religion, Brigham Young University, Provo, Utah.

Yinger, J. Milton

1957 *Religion, Society, and the Individual.* New York: MacMillan.

1965 *Toward a Field Theory of Behavior,* New York: McGraw-Hill.

1970 *The Scientific Study of Religion.* New York: MacMillan.

Yorgason, Laurence M.

1970 Preview of a Study of the Social and Geographical Origins of Early Mormon Converts, 1830–1845. *BYU Studies* 10:279–283.

Young, Kimball

1954 *Isn't One Wife Enough*? New York: Henry Holt & Co.

Zablocki, Benjamin D.

1980 *Alienation and Charisma: A Study of Contemporary Communes.* New York: Free Press.

Zald, Mayer N. and Robert Ash.

1966 Social Movement Organizations: Growth, Decay and Change. *Social Forces* 44:327–341.

Zinn, Howard

1981 *A People's History of the United States.* New York: Harper & Row.

# Index